Radical TAROT

ALSO BY CHARLIE CLAIRE BURGESS

Fifth Spirit Tarot:
A 78-Card Deck and Guidebook

All of the above are available at your local bookstore,
or may be ordered by visiting:

Hay House USA: www.hayhouse.com®
Hay House Australia: www.hayhouse.com.au
Hay House UK: www.hayhouse.co.uk
Hay House India: www.hayhouse.co.in

***

Radical TAROT

Queer the Cards, Liberate Your Practice, and Create the Future

CHARLIE CLAIRE BURGESS

HAY HOUSE, INC.
Carlsbad, California • New York City
London • Sydney • New Delhi

Published in the United States by: Hay House, Inc.: www.hayhouse.com®
Published in Australia by: Hay House Australia Pty. Ltd.: www.hayhouse.com.au
Published in the United Kingdom by: Hay House UK, Ltd.: www.hayhouse.co.uk
Published in India by: Hay House Publishers India: www.hayhouse.co.in

Cover design: Claudine Mansour
Interior design: Nick Welch
Interior photos/illustrations: Charlie Claire Burgess

Cataloging-in-Publication Data is on file at the Library of Congress

Tradepaper ISBN: 978-1-4019-7147-2
E-book ISBN: 978-1-4019-7148-9
Audiobook ISBN: 978-1-4019-7149-6

10 9 8 7 6 5 4 3 2 1
1st edition, September 2023

Printed in the United States of America

*To the radicals of the past who
made my present possible,
and to the radicals of the present who
are fighting for our future.*

CONTENTS

FOREWORD

Charlie and I became acquainted through the larger queer tarot community that has come out of the margins and into the online spotlight since the 2010s. I'd been writing my "Queering the Tarot" series that got turned into the *Queering the Tarot* book. Charlie had successfully kickstarted the first run of their *Fifth Spirit Tarot*. As a result, we were both invited to participate in the 2020 Searcher's Solstice Conference, held by Nick Kepley of the *In Search of Tarot* podcast. We were on a panel about gender in tarot, and Charlie blew me away every time they spoke. As a speaker, they managed to spill compassion and brilliance from every pore as we talked about difficult topics as three nonbinary tarotists.

This is the essence of Charlie as a writer. Scores of knowledge, love, and passion burst forth in these pages. In conversation about this book, Charlie and I talked about the dialogue around these modern, radical explorations of the cards. Charlie offered this: "Queering isn't an end goal with a final destination, but an ongoing reflexive process that each reader has to engage with individually and continuously." Charlie walks that walk with *Radical Tarot*. This book is a vital jumping-off point for conversation, contemplation, and change-making of your own design.

When I first learned how to read tarot, I taught myself based only on the art and my reaction to it. Tarot felt like a deck of secrets eager to reveal themselves to me this way. (I would be tickled pink years later to learn that *Arcana* translates to "secrets.") For the next step in my journey, I bought a few books I was told were the tarot standards. What I learned about the first couple of cards made sense. I could use the books when I pulled spreads. Most of the time it went fine. But . . .

I began to run into trouble that was difficult to shake even as my card-reading skills grew. Writings on the Court Cards, The

Emperor, and even The Lovers left me cold. I couldn't find value in the kind of world a standard tarot deck presented (according to these books) that mirrored so much of the pain in my existing world. These readings were helpful from when I was butting up against the bad things I knew existed. Yet these old-fashioned decks and books were never going to help me imagine a better world, let alone move me toward it.

When I started writing about tarot myself, I was so underresourced that I often felt like I was making it all up. And that's fine. As Charlie pointed out to me, tarot is all made up anyway. Yet it's very isolating to look at an entire library's worth of books you can't relate to about a subject you love. *Radical Tarot* is a necessary addition to the catalog and frankly, to the world. Where I struggled with compulsory heterosexuality in how The Lovers were typically framed, Charlie immediately dives into how important community and friendship are to this card. Where I was frustrated reading gendered, hierarchical take after gendered, hierarchical take on the Court Cards, Charlie kicks their Court Cards chapter off with the, ahem, killer title, "The King Is Dead. Long Live the _____." And it only gets more radical from there.

Radical Tarot outlines a process you can go through time and time again in order to do radical work. Queer or not, you will begin to understand why this modern twist on tarot serves each of us and, more importantly, the world. Combining sociopolitical theory, queer theory, and plenty of tarot prowess, Charlie creates that better world I longed to see in a tarot book when I started. This book holds space for our potential, rage, and joy. It will call you in, call you out, and make you laugh. You will be transformed. In that, this book is a tease, a dare, a flirt, a call-to-action. The challenge has been set. Can you meet it?

Cassandra Snow
Author of *Queering the Tarot, Queering Your Craft,*
and *Lessons from the Empress*

INTRODUCTION

I bought my first tarot deck from a mall bookstore in Birmingham, Alabama, in 2002. The deck was the classic Rider-Waite* in the yellow box, and I was a budding bisexual teen witch in the Bible Belt with Goth aspirations, so deep in the broom closet that I was halfway to Narnia. Like many queer kids who grew up internalizing the message that they were wrong, sinful, broken, or generally Hell-bound, I was on the search for something else to believe in. Each book I picked up on Wicca or crystals or astral projection was a potential portal into a different world, one where someone like me could be powerful, be loved, belong, or at least be okay. That's what brought me to those dusty, understocked metaphysical shelves, exiled between the fellow taboo topics of manga and erotic fiction in the far reaches of the bookstore, to the Silver RavenWolf teen witch grimoires and the yellow Rider-Waite pack with its red-robed Magician singing to me through its veil of shrink-wrap. *If something as controversial, as forbidden, as magic can exist*, I thought, *then maybe I can too.*

I took that tarot deck home, and for one magical year of hormone-fueled revelation, I cast spells and read cards and even kissed a few girls. If I did it all with more enthusiasm than skill or knowledge, that's because my only guides were Willow from *Buffy the Vampire Slayer,* one burned Ani DiFranco CD, and the cryptic little white book (LWB) that came with my tarot deck. I pilfered powdered herbs from my mom's spice rack for my midnight candle spells. I pulled Celtic cross after Celtic cross spread because it was the only spread I knew of. I intrepidly puzzled through those unnecessarily large, beginner-*un*friendly spreads with the LWB in hand, more hindered than helped by keyword descriptions such as, "The Hermit—Prudence, also and especially treason."[1]

---

* In the 21st century, readers refer to this influential deck as the Rider-Waite-Smith (RWS) or Waite-Smith to give much-deserved (and long-deferred) credit to the artist, Pamela Colman Smith. I'll call it RWS in this book unless referencing the title of a specific edition of the deck, as I am here.

You could say my queer magical awakening was guided more by stubborn determination than by spirit guides.

Eventually, though, I stopped reading the cards as often. Things weren't going well, a mix of typical teen drama and more serious struggles with depression and self-harm. For months, my readings were populated by Towers and Devils and people backstabbed by an entirely unnecessary number of swords. Instead of being helpful, all those grim readings did was dump a big, fatalistic pile of salt on my wounds. I didn't know how to help myself, and the future the cards showed me seemed bleak. So one day, I gathered up my tarot deck and witchy books, drove to the same mall bookstore with the metaphysical section that once seemed a portal to another world, and threw them all into a dumpster behind the food court. Believing in magic had simply gotten too hard.

I had wanted to see love in my readings, happiness and stability and joy. I wanted reassurance, but what tarot gave me was reality. What I didn't know then was that the cards show us shitty, scary things simply because those things exist. They're part of life, and tarot is a mirror of life. If the deck didn't have those scary cards, ones that speak to loss and strife and trauma, then it wouldn't be of much use, would it? If tarot was all love and light, then it would only tell half the human story. Instead, this wonderful deck with its 78 cards speaks to every human experience, every emotion, good and bad and ecstatic and unfair, and that's what makes it work. That's what makes it special. It shows us everything, even the hard stuff we don't want to look at, and that's how it helps us grow.

For the next decade of my life, I didn't read tarot, cast spells, or date girls. I did the things I was supposed to. I lived as a cisgender, straight woman. I went to college and grad school. I wrote and published short stories. I got a day job that turned into a career that I was good at and enjoyed. I made wonderful, stalwart friends and even had a couple of good boyfriends who I still care about. At the same time, by the age of 25, I had been sexually assaulted more times than I can count on one hand. In grad school, I landed in a brief but abusive relationship. I started drinking heavily to cope with my undiagnosed and swiftly compounding PTSD. Still, I made good grades, graduated with my MFA, landed jobs, earned promotions, and garnered publications. Eventually, I met the man who would become my first husband and entered my second abusive relationship. *I've made it*, I thought. *Now I can be happy.*

At 29 years old, I had a husband, a career, and a house in the suburbs, and I was deeply unhappy. I was also deeply in denial. I never stopped to ask *why* I was making the choices I made, never paused to check in with how I felt and what I truly wanted, never thought to consider that there may be other options. I was living an unexamined life, chasing a blueprint for someone else's happiness and mistaking it for my own.

Then, one Saturday, 12 years after my first tarot deck's untimely dumpster burial and four years into an abusive marriage, I went to a Renaissance fair. Afterward, a new friend gave me a tarot reading on the back of a milk crate, and my whole life changed.

In the safe space for introspection that the reading created, aided by my friend's gentle-but-real interpretations, in the faces of the very same scary cards that drove me away from tarot once before, I was finally able to push past my own denial and realize the truth of my experience: I was not okay. And I needed a divorce.

The next morning, I bought my second tarot deck—an Albano-Waite, a version of the Rider-Waite-Smith (RWS) with wildly vibrant, almost psychedelic colors.* Two months later, I left my husband and moved out. I was 30 years old, struggling financially, living in a rented room barely larger than my full-sized bed, sharing a bathroom with three 20-year-olds, and getting a divorce. And I was beautifully, expansively happy.

I haven't stopped reading since.

That was 2016—not so long ago, but it seems like eons. With that pack of cards, I learned to read tarot in a new way. I taught myself with all the resources I didn't have access to as a teen: classic tarot books by legends such as Rachel Pollack and Mary K. Greer, and the blogs, podcasts, and social media posts of hundreds of people who were exploring tarot just like me. As a creative writer and lifelong reader, I noticed the classic narratives and character

---

* The significance of the fact that this was essentially a rainbowed version of my deck from high school is only hitting me now.

archetypes in the cards and how they speak to the human soul by telling us the story of ourselves, just like a good book does. I saw how card keywords and interpretations varied, sometimes widely, from source to source, so I started writing my own. I developed a personal relationship with the cards that was based on tarot fundamentals but was also adaptive, a practice that prioritized observation, intuition, and curiosity over prescription and portent. I started thinking about the ways we create meaning of our lives, spinning our own personal mythologies. I started thinking about the power and constraints of narrative, and how our assumptions and conditioned beliefs limit our potential futures.* Then, as my life started to change in remarkable ways, as I started healing and discovering who I wanted to be, as I began to feel truly happy, I realized that tarot doesn't tell the future. It helps us *create* it.

Since then, I've read tarot professionally in coffee shops and metaphysical stores, by appointment and random walk-in, for big parties and corporate events with a hundred people rotating through my table. I've taught tarot to hundreds of students in private workshops, witchy shops, and multiweek classes at the local community college. I've written tarot zines and produced a tarot podcast called *The Word Witch*. And I created my own tarot deck, *Fifth Spirit Tarot*. It's the deck I wish I'd had as a teen, a deck specifically for queer folks and others on the margins like me.

Since 2016, I also finalized that divorce, quit my job, gave away all my stuff, moved cross-country, fell in love, started my own business, figured out how to draw, realized I'm nonbinary, changed my name and pronouns, started therapy for PTSD, and remarried—this time to a certain tarot-reading friend who happened to read my cards one night after a Renaissance fair.

So how does tarot help us create such radical change in our lives? Is it witchcraft? Sorcery? Ask five different readers and they'll give you five different answers, but if you ask me, I think the magic of tarot lies in the simple and phenomenal art of *listening*.

The first time I practiced tarot as a teen was concurrent with my first queer awakening, and the second time ushered me into fully uncovering and embracing the fullness of my sexuality and

---

* Conditioned beliefs are the beliefs that we have been taught or internalized from culture, religion, family, or other external sources. However, they are not necessarily true, intrinsic, or applicable to us.

gender identity. Not because tarot *makes* you gay (although I do believe it's essentially queer—more on that later), but because reading the cards inevitably brings us closer to our authentic selves, no matter your sexual identity or gender. Developing a personal tarot practice requires paying attention to our lives and listening to our inner voice, which naturally aligns us more and more with our truth and authenticity. On top of that, working with the cards develops our intuition muscle, making it easier to access the vast libraries of our internal knowledge, buried down deep within us where our conscious minds don't usually go. Every time we pull a spread, we make a tiny commitment to understanding ourselves better and to navigating our lives in alignment with our truest and fullest selves. It would be hard to practice tarot and *not* radically change your life.

The magic of tarot comes from our engagement with it. Used one way, the way I used it as a teen, tarot is a fatalistic augury that snaps closed on our future like a leg in a trap, frightening us, disempowering us, and hampering our free will. Used a different way, tarot becomes a door to possibility, a wild and gentle space for listening and exploration, a window to formerly impossible perspectives on *what is* and *what else could be.* Magic was once defined by a notorious magician as enacting change through the power of will,* something that tarot certainly helps us to do. The word *magic* is also used to describe change that occurs through unknown means, and divination is, in one sense, seeking knowledge of the unknown. It turns out that tarot, this queer tool of the liminal and the unknown, of ordered cards and chaotic shuffle, of meaningful randomness, of creating change, is magic after all.

This book offers a way of conceiving of tarot—and by extension, ourselves and this radically connected human life—as magical, practical, spiritual, and *alive.* Radical tarot is a way of working with the cards that is explicitly queer, curious, intersectional, expansive, inclusive, transformational, nonbinary, and creative.** It's part learning the tarot, part queering the tarot, and part guide to revolutionizing your own life.

---

* "Magick is the Science and Art of causing Change to occur in conformity with Will."—Aleister Crowley, *Magick in Theory and Practice* (New York: Dover, 1976), xii.

** Creative as in imaginative, as in relating to the act of creation, and as in generative of further creativity and creation.

This book is also the result of the innumerable tarot readers, fiction writers, philosophers, poets, activists, healers, teachers, and friends who I have learned from, and the people they have learned from, and so on back through time, an uncountable lineage filled with cross-pollination. It includes comparative mythologist Joseph Campbell, whose thoughts on archetype, narrative, and belief have left an indelible imprint on me, ever since I first lifted *The Power of Myth* from my mom's bookshelf; Rachel Pollack, whose *Seventy-Eight Degrees of Wisdom* cracked open the tarot for me and revolutionized my understanding of the cards; tarot teacher Lindsay Mack, whose podcast *Tarot for the Wild Soul* gave me permission to rewild the tarot at a sensitive time when I otherwise may have abandoned it again; and my therapist Charmagne, who introduced me to the concept of the dialectic and inadvertently handed me the key to understanding tarot's duality as nonbinary. It also includes adrienne maree brown's kaleidoscopic visions of shaping futures through change in *Emergent Strategy*; José Esteban Muñoz's queer utopian philosophy; Kate Bornstein, Audre Lorde, Alok Vaid-Menon, and my spouse, Aaron; and every other queer theorist, gay poet, and gender outlaw who proves every day that there is more possibility, resiliency, and visionary power in the human spirit than I was ever taught to believe.

In other words, a radical tarot is a collective creation, not a solo one. This book is but one iteration of the continuing work to queer the tarot and liberate the future, but one reflection of this glitteringly multifaceted and ever-changing pack of cards. I may be writing these words, but *you* are part of radical tarot's continued co-creation.

PART 1

TOWARD A RADICAL TAROT

Chapter 1

A RADICAL TAROT MANIFESTO

Radical is a loaded word. It's thrown around by political parties to divide voters, wielded by media to get clicks, and leveraged by the powers that be to demonize anyone who challenges the status quo. When I use the word *radical* in this book, I don't mean it to connote a particular political standpoint. However, this book certainly is political in that it is unabashedly queer, intersectionally feminist, anti-racist, anticapitalist, environmentalist, and invested in creating better, more equitable, more sustainable, more liberated futures for us all. As Black feminist activist and poet Audre Lorde so famously said, the spiritual *is* political.[2] Our belief systems and the tools we use to understand ourselves inform our sense of right and wrong. They give us permission to sit back and do nothing, or they drive us to fight for a better world for everyone. That's a political thing.

So the tarot does *of necessity* encompass the political, and a radical tarot is no exception. When I say *radical*, I mean radical in the sense of conscious progress and change. Radical in the sense of boldly deviating from and questioning the norm. And radical in the sense of the word's lesser known meaning as "of, relating to, or proceeding from a root."[3] A radical tarot, or a practice of using tarot radically, is interested in getting to the roots of things—the roots of our individual values, desires, dreams, and truths; the roots of our fulfillment and our longing; the roots of our strife, grief, pleasure, and bliss; and the roots of the oppressive systems that surround us, dictate our survival, and compromise our free will. A radical tarot endeavors to examine these roots and plant better ones. In being both foundational and progressive, rooted and revolutionary, the word *radical* captures a nonbinary complexity that sits at the heart of this approach to tarot and, I believe, at the rooted heart of tarot itself. To these ends, I offer you three core values for cultivating a radical tarot:

The tarot is queer.

The archetypes are alive.

Tarot does not predict the future; it helps us create it.

Also note that I said *a* radical tarot, not *the* radical tarot. That's because, as you'll discover in the following pages, there is *no definitive tarot*. Especially no definitive *radical* tarot. There are a million radical ways to read the cards, and this book's hope is to offer a starting point for discovering *your* radical tarot.

1. THE TAROT IS QUEER

I'm not the first queer misfit to be drawn to the metaphysical section of the bookstore. There is a long history of queer folks and other marginalized people turning to tarot, folk magic, witchcraft, and other sources of fringe wisdom for help, solace, and survival outside the safety and privilege of the mainstream. Spells have been cobbled together from scraps of memory and whatever's in the kitchen cabinet in times of need. Fortunes have been told with a tattered pack of cards to find guidance when all the guides have turned their backs. Old gods and new gods and DIY queered gods have provided the comfort, confidence, and faith to keep going, love ourselves, and create our own communities outside of the bounds of the norm.

If we go back to the original meaning of the word *queer*, it basically means odd, weird, or strange—terms the mainstream frequently applies to those on the margins as well as to those who involve themselves in the metaphysical, who read the cards. No one knows for sure who was the first person to use tarot for divination, soul-searching, or self-knowledge, but whoever they were, I bet there was something queer about them. Maybe there's something queer about you too. Maybe you're searching for the same things I was in that long-ago bookstore, things that many before me have sought in the deck's shuffle. Things like belonging, affirmation, safety, empowerment, answers, hope that there's more to life than this, and maybe even the ability to change your cards.

Tarot exists within and deals with the queer space of the liminal and the unknown. When we shuffle the deck, not knowing what cards we'll turn over, when we ask the question that we don't know the answer to, and when we tune in to our intuition through the paper windows of these archetypal cards, we are briefly stepping outside the world of the known and into the magic of mystery. As a tool of the margins, tarot helps us stand briefly outside our own lives, outside our conditioned beliefs and value systems, outside the false paradigms that we accept as truths, and examine them from new perspectives. It helps illuminate our assumptions and ask *what else* could be true.[4] It is in this rich liminal space between the known and unknown, where the strange can become normal and the normal strange, that we can grow, discover, and transform in radically liberated ways.

To access this space, we have to let go of our assumptions, open our minds, and get curious. We can't insist on rigid card meanings, definitive answers, and indisputable truths, and instead must prioritize intuition, learning, complexity, mystery, and the inevitability that even this will change.

Historically, *queerness* has been defined by the status quo as that which is strange or dissimilar, situating it on a dichotomy of *same* versus *other*, *us* versus *them*. But a radical tarot rejects this false binary, along with *all* false binaries—good/evil, light/dark, male/female, happy/sad—and approaches tarot and life in an essentially nonbinary way. To these ends, it reenvisions tarot's principle of duality and the story of the Major Arcana as an essentially queer journey from binary thinking to nonbinary thinking,* from fractured simplicity to holistic complexity, from separation to connection. This situates queerness and tarot not as something defined by what they are in opposition to but characterized instead by what they welcome and envelop, which is fluidity,

---

* Binary thinking, also called dichotomous thinking or polarized thinking by the American Psychological Association, is the tendency to think in oversimplified extremes of polar opposites, ignoring the complexity and nuance of the world.

complexity, transformation, multiplicity, acceptance, ecstasy, integration, wholeness, and change.

Since tarot is essentially queer, this also means that it can only be defined by the practitioner using it, not by anyone else, and not by this book. The aim of this work is not to categorize or codify tarot but to liberate it for individual and collective discovery and transformation.

2. THE ARCHETYPES ARE ALIVE

Archetypes are models of behavior and virtue that we see repeated in art, literature, and culture throughout history as well as in movies and media today. You know them already: the warrior, the maiden, the trickster, the witch. The gym bro, the diva, the gay best friend, the rebel. They're also in tarot: the Emperor, the Empress, the Magician, the Hermit. For better or worse, these characters are projections of ourselves, our cultural values, and our psychology coalesced into human shapes, which means they can tell us a lot about how and why we think the way we do. They're one of the reasons that tarot possesses its uncanny ability to reflect our lives and our inner workings, and to speak to our hearts and minds the way it does. The archetypes are pieces of our human consciousness, and the tarot tells us the story of ourselves.

The archetypes aren't set in stone, however, and neither is tarot.* The archetypes will be different for each of us because they're not static, external entities; rather, they are aspects of our own psyche. They're human thought-forms, impressions of our values, beliefs, and collective wisdom, changing, morphing, dying, splintering as our knowledge, culture, and ideals change. They're made *by us, from us,* so they must evolve as we do to reflect us as we are. An archetype that doesn't evolve isn't an archetype; it's a statue. A tarot that isn't responsive and reflective isn't a tool; it's a relic. Archetypes influence how we see ourselves and the world around us in myriad subtle and obvious ways; they can influence

---

* This take on archetype both extends from and departs from the two most well-known ideas of archetype: Plato's concept of the ideal form and psychoanalyst Carl Jung's concept of the inherited "primordial image" that dwells in the unconscious and shapes human behavior. Whereas Plato and Jung focus on a supposed "original" ideal model that all proceeding iterations extend from, I don't consider archetypes as inherent and static but as created by culture, history, narrative, and personal experience.

our personalities, life choices, and beliefs about ourselves. When we perceive tarot and the archetypes as external, immutable truths, we mold ourselves into roles that weren't made for us, and that's when we lose touch with the root of what tarot actually is.

This is especially true when those commonly held cultural values, those dominant archetypes, don't include us. Tarot art has historically been composed of white, thin, cis-heteronormative, able-bodied, presumably wealthy, and privileged people (literal Kings and Queens!). This singular view shuts out people of color, people with larger bodies, LGBTQIA2S+* folks, people with disabilities, the working class, people experiencing poverty, and other marginalized groups. When we look at a tarot card, the first thing we respond to, even before archetype, is image. What message does it send to a young Black kid when everyone in their tarot deck is white? What messages does it reinforce when a woman pulls the Empress and the guidebook reads like a conservative treatise on women's roles from the 1950s? What does it do to a queer person when they're constantly having to read around the cis-heteronormative guidebook interpretations, the conventionally beautiful cisgender bodies, and the heterosexual relationships that are still predominantly represented in tarot art even today? How does it make a disabled person feel when visible disabilities are used in card art to metaphorically represent weakness?

In recent years, tarot readers, teachers, writers, and deck creators have been addressing these problems and revolutionizing tarot in beautiful and exciting ways, spearheaded by independent artists and authors from the very marginalized communities that most tarot decks ignore.[5] Traditional decks like the RWS and the Tarot de Marseille have been re-created with same-sex Two of Cups cards and greater racial representation. Queer decks have played with gender expression, made the Lovers card polyamorous, and brilliantly renamed the gendered cards with

---

* LGBTQIA2S+ stands for Lesbian, Gay, Bisexual, Transgender/Transsexual, Queer, Intersex, Asexual, and Two-Spirit. The plus sign indicates that a great number of queer identities are not covered in this initialism, such as nonbinary and pansexual, and acknowledges that queerness is too expansive to be contained in one umbrella term. I personally love the ambiguity of the word *queer* to describe all the expansive varieties of and possibilities for gender identity and sexual orientation, which welcomes anyone who is not both heterosexual and cisgender into its embrace. However, I acknowledge that this can't replace the affirmation of being specifically and precisely named and included. I also want to note that the words we use to describe our identities change over time as we grow and learn more about ourselves and each other, so LGBTQIA2S+ will undoubtedly continue evolving.

expansive nongendered titles. There are decks that are fat-positive, sex-positive, and kink-positive. Tarot is undergoing a rebirth, and it's a different-looking phoenix this time.

But it's not enough to change the art; we must also change the way we *think about the cards*. In a radical tarot, we recognize that the archetypes are *alive*. The archetypes and the tarot itself are presently in the act of transformation and co-creation, as they always have been and always will be. From tarot's very beginnings as a fancy deck of playing cards to the first writings on its occult and divinatory use centuries later, tarot has always been a human invention in meaning-making—which is to say that *the tarot is all made up*. Instead of fabricating false mystical lineages, as pretty much every piece of writing on tarot did prior to modern times, or forcing appropriative spiritual correspondences, as numerous white, Christian tarotists have done with the Jewish Kabbalah, we can instead embrace and celebrate the fact that tarot is entirely an exercise in make-believe, which is to say it's an exercise in *making meaning*. Knowing this, we become empowered to question standard definitions and make our own card meanings that resonate in our cells and our soul. Tarot's archetypal framework makes it ideal for doing this work, as it helps us to identify, examine, and deconstruct false paradigms and conditioned beliefs and then create newer, better, truer ones. This is part of the work of *queering*. As Cassandra Snow declares in their groundbreaking book *Queering the Tarot*, "Queering anything is about reclaiming it, making it your own, and subverting it to fit comfortably in your community."[6]

Every time we shuffle the cards and pull a spread, every time we consider the archetypes and how their energies are showing up in our lives, every time a meaning we hadn't thought of before pops into our heads, we are changing the tarot—even as it changes us. The card interpretations set forth in this book should therefore be read as suggestions, not instructions, because *they will change*, and because no one can truly know your archetypes or interpret your cards but you.

My goal in this book is threefold: first, to offer queered, updated, nongendered and any-gendered models of the cards and their archetypes. Second, to demonstrate how the cards can act as portals for radical reflection, self-discovery, liberation, and change. And third, to empower you, the seeker, to do your own exploration, deconstruction, and deep listening, and thereby discover your own unique relationships with the cards. That way, you can create your own living tarot, and it will live and breathe and change with *you*.

3. TAROT DOES NOT PREDICT THE FUTURE; IT HELPS US CREATE IT

Whether with cards or tea leaves, bones or stars, ever since we humans grew brains big enough to fear the unknown, we have attempted to divine the future using patterns around us in the world. The variety of divinatory methods we've come up with is remarkable, from the whimsical (divination with spiderwebs) to the macabre (reading animal entrails) to the more practical methods using ready-at-hand objects like dice and playing cards. Skeptics will say that divination is merely humans being skilled at creating meaning from chaos. I say that humans are extraordinarily resourceful and naturally intuitive, and that if the meanings we find in a teacup or a pack of cards or the eastern sky are *useful* to us, then, well, pass the telescope.

Going deeper, though, our human lives hang in the tension between order and chaos. If you think about it, chaos is the variable that creates the future. If everything were controlled and ordered, nothing would ever change and we'd be able to predict the future with unerring and boring accuracy. Chaos inserts the necessary uncertainty to allow the improbable and extraordinary to happen. It was chaos that unfurled the first genetic mutation, and the second, and the trillionth, that brought the first land creatures crawling from the primordial soup. It was chaos that crafted the first avian wing, that evolved us hairy mammals into fancy-brained Homo sapiens peering at a hand of tarot cards and wondering if the randomness meant something. It is both order and chaos that connect the past and the future and that connect us all with each other, with nature, with every creature now alive, once alive, and not yet alive into a vast system of energy and cause-and-effect that our human minds can't possibly understand but that we *can* sense and that we are a part of regardless.

If our divinatory systems attempt to make meaning from chaos, then maybe they're onto something.

Tarot embraces the act of chaos in the shuffle and the random card pull, the creative meaning-making that arises from interpretation, and the queer possibility of change that the reading cracks open. A radical tarot does not approach the cards to tell the future, but to create it. *Telling* casts the future as something that can be finitely told, implying a predetermination and immutability that ignores the chaos of the unexpected and robs us of the ability to change. *Telling* the future diminishes our potentialities to a fixed outcome that either lulls us into complacency or looms forever in the distance. *Creating* the future, on the other hand, shifts the agency for change into our palms every time we bridge the cards. It opens the way for exploration and response, and empowers us to become active participants in piloting our lives. Creating the future is not *controlling* the future; rather, it is an act of conscious co-creation with the order and chaos of the universe. Creating the future emphasizes agency instead of fatalism, curiosity instead of control, experimentation instead of perfectionism, imagination instead of prescription.

When we pull cards in future positions, we are not divining fate but divining our own emotions, patterns, narratives, hopes, and fears, because these are the subconscious influences that create our present reality and shape our future trajectory. Picture life as a cart rolling down a hill: the cart has momentum and inertia, and without guidance it will keep on rolling in the direction that gravity sent it, for better or for worse. Tarot helps us become aware of the terrain of that hill and the speed of the cart, and of the fact that we're in a wildly rolling cart at all, and tarot helps us figure out how to stop screaming and consciously steer the cart in the best direction. We do this by deciding to take conscious actions to heal, adjust, tend, shift our inner narrative, break toxic cycles, and to cultivate pleasure, empathy, confidence, connection, love. In other words, instead of placidly rolling downhill, we can use tarot to become aware of what needs our attention, decide to do something about it, and redirect our trajectory.

In physics and in psychology, there is something called the "observer effect," which means that the act of observation changes the observed object, even if minutely. Pulling a tarot card draws our attention to a certain emotion, fear, thought, or behavioral tendency within us, and by observing that part of ourselves, we start becoming aware of how it influences and directs our lives. If we pull Death, perhaps that day we will have heightened awareness of what is ending or transforming in and around us, and we will be better able to accept it or ease it on its progress. If we pull the Emperor, maybe we will remember to have confidence and believe in our own authority as we meet adversity. If we pull the Page of Cups, we might be reminded to look at the world with a sense of wonder, curiosity, and play, and end up making a creative connection we otherwise would not. Through the simple power of awareness, we think or act or perceive slightly differently than we would have otherwise. The observation has changed the observed—and the observer.

Already, we're creating the future.

Tarot works in ways that are psychological and scientific, but it is also metaphysical. I've experienced too many uncanny and remarkable things to believe there isn't some magic in the sortilege*: when I pull the exact card that reflects and affirms the emotion I'm feeling, every time; when the same two cards appear in all my spreads on a particular topic, across days and different decks, until I finally listen to them; when a reading yields the exact advice required to solve a problem; when it calls me on my bullshit frankly, as a best friend would; or when I watch the themes in the cards unfold over weeks and months, met by synchronicities, chance encounters, and intuitive nudges along the way, as the design clicks into place. The tarot works in ways that are too inexplicably precise and intelligent to diminish it to a 78-part inkblot test.

There's something more at work when we read the cards, something that includes but is not limited to observer effect and projective psychology. Some say our hands are moved by guides

---

* Sortilege is the practice of divination by choosing cards or other items, such as stones or slips of paper, at random. Perhaps the oldest form of divination known to humankind, sortilege was used in ancient Egypt and Rome and is mentioned in the Hebrew Bible/Old Testament (1 Samuel 14:41).

or spirits, or that psychic gifts lead our fingers. But I believe it goes back to that web from earlier, to that magnificent tension between order and chaos that shapes and connects all existence—to the remarkable cascade of a little change.

When we shuffle the cards, we open to the unknown and introduce randomness into the pattern. We court a little bit of chaos using a deck made of order. Perhaps the cards that come to the table are a thread of that vast interconnected web, a sliver of the code, a mirror of the macrocosm in the microcosm. In the reading of the spread, we attempt to find the order once again through the search for meaning. We then go forth with deepened intuition and expanded insight, shifting the ordered trajectory ever so slightly, spinning off tiny whirlpools of change, a partici-pant in that giant cosmic dance of order and chaos.

That's divination.

In a radical tarot, we work with the cards to be active partici-pants in our own lives and in the larger entangled web of life. In queering the cards and expanding the archetypes, in deep listen-ing and curiosity, in claiming the agency for change, we each can enact more inclusive, supportive, equitable futures. A radical tarot acknowledges that we are always working within numerous inter-connected systems—of the natural world, of privilege, of oppres-sion, of society, of economics, to name a few—which affect the trajectories of our lives and over which our control is limited. But even these systems can and do change, and we have the power to hasten and direct that change by taking actions in our own lives to be in right relationship* with the Earth and the greatest collective good. A radical tarot seeks to create better futures for ourselves *and* for the collective, particularly in terms of social and environmental justice, and in fact regards this as a responsibility that every card reader and magic-maker carries. We begin this work using the same methods outlined above: by engaging with mystery and opening to new perspectives, by deep listening and becoming aware, and by taking conscious action to create change.

If we all did this work, imagine what radical new futures we could create.

---

* "Right relationship" is the Quaker principle of living in harmony with the health and well-being of the Earth and all its creatures. I have encountered other iterations of the idea in the works of tarot teacher Lindsay Mack and writer and activist adrienne maree brown, all of which center interconnectivity, interdependence, and seeking mutual harmony.

Chapter 2

NO ORDINARY DECK: WHAT IT IS, WHAT IT'S NOT, WHAT'S IN IT

A BRIEF HISTORY OF A SEARCH FOR MEANING

The Major Arcana has been interpreted in many ways over the centuries: as the legendary Book of Thoth, as the secrets of the Kabbalah, as a medium for talking to spirits, and as the keys to personal empowerment. In truth, these 22 cards were created in 15th-century Italy for a noble family who really liked card games. Between 1420 and 1445, Filippo Maria Visconti, Duke of Milan, commissioned a series of allegorical cards that would function as trumps, modifying the then 52-card playing deck into a new game that would come to be called *tarocchi*.* The hand-painted cards showed scenes from Christian allegory and the Renaissance interests of the time, including references to astronomy, alchemy, and the socio-political climate of Italy. Originally called *trionfi*, or "triumphs," because they would triumph over other cards in game play, these trumps would eventually evolve into what we know as the Major Arcana today. In case you're wondering, I hear the game of tarot was played similarly to bridge.[7]

---

* The Duke of Milan commissioned at least two decks, with the first possibly commissioned as early as 1414 but likely in the 1420s, and a second in the early 1440s (Farley, *Cultural History of Tarot*, 35–36). A third deck, known as the Visconti-Sforza, was created for Filippo Maria Visconti's successor and son-in-law Francesco Sforza and his wife Bianca Visconti around 1450 (Farley, 38–39; Kaplan, *Encyclopedia of Tarot*, 106–107). The Visconti-Sforza deck is the most complete of the surviving early tarot decks and became the archetypal blueprint that most later tarot decks followed.

There's no record of tarot being used for divination or mystical purposes until over 300 years later, when a handful of 18th- and 19th-century French occultists—namely Antoine Court de Gébelin, Etteilla (Jean-Baptiste Alliette), and Éliphas Lévi (Alphonse Louis Constant)—decided that the Major Arcana was an ancient text that held the secrets of mystical human knowledge, applied their Christianized Kabbalah to the cards, and waxed it all with a gloss of appropriated Egyptian flavor.* Their probably well-intentioned but definitely problematic esoteric musings stuck, catching hold of the occult imagination and resulting in a lengthy catalog of tarot books and decks linking the tarot to the fabled Book of Thoth, hieroglyphics, Hermeticism, Kabbalah and the Tree of Life, Neoplatonism, astrology, numerology, Hindu cosmology, Rosicrucian mysteries, and much more. We can see the visual evidence of this legacy of imagination—and appropriation—in two of the most popular tarot decks today, the RWS and the Thoth tarots. On the one hand, the variety and complexity of the theories that have surrounded tarot since the 18th century are a testament to the versatility and strange magnetism of this pack of cards. On the other, we must reckon with the appropriative aspects of tarot and ensure that we do not perpetrate the same mistakes.

Much value can be found in connecting tarot with different spiritualities and metaphysical systems, but as 21st century tarot practitioners we must be more conscious than our forebearers and be vigilant of what is ours to use, and what is not. As a white, Protestant-raised American, I don't use the Kabbalah or the Tree of Life in my tarot practice because they are outside my heritage and culture, and because I haven't put in the hours of devotion and reverence that it would take for someone like me to even begin to understand these systems. I do, however, use tarot with systems I have studied and continue to study, including astrology and numerology. Drawing connections between the Major Arcana cards and stories from Greek and Roman mythology, Celtic legend,

---

* Though the occultists' theory of the tarot as an ancient Egyptian mystical artifact is patently false, there is some truth to the deck's Egyptian origins. The Major Arcana and the game of tarot originated in Renaissance Italy, but the four suits that we now call the Minor Arcana were essentially identical to the regular Italian playing cards of the time (Decker, DePaulis, and Dummet, *A Wicked Pack of Cards*, 29). European playing cards, in turn, were an evolution of 13th- or 14th-century playing cards from the Mamluk Empire of Islamic Egypt (Farley, 12–13). In short, tarot was never an ancient Egyptian repository of sacred knowledge, but it is a descendent of an Egyptian pack of ordinary playing cards. I suspect the occultists' Egyptian speculations were purely coincidental.

European folktales, and literature is also a great source of passion and understanding for me. And although I wouldn't call myself a Christian anymore, I think the evangelical Christian imperialism of the globe means we all get free rein on the Bible. I am certainly not the arbiter of cultural and spiritual appropriation, but I believe it is important that any radical tarot practice involves awareness of tarot's legacy of appropriation and the continual commitment to not do harm. As responsible tarot practitioners, we have to ask ourselves the hard questions.

Luckily, that's what tarot does best.

The history of tarot is a history of the often misguided but incredibly human search for meaning. For centuries, seekers and thinkers have applied their fascinations, obsessions, dreams, and beliefs to these cards, evolving them anew with every passing era. In the 18th and 19th centuries, tarot was all about Egyptomania, Cabala (Christianized Kabbalah), and secret magical societies acting out supposedly ancient rituals. In the mid-20th century, tarot shifted to embrace the power of positive thinking, second-wave feminism, Wicca, and hippie multiculturalism. Now in the 21st century, tarot is changing again, this time into a liberatory tool informed by social justice, intersectional feminism, anti-racism, decolonization, and queer theory. The tarot in every century is a product of its time and culture, becoming a repository of our values, beliefs, and hopes as well as our cultural norms, prejudices, and biases. Tarot's very utility lies in this reflexive ability, making it an invaluable tool for deconstructing our narratives, questioning our social codes, consciously directing our lives, and improving this world we live in.

The tarot isn't an ancient reservoir of secret knowledge and wisdom *or* a magical fortune-telling tool—it's a 600-year-old expansion pack for a card game. But its cards bear the evidence of centuries of the human desire to find meaning. Their pictures act like a cipher that the human brain can't resist puzzling out, tempting us into folly or leading us to self-realization. Like a Rorschach test that we cast our subconscious images upon, the cards have an uncanny way of revealing our internal fascinations and machinations, externalized onto its paper mirrors where we can observe and examine them. And if we can learn what's going on beneath the surface of our consciousness, where our assumptions and prejudices lie as well as our truth and our power, then we can do something about it. We can change the story.

Whatever knowledge, whatever secrets, whatever wisdom the tarot holds, we give to it. *You* give to it.

And that's a kind of magic, indeed.

THE MAJOR AND MINOR ARCANA

If you know about tarot, you know the deck is split into two main sections: the Major Arcana and the Minor Arcana. The Major Arcana, or "Greater Mysteries," consists of 22 cards that provide a road map for the soul's journey to enlightenment—or so they say. The Minor Arcana, or "Lesser Mysteries," contains the rest of the 56 cards in the deck, divided into four suits. The suits go by several names, but here I use the most common ones today: Wands, Cups, Swords, and Pentacles. These four suits are then composed of 10 numbered cards and 4 face cards, or "Court Cards," each. In this book, I give the Court Cards their own section independent of the rest of the Minor Arcana because they function in their own distinct way.

There are lots of ways to theorize the arcana, but one is to think of the Major Arcana as the macrocosm and the Minor Arcana as the microcosm. The Major Arcana tells us the story of our lives, our selves, our society, and our personal journey in broad strokes. It's more concerned with the big ideas and philosophical concepts, with making meaning and building our personal narrative, while the Minor Arcana provides the practical details of living. The Minors show us the experience of daily existence: our passions and desires, our emotions and intellect, our labor and purpose. If the Major Arcana is the story of a life, the Minor Arcana is the actual living of it. Historically, tarotists have considered the Major Arcana to be "better" or "higher" than the Minor Arcana (hence "major" and "minor"), but that's not true for me. *Both* are necessary and important in equal but distinct ways.

THE FIVE ELEMENTS

Another way to work with tarot is to think of the Major Arcana and each of the four Minor suits as corresponding to one of the five classical elements. In this model, Wands usually correspond to Fire, Swords to Air, Cups to Water, and Pentacles to Earth. That leaves the fifth suit of the Major Arcana, which corresponds to the fifth element, or *quintessence*, of Aether or Spirit.* I use this method because it's relatable and intuitive (we all know what earth is, but maybe not a pentacle), and because it lends itself to nonhierarchical interpretation. When we conceive of each suit as an element, we can also relate to them as essential parts of the natural world.

Fire is the sun that shines light and life onto the Earth and the energetic spark that animates our bodies, so Wands correspond to the energetic realm of action, passion, aspiration, and purpose. Water is the ocean in which life on this planet was born, the quenching liquid we depend on for survival, the blood in our veins and tears in our eyes, so Cups correspond to the emotional domain of feeling, connection, and the intuition that arises from our subconscious depths. Air is the breath in our lungs and the medium of sight, and so Swords are the mental space of our thoughts, intellect, perception, and communication. Earth is the element of the terrestrial planet itself, of fertile soil and solid rock, of nature and flesh and all manifest creation, and so Pentacles are the material realm of resources, wealth, labor, routine, and the ways we build a stable and supportive life. Aether, or Spirit, is the feeling we have of something bigger, the human desire to touch God, the way we synthesize the stuff of our lives to find meaning—the reason you picked up a tarot deck.

Just as we need all the elements to live, so too do we need all the suits in some combination. Esoteric tarotists have traditionally assigned a hierarchy to the elements, usually ranking the Pentacles lowest or most basic, the Wands highest or most elevated, and with the Major Arcana reigning supreme. But in a radical tarot, we have no use for hierarchy. No element or suit holds precedence

---

* The fifth element isn't just a movie starring Bruce Willis and Milla Jovovich. It's a metaphysical substance that originates in Greek mythology as the stuff gods breathed, was developed by Plato and Aristotle into the element that fills the celestial spheres (the heavens), was adapted by medieval alchemists as a universal medicine, and was later thought by scientists to conduct light from the stars and to supply the planet with gravity.

over any other; each suit has its vital roles and functions. Moreover, no suit exists in a vacuum; they intertwine and support each other in myriad ways.

NUMEROLOGY AND SEQUENCE

Similarly, the numbering of the cards appears to contain an ordered progression, but in practice life does not unfold linearly. Some of us are forced to grow up faster than others. Things happen that aren't supposed to. Success and grief, joy and pain come at odd and often unpredictable intervals. Practically, we don't move through the Major Arcana from 0 to 21, nor do we progress through the Minor suits from ace to ten. We linger in some cards, waiting for change or closure. We leap clear past others, moving diagonally and circuitously. We think we're done with the experience of one card, and then we're sent right back to stew in it again. There is an order to the cards because it suits a narrative, but this sequence isn't set in stone,* and there's no reason that a very radical tarot practitioner couldn't reorder the cards altogether, moving them about to find an order that suits their own story better.

Much of tarot interpretation does come from the numbers on the cards, however, so the numbers aren't without meaning in practice. When I work with the Minor Arcana, I think of the cards as a matrix of element and number, with the numbers corresponding to the following:

Ace - potential
Two - balance
Three - expansion
Four - structure
Five - challenge
Six - harmony
Seven - complication
Eight - movement
Nine - culmination
Ten - completion[8]

---

* The numbering and sequence of the cards wasn't standardized until the Tarot de Marseille found its form in the 17th and 18th centuries. In the very earliest tarots, the Visconti-Sforza decks, the cards were unnumbered (and unnamed), so there's no way to determine any "original" order with certainty.

BRIDGING DUALITY

For a long time, occultists and those who use tarot for spiritual work or self-development have ascribed a duality to it, with some cards being "feminine" and others "masculine." (Don't worry, we'll demolish the gender binary in the next chapter.) The concept of duality is a core one in metaphysical systems of thought, harkening all the way back to Plato, Pythagoras, and Laozi (Lao Tzu). The general and much simplified idea is that the universe is all one big holistic thing, sometimes called *God*, and before we are born we are nestled in it, one with it, indistinguishable from it. But once we are born, we suddenly feel separated from it. A result of our human consciousness is that we have knowledge of difference and separation. Our ability to perceive ourselves leads us to mistakenly think our minds are separate from our bodies. We desire connection with our fellow humans and with the God of our understanding, but the knowledge of our essential disconnection brings us great pain. This pain leads us to perceive *everything* as difference and separation, *everything* as opposition. When we experience one thing, its opposite is always suggested. When we feel acceptance and belonging, we are also aware of its lingering twin: the specter of disapproval and shame. Instead of finding a way to reconcile the two, to balance our desire for connection with our fear of disconnection, we spend our lives chasing the highs for fear of the lows. We run around as only half of ourselves, acknowledging only half of our experience, unintegrated. The goal of most of the occult sciences is to unify these dualities and become one again. Modern psychology also acknowledges this perceived duality between mind and body, self and other, feeling and thought, connection and disconnection, and it is the work of many therapies to bridge these gaps.

If we spend a little more time with the concept of duality, however, we discover that *duality is an illusion*. If everything in the universe is connected, if we are all part of God, then it's only our consciousness and our ego that convince us of separation. We have always been both, always been all, always been whole. This does not mean difference doesn't exist—it does, and difference is wonderful. Audre Lorde wrote, "It is within our differences that we are both most powerful and most vulnerable," and she urged us to claim those differences and use them "for bridges rather than as barriers between us."[9] So the goal, whether of tarot, the occult sciences, or psychology, should not be *sameness* but unification of the self in all its authenticity. As social justice activist and author Sonya Renee Taylor reminds us, "Rendering difference invisible validates the notion that there are parts of us that should be ignored, hidden, or minimized, leaving in place the unspoken idea that difference is the problem and not our approach to dealing with difference."[10] When we force people into gender binaries, roles, and boxes, we do it out of a fear of difference, which is tantamount to a fear of *being* different, which is essentially a fear of disconnection. So, paradoxically, to become unified—me as myself, you as yourself, and us with each other—we must first embrace our differences. To embody our wholeness, we must accept all our fractured bits and pieces, all our complexities and contradictions. To experience connection, we must transcend the fear of disconnection by accepting its possibility.

In large part, this is the goal of the tarot, to reconnect us to ourselves and each other, to transcend dualities, to guide us on a queer journey to nonbinary thinking.

Chapter 3

NO BOSSES, NO BINARIES: TAROT BEYOND HIERARCHY AND GENDER

BREAKING THE GENDER BINARY

When we assign genders to intrinsic human qualities like emotion, intelligence, compassion, strength—capabilities that are present in every single one of us, regardless of gender—we create a rift *in between* people and *within* people. We tell one huge part of the population that they must embody certain qualities above all else or be deemed unnatural and unlovable, even while we tell another huge swath that they must *suppress* those very same qualities lest they be considered unnatural and weak. Let us be clear that *unnatural* in these contexts has nothing to do with nature, and everything to do with fabricated societal norms. We pit ourselves against each other—and against our authentic selves—in our attempts to conform, enforce, or rebel against these norms, all while our natural human birthright to explore our truths and self-define our identities is stolen from us by a made-up social construct that none of us ever signed up for. This is the violence of the gender binary, and its violence runs deep.

When we assign genders to tarot cards, calling half of them *feminine* and the other half *masculine*, we reinforce that violence. The Empress's sensuality, creativity, and nurturance are not *feminine*; they are capacities that exist in *all of us* regardless of gender. The Emperor's strength and authority are not *masculine*; they are attributes we each possess in our own diverse ways. Likewise, the discernment and wisdom of the Queen of Swords is accessible to all of us, and the emotional intelligence and compassionate leadership of the King of Cups is alive in each of us. When we teach ourselves that any of these qualities are essentially masculine or feminine, we harm and hamper our ability to fully embody them. When we give the caveat that the masculine and feminine exist in all of us, and then we continue to employ these terms in the same old stereotyped ways, we still only perpetuate the oppressive gender binary and further its harm on ourselves and others.

Besides, if these masculine and feminine qualities and capacities exist in all of us regardless of gender, then *why do we gender them at all?* Many arguments trace back to tradition—the masculine/feminine metaphor can be found in alchemy, hermeticism, Platonism, Kabbalah, Christian mysticism, and more—but just because something is *old* doesn't mean it's *good*. Take monarchy, for example: old, but not good. Slavery? Been around since before the Old Testament. Definitely not good. Treating illness with leeches and bloodletting? A classic. But five out of five doctors agree: not good. We do not have to keep using the masculine/feminine duality in tarot just because it's traditional and established. In fact, when the masculine/feminine duality is deployed in tarot and in most of the above systems, it's used as a *metaphor*. Like an adult version of the "put the square peg in the square hole" game for toddlers, human genitals and heterosexual intercourse are used as a lazy shorthand that roughly translates to "two things that are dissimilar but complementary." So instead of reducing the mysteries of the universe to missionary style, why don't we do as my friend and colleague in nonbinary tarot Nick Kepley recommends: *say what we actually mean.*[11]

Instead of saying the Magician has masculine energy, we could just *describe* the Magician: bold, active, daring, creative, clever. Instead of saying the High Priestess has feminine energy, we could just *describe* the High Priestess: wise, contemplative, intuitive, mysterious. Working with duality is part of tarot, but there is absolutely no reason we must use the gender binary to do it. You also won't see the terms *"divine* feminine" or *"divine* masculine" applied to any cards in this book, because elevating the gender binary to the status of actual *divinity* not only perpetuates this violent falsehood but sanctifies it—along with the cissexism, transphobia, heteronormativity, misogyny, gender-based violence, and the harmful gender roles it entails—to the level of godliness. Why should the gender binary be our god? Surely, we can access better gods than that.

We could go a step further and rename the cards with nongendered titles, and I suggest some for each Major Arcana card under the heading "Alternative Names" at the top of each chapter. I also offer alternate names for the Court Cards based on my own relationship with them. You are welcome to use the names I offer in your practice, but as in all other things tarot-related, I recommend that you explore your own renamings based on your personal relationship with the cards. They don't have to be catchy or literary—they just have to be true to *you*.

You'll also notice that I use the third-person pronoun they/them/theirs in the singular sense to refer to the people in the cards,* except in some cases when I'm referring to an actual person, in which case I will use their affirmed pronouns. I employ they/them/theirs to open the possibilities for each card to envelop many genders, *any* gender, or no gender at all.

This doesn't mean that the cards cannot speak about gender to you as an individual. I've had many a conversation with the Magician about my nonbinary gender, and I've known people who have partnered with the Empress or Emperor to heal wounds they have around femininity and masculinity. These are beautiful and valid ways to work with and explore gender in the cards! *And* the cards have no intrinsic gender. By liberating the cards from

---

* The singular *they* is not new; it has been in use for at least 600 years to refer to a singular person of unknown or indeterminate gender, or when gender is not important. Shakespeare and Jane Austen used singular *they*. Also, for those who protest that *they* is plural and that English can never change, consider this: the second-person pronoun *you* used to be exclusively plural, and *thou* was the second-person singular pronoun. Now *thou* is the stuff of period dramas, and no one bats an eye at the singular *you*—even though it is still used with plural verbs ("you are"). *What does thou think of that?* (Cody Cottier, "People Have Used They/Them as Singular Pronouns for Hundreds of Years," *Discover Magazine*, Jan. 4, 2021, https://www.discovermagazine.com/mind/people-have-used-they-them-as-singular-pronouns-for-hundreds-of-years.)

the masculine/feminine binary, we liberate them to more freely make themselves known to us all.

THE FOOL'S JOURNEY TO ~~ENLIGHTENMENT~~ NONBINARY THINKING

Remember when I said tarot doesn't make you gay? It doesn't make you nonbinary either. But it *can* help us discover the ways we've been living in binary boxes and bust out of them. The gender binary is not the only binary in the world. In Western society we think in all sorts of extreme dichotomies. Politics divides communities into ideological factions of *us* versus *them*. Whichever side we're on is good; the other one is evil. We must be right 100 percent of the time, otherwise we're unforgivably wrong. Beauty must be flawless. Ugliness must be eradicated. Happiness must be constant. Sadness must be vanquished. Performance is expected to exceed expectations. All people, all opinions, all actions, all decisions, all things are good or bad, and there is no in between.

But tarot *lives* in the in between. The liminal. It straddles the borders and swims in the gaps. Its magic happens between the random shuffle and the ordered spread, between uncertainty and certainty, unknown and known. Its visual symbolism invites us into free association, intuition, curiosity, and play, instigating thousands of meanings and defying definition into a singular one. When we lay one card next to another on the table, we are confronted with a juxtaposition of potentially dissimilar things, and then our brains get to stretch and puzzle and make connections and meaning out of it. Psychologist and tarotist Arthur Rosengarten explains it this way: "In Tarot, a vision-based image language, ideas including the laws of opposition are expressed pictorially and can be perceived and interpreted at *simultaneous levels of reality* [emphasis added]."[12] In other words, two supposed opposites can be true and present at the same time. This is the idea of the dialectic in dialectical behavioral therapy (DBT), that the experiences we think of as mutually exclusive—happy/sad, love/hate, comfort/discomfort, certainty/uncertainty—can coexist and, in fact, *do* much of the time.

No human is *only one thing*. No person is an either/or. Identity, experience, and reality are all much more complex than that. We can be happy and sad at the same time. We can be wrong and right simultaneously. We can be hurt and still love the person who hurt us. We can be a mom and a dom. We can be femme one day and masc. the next. We can be afraid and still courageous. We can be soft and be strong. We can change our mind. Queer grandaddy Walt Whitman said it best: "Do I contradict myself? / Very well then I contradict myself, / (I am large, I contain multitudes.)"[13]

Tarot is composed of bunches of dualities. We find them in the iconography: repeating sets of pillars, contrasting colors, pairs of creatures, the sun and the moon. We can locate them using numerology: even and odd, repeating numerals, multiples of two. We can find them in the elemental polarity of fire and water, earth and air. We can even think of the pairing between spread position and card as a duality of juxtaposition. But the *purpose* of tarot—or at least, the purpose it seems to lend itself to, and the purpose we can give to it—is to guide us on a journey of *bridging* dualities, synthesizing dichotomies, and discovering spectrums of meaning and experience beyond the binaries we've been boxed into. Because tarot isn't binary. It doesn't have two suits; it has five. It doesn't have 2 cards; it has 78. What appears as a dualism is in fact a spectrum. What appears as a binary is a multiplicity.

This story is told visually through the Major Arcana, even before the occultists got their hands on deck design. We see it in the cycling of the Wheel of Fortune, in the human and lion coexisting in Strength, and in the Moon's middle path between two pillars. We see it in the Tower's crumble and the World's dance and Judgment's crowd rising from the *boxes* of their graves. As we'll find as we delve into each card, the Major Arcana takes us on a journey from binary to nonbinary thinking, from simplicity to complexity and back again. It shows us the boxes so we can transcend them. It presents us with dualities to blend and bridge them. Even the linear structure of the Major Arcana (and the Minor Arcana) is revealed to be an illusion, collapsing into circles and cycles by the end. The end, which is also the beginning.

In this interest, I offer a reconceptualization of the classic three lines of the Major Arcana. There is no "right" way to organize the cards, no "correct" theory of their meaning, but a popular and resonant method is to take the suit's 22 cards and divide them into three lines of seven, with the Fool standing on its own as the "protagonist" of the journey. Or, as I like to think of them, as the consummate radical, the rebel soul, leaping bravely toward each new card's horizon. I first encountered this arrangement in Rachel Pollack's *Seventy-Eight Degrees of Wisdom*, where she names the first seven cards the "conscious" line, the second seven the "subconscious" line, and the final seven the "superconscious" line.[14] The lines I lay out below are indebted to her work.

Line 1: Creation

Cards one through seven of the Major Arcana, from the Magician to the Chariot, are where we encounter the most rigid archetypes and roles in the deck—at least on first glance. Here, we find many of the societal constructs that are presented to us as facts by the status quo, including gender roles, authority and the rule of law, institutionalized religion and academia, and the triumph of productivity and advancement. But in a radical tarot, we take these as opportunities to investigate and challenge these norms and constructs, and to liberate and queer them for ourselves. We encounter our own willpower and mystery, our inner voice and agency, our bodies and creative capacities, our autonomy and interdependence. We discover our ability to self-define and self-direct, and by the last two cards, we are well on the journey of becoming.

Line 2: Transition

The second seven cards, Strength to Temperance, launch us into a journey into our deepest selves as well as far outside our fences. The crux of this second line is the queer process of entanglement and change. We meet our wildness and our difference, our weirdness and our otherness. We get comfortable with being uncomfortable, with being inconvenient, with being confused.

This middle line is a middle space of transition and uncertainty, when we've left the safety of the known and haven't yet reached the shore of the next. Here, we do the hard work of facing our fears and unlearning everything we thought we knew. We face our pasts, get stuck, get hurt, feel misunderstood. We grieve, release, and disintegrate. In this in-betweenness, we engage the messy work of transformation.

Line 3: Liberation

In the last line, from the Devil to the World, we are ready for a revolution. Here, we tear down the ideological structures and systemic beliefs that harm us and control us. We become accountable for our agency in our own lives and our collective well-being. We unmake our worlds and dream our next creation. We pass through oppression and horror into hope and joy. We meet unknowns without fear. We embrace our authentic selves even as we transcend our individualism, feeling into our place in the enmeshment of all life. We rise up for a better existence, bridge possibilities into realities, and liberate our power to create the future.

And then the journey starts again.

In the following chapters, we'll delve deep into each Major Arcana card, digging into the roots of their iconography and interpretation while we simultaneously envision their radical capacities for liberation. We'll interrogate what the cards can tell us about the way things have been and the ways they could be, with the magic of a little change. You may encounter ideas that challenge you or card interpretations that don't resonate with your own, and that's okay! In fact, it's more than okay: it's beautiful. If you disagree with what I offer here, ask yourself why and chase it to the roots. Unwind your own understanding. Germinate your own tarot. I invite you to join me on this queer journey of interrogation and expansion, deconstruction and revolution, because that's how we co-create a radical tarot—and a liberated future—together.

PART 2

THE
MAJOR ARCANA

THE FOOL: THE RADICAL WHO DREAMS CREATION

Alternative Names: the Jester, the Wanderer, the Dreamer, the Anarchist, the Radical

Domains: possibility, surprises, imagination, leaps of faith

The first time I picked up a tarot deck, I felt like a fool. Aside from having been raised in an environment where tarot was the devil's work, everything I'd learned about logic, reason, and probability told me that what I was doing was irrational and silly, that finding meaning in a random card pull was an exercise in confirmation bias, and that I was tripping down the path of folly. But I shuffled anyway. I pulled a card.

The Fool enters whenever we do something that conventional wisdom finds foolish. Maybe that thing is believing in magic, or falling in love quickly, or quitting your day job, or picking up this book. The Fool is the reckless urge to try it anyway, the inner voice that says *why not?*, and the idealistic hope that floats the heart into believing things will work out. The Fool is the antidote to society's cynicism, unafraid to embarrass themself in the pursuit of living. While the world rolls its eyes in judgment, the Fool shrugs it off with a laugh and cartwheels into the next adventure.

Alternately depicted in the rags of a beggar or vagabond, the bright costume of a court jester, or the fanciful robes of a wanderer with not a care in the world, the Fool has many faces and even more interpretations. Some read the card as one of innocence, optimism, and new beginnings, characterized by a big-hearted trust in the universe that can lead to folly or to miracles. Others work with the card as one of randomness, primordial chaos, and ultimate possibility. For still others, this card is a warning against naivete, recklessness, and silly mistakes. These are indeed all faces of the shape-shifting and effervescent Fool, but for a radical tarot, we need to first dig down to the root in order see what soil we're planted in.

The earliest tarot Fool is pantless and dressed in beggar's rags, with feathers in their hair and a club or "foolstick"[15] leaning on one shoulder. Their garb is meant to identify them as an outcast from society and an object of public derision. However, in the game that was played with tarot cards, the Fool was the wild card, able to be dealt in place of any card in the deck, giving this lowly card a great deal of power. Considered in one light, this momentary elevation of a Fool, the lowest of the low in society, to the place of a King or an Emperor seems deliciously subversive, turning the rules and power structures on their heads. A similar thing occurred in medieval Europe during feasts of misrule, carnival-like festivities that temporarily inverted the social order, situating those of lowest rank at the top for a day, mocking religious and political leaders, and flouting customs of propriety. The name of one such festival was the Feast of Fools.

But this toppling of hierarchy and norms was only momentary. Canadian philosopher Charles Taylor observes that "the festivals were not putting forward an alternative to the established order. . . . The mockery was enframed by a [sic] understanding that betters, superiors, virtue, ecclesial charisma, etc. ought to rule."[16] Beneath the drinking, cross-dressing, and rule-breaking, such feasts of misrule were primarily a tool of control, designed to let the lower classes blow off steam, allow the God-fearing populace to indulge their desires for a time, and ultimately reinforce the prevailing order.* Likewise, the tarot Fool's wild card status didn't truly make it the most powerful card in the deck. It made it valuable, certainly, but also expendable. If you didn't want to sacrifice a higher-ranking trump to the trick, you could play the Fool in its place. In France and Germany, the card is called the Excuse for this reason.[17] The Fool, as an archetype and a wild card, functions outside of the system, opposed to the system, mucking up the plans. The anarchist but also the patsy.

In the Tarot de Marseille and other decks, the Fool acquired a different identity. No longer a beggar, the Fool became a court jester decked with bells. It might seem that, as the jester, the Fool would be simply a target for mockery, but the court jester's role was complex: they were the entertainment and the butt of the joke, but they were also one of the few people who could mock kings and popes without consequence. Part of the jester's role, in fact, was to act as a foil to these rulers, humorously pointing out their foibles and hypocrisies and keeping them humble. At the same time, the archetypal jester provides the levity and comedic relief we regular people need to fight through life. Think of modern-day comedians like Jon Stewart, Stephen Colbert, and Trevor Noah: all funny people who mock the establishment, revealing its weaknesses while making us laugh, all the while keeping our eyes on the important things. One could say that the highest function of comedy is to help us deal with tragedy, because otherwise we'd probably just never deal. Comedians serve as the wise Fool, the sly jester speaking truth to power through a punchline, helping us all to laugh—and keep from crying.

The last major evolution of the Fool in card art was as the floral-robed innocent walking off a cliff, popularized by the rose-sniffing Fool of the RWS Tarot. The figure's brightly printed outfit suggests a carnivalesque attire, and they carry a hobo's bindle that recalls the card's roots as a vagabond. The major difference

---

* Interestingly, these Feasts of Fools were outlawed in many places starting in the 15th century, around the same time that the first tarot decks were created.

here is the addition of that cliff: that sense of impending doom or obvious folly. When tarot newcomers lay eyes on this version of the card for the first time, it almost always makes them nervous. That, along with the name The Fool, has them quickly second-guessing any decision they've made and belief they'd trusted, lest they be made a fool.

That's part of the Fool's wry humor: the inversion of the order of things, one's personal world suddenly upside down. I don't believe the purpose of the Fool is to caution us against a bad choice, however, but instead to make us question those hierarchies and paradigms that rule over our lives. Indeed, the Golden Dawn* system that birthed this version of the Fool situates the card as representing the highest level of consciousness.[18] Valentin Tomberg, presumed author of the anonymously written *Meditations on the Tarot*, calls the Fool, "the alchemical work of the union of human wisdom, which is folly in the eyes of God, with divine wisdom, which is folly in the eyes of man, in such a way that the result is not a double folly but rather a single wisdom which understands both that which is above and that which is below."[19] A. E. Waite himself says of the cliff that the Fool approaches, "The edge which opens on the depth has no terror; it is as if angels were waiting to uphold him, if it came about that he leapt from the height."[20]

Though the image makes us feel foolish or afraid, it is only our perception that holds us back. But our perception that the unknown is rife with danger, that we must keep to the safety of the beaten path of how things have always been done, that we must never take a step without knowing exactly what waits beneath us—that's what's truly foolish. The Fool doesn't warn us away from that cliff but encourages us to be wise enough to take the leap even though we might land splat on our face.

So this is our Fool: a little bit reckless, a little bit idealistic, ready to belly flop in the pursuit of truly living. This Fool doesn't buy into the establishment's promise that narrowly adhering to society's codes and norms will ensure happiness. This Fool doesn't care about climbing career ladders or social hierarchies, hoarding

---

* The Golden Dawn was an influential society of ceremonial magicians in Great Britain in the late 19th and early 20th centuries, of which RWS Tarot creators Arthur Edward Waite and Pamela Colman Smith were members.

wealth or public opinion. This Fool isn't afraid to be laughed at as they stumble down the path to joy, and they'll just as quickly crack a joke at their own expense as hurl a brick through a window for the revolution.

For a radical tarot, we might think of the Fool as *the* radical. This is the agent of change and spontaneity; these are the capers, mistakes, and surprises that catalyze living; this is the chaos and inherent possibility from which the future is born. The Fool has old associations with chaos and anarchy in that fools traditionally don't give a fig about the rules. In other words, they're *ungovernable*. And that's what our Fool asks us to become as we wander down the arcana's alleyways and hedges: to stop following the rules just because they're rules; to think deeply, critically, and freely about the beliefs and values we hold to be true; to reclaim our agency, intuition, and personal and collective power; to be mad enough to fight the structures of abusive power and to be foolish enough to believe in a different and better—dare I say utopian—world.

In *Cruising Utopia*, a text that is not about tarot but is central to my understanding of it (and of life in general), queer theorist José Esteban Muñoz insists that utopia—imagining it, striving for it, failing at it—is not naive or foolish but is instead vital to enacting a queerer and more equitable future.[21] The point of utopia isn't perfection or pragmatism; it's imagining, dreaming, and experimenting our way into a better world. In a radically Fool-esque move, we must be bold enough to step outside of what Muñoz calls "straight time," the linear orderliness of social roles, capitalism, and the status quo that convinces us the here and now is all there is; and into "queerness's time," which is an expansive, nonlinear, and ecstatic space, open to potentiality and movement and oriented toward the horizon.[22] Straight time is the cliff of the known and regimented world, and "queerness's time" is that yawning space of unknown potential waiting just beyond the lip's edge.

That's the Fool's space. That's the tarot's space. It's believing in better despite the cynicism of the status quo. It's a queer perspective on the outside of the establishment's straight-and-narrow view. It's a future potentiality pressing into the present, if only we can open our minds to imagine it.

The Fool gives us the daring to take that leap. It doesn't promise that it'll all work out, because the Fool knows that nothing is certain, not popes nor kings nor law and order, but it doesn't promise it *won't* work out, either. The fact is that we can't always cling to the sure thing in life—that would be a small life, indeed. We must take risks to grow and make mistakes to live. And if failure does come our way, the Fool reminds us that the biggest fails can lead to the best innovations, and that a healthy sense of humor goes a long way.

That's the attitude we need to begin the tarot's radical journey, after all. This mind-expanding, soul-spelunking, reality-bending pack of cards requires us to enter as the vagabond, ready to wander any path; as the jester, unafraid to be a fool in the pursuit of life; and as the dreamer, tripping off cliffs into utopia.

THE MAGICIAN: THE ALCHEMIST OF SELF AND FUTURE

Alternative Names: the Conjurer, the Trickster, the Artisan, the Alchemist, the Witch

Domains: willpower, action, inspiration, individuality, creation, cleverness, skill

If we take the Fool to be the wide-open spirit of imagination, spontaneity, and possibility, then the Magician harnesses that wild potential and, through their attention and skill, manifests it into reality. In modern decks, the Magician is usually depicted in the robes of a sorcerer or ceremonial magician, the kind that casts magic circles and summons spirits, or sometimes as a witch at their altar. On their table are representations of the four Minor Arcana suits or the four classical elements of earth, air, fire, and water, which are the magical tools or raw materials with which they weave their magic. With these, the Magician receives the Fool's potential, rolls up their sleeves, and gets down to the business of bringing that potential into the world. As Jungian tarotist and author Sallie Nichols describes it: "The Fool may bring us seemingly impossible dreams, but the Magician will get them up on the table for consideration. It is he who helps us to make our dreams come true."[23]

Also like the Fool, the Magician has a trickster side. For most of tarot history, the card has not illustrated a magic worker but a common conjurer or street entertainer, the kind who coaxes money out of the pockets of passersby with card tricks and sleight-of-hand. In some of the earliest decks, as well as the Tarot de Marseille, this card shows a performer in the act of the infamous cup-and-ball trick. You know the one: the trick where the magician puts a little ball under one of several cups, shuffles the cups around the table, and then asks you to point to the cup with the ball under it, only to reveal the ball has disappeared (and then keeps the money you bet on it). It wasn't till much later that our clever street conjurer became the serious worker of high magic as envisioned by Éliphas Lévi in 1855 and immortalized by A. E. Waite and Pamela Colman Smith in 1909. In this version of the Magician, the character loses some of their cunning and trickery, apparently trading it for status and power.

Personally, I'm partial to the common conjurer Magician. The kind of ceremonial magic suggested by the later Magician feels too stuffy and rule-bound for a radical tarot. It's the stuff of rigid hierarchies, formulaic rituals, and archaic grimoires that caution that women should never lay eyes upon their pages lest they contaminate them with the proximity of their menses. (Yep, that's a real thing in an actual grimoire.*) Our radical Magician, on the other hand, is scrappy and creative, a fast talker with a mind for innovation and scheming, the kind of person who has the vision to perceive the potential in the simplest things and the wily skill to draw it into reality. I lived in New Orleans for a little while, and every time I'd pass through Jackson Square I'd find myself in awe of the street performers. Dozens would set up there daily, painted head-to-toe in bronze, break dancing on a cardboard box,

---

* It's the 18th century *Grimorium Verum*, in case you were wondering. (Misha Magdalene, *Outside the Charmed Circle: Exploring Gender & Sexuality in Magical Practice* (Woodbury, MN: Llewellyn, 2020), 96.)

slinging tarot cards on a fold-out table, or blowing jazz on a trumpet. Some were locally famous and had been performing in the square for years or decades. I admired not only their skill but their moxie and dedication, the character it took to carve out their own nontraditional path in the world and the nerve to do it day after day.* That's the kind of Magician I want: someone not only with willpower but with *vision*, not only skill but *inspiration*, not only action but *tenacity*.

This reminds me of something my MFA thesis adviser, Tony Earley, told me when I was close to graduation: "I know you have the talent to be a great writer," he said. "What I don't know is if you have the dedication." While, yeah, that compliment-insult cocktail burned on the way down, a decade later I'm grateful for Tony's words. Because he was right: after graduation I scarcely wrote a thing for five years. I lacked the follow-through to sit down every day and work at my craft. Maybe talent is something you're born with, but skill is something you work at, and talent's nothing without skill. In regard to the Magician, Rachel Pollack says something similar: "Unless we make something of our potentials they do not really exist."[24] The Magician is where we take that potential, that talent, idea, dream, or inspiration, and get down to the work of *doing*.

But how do we achieve this doing? How do we get from the potential of the Fool to the skilled creation of the Magician? A key lies in the card image itself. Whether you're looking at the Tarot de Marseille or the RWS or many decks before, after, and in between, the figure in arcanum number one *uses both hands*. (Ani DiFranco, anyone?) In the RWS, the Magician lifts a wand to the sky with one hand and points down to the ground with the other, a stance that Pollack likens to a lightning rod: with the upraised wand the Magician attracts the divine spark, and with the down-pointed finger they ground it into material reality.[25] In Marseilles decks, the figure holds a wand in one hand and a ball in the other, perhaps distracting the eye of the viewer with the wand while performing some sleight-of-hand with the ball, again

---

* I must acknowledge that some street performers turn to busking (performing on the street for tips) out of financial necessity, not out of a personal choice for a nontraditional artist's path. Without romanticizing what must be an often difficult and thankless occupation, busking requires nerve and ingenuity whatever way you slice it, and that's worthy of admiration.

using both hands to execute their magic trick. The name of the Marseille card is also interesting because it is not called the Magician but *Le Bateleur*, the Juggler. A Juggler, someone whose hands are brisk and dexterous, constantly catching and throwing, receiving and projecting, again and again in the endless gravity-defying loop of juggling. The RWS Magician's hands, too, suggest this flow of receiving and projecting, catching the figurative lightning with one hand and directing it with the other. In both cards we also see a lemniscate, or infinity sign, present in the brim of the Juggler's hat and floating above the head of the Magician, which is a symbol of the infinite cycling of energy, of receiving and projecting, of inhale and exhale, of inspiration and expiration.

Let's consider inspiration for a moment before returning to the Magician's hands. *Inspiration* is a keyword often ascribed to this arcanum, and the word has multiple meanings. It's the creative stimulation that we call "being inspired," and it's also the drawing of breath into the lungs. If we break it down, the word's root is in fact *spirit*. When we are inspired, which the Magician signifies, we are literally *being filled with spirit*. Valentin Tomberg, author of the anonymously published *Meditations on the Tarot*, relates the Magician to what he calls the experience of "spiritual touch," saying, "Spiritual touch (or intuition) is that which permits contact between our consciousness and the world of pure mystical experience."[26] This is that tactile moment when something new brushes against our consciousness but before we understand it fully, when we feel the buzz of static electricity but before the spark jumps the gap.

This sense of touch, of contacting something indefinable and perhaps divine, is also related by Sallie Nichols, who compares the Magician to the finger of God reaching toward Adam in Michelangelo's famous *Creation of Adam* on the Sistine Chapel ceiling, and to Rodin's sculpture *The Hand of God*, which shows Adam and Eve emerging from the primordial clay of God's hand.[27] This is a point of contact, a transfer of inspiration, energy, or life force, but also a *making*, an emergence or becoming from the raw stuff of creation. Nichols compares the Magician to the alchemical spirit Mercurius, who indeed is related to the Magician's predecessor

Mercury/Hermes,* and who the alchemists referred to "as both 'the world-creating spirit' and 'the spirit concealed or imprisoned in matter.'"[28] The Magician, then, is the creator as well as the created, the liberator as well as the one in need of liberation.

This is our touchstone (no pun intended) for a Magician in a radical tarot. When we work with this card, we are not merely exerting our will into the world, not simply casting an external creation. We are possessed in the act of *co*-creation with the forces of the Earth, the cosmos, the collective, or the divine, with powers both inside and outside ourselves. We are engaged in an internal alchemy of the self, wherein we are the raw material and the instrument, the cause and the effect, the process and the product. Implicit in this model is the imperative that we *must become active in our own liberation* because it won't happen without us. We must liberate ourselves to create a liberated world.

There is an idea in magic and alchemy of "as above, so below," which we can see indicated by the position of the Magician's hands: one pointing up, the other down; one held higher, one lower. This is the concept of the microcosm and macrocosm, the idea that the small reflects the large and vice versa, that our daily actions and patterns both affect and are affected by the motion and weave of the larger collective patterning. When magicians, witches, and magic workers cast spells, they are working with this principle. If you've ever set an intention, performed a visualization, or done manifestation work, you have worked with this principle. Social justice facilitator adrienne maree brown, who is themself a tarot reader and self-proclaimed witch, also works with this principle in her activism organizing, relating it to the natural phenomenon of fractals**: "When we speak of systemic change, we need to be fractal. Fractals—a way to speak of the patterns we see—move from the micro to macro level. The same spirals on seashells can be found in the shape of galaxies. We must create patterns that cycle upwards."[29] According to brown, to create

---

* Mercury/Hermes is the Greco-Roman messenger god of merchants, communication, trickery, and boundaries, who himself carried a kind of magic wand, the caduceus.

** Fractals are repeating patterns that display self-similarity from small to large scale. They can be found in frost crystals, algae, ocean waves, blood vessels, and elsewhere in nature.

widespread systemic change, to enact better and more equitable and liberated futures for us all, we must start small.

That is the world and work of the Magician. We begin with the tools on our table, the skills at our fingertips, the energy and networks and ideas that we can harness and put to work. We begin in our personal lives and build outward. That's not small; it's revolutionary.

The Magician's rallying cry could very well be these words from brown's mentor, social activist and feminist philosopher Grace Lee Boggs: "*Transform yourself to transform the world.*"[30] This is similar, I think, to what José Esteban Muñoz meant when he wrote, "I attempt to inhabit a queer practice, a mode of *being* in the world that is also *inventing* the world [emphasis added]."[31] The Magician teaches us that we enact what we want to see in the world by enacting it in our own lives, through our own queer practice and personal transformation. Like a street performer donning their costume, we invent ourselves to invent the world. Like a witch at their altar, we are the transformer and the transformed. We create with our own becoming. We make our magic with both hands.

The Magician appears during times of inspiration and creative potential, when a new idea or motivation may spark us into action. They can signal the beginning of something, and we are invited to take actual, tangible steps to initiate the process of this new thing. If we're not feeling inspired, the Magician directs our attention to the tools, resources, and skills at our disposal. Are we using our full toolbox, or what do we need and how can we get it? Don't forget the Magician's trickster side: the situation might call for some cleverness and cunning. But most of all, when the Magician appears, they ask us: What are we creating with our talent and potential, our words and actions? What futures are we patterning as we move through the world? The things we do and make in the world, the ways we move and interact in the world— they matter. *You* matter. The microcosm of your life ripples outward, spirals upward into the macrocosm of the collective. Now, in this moment, you are creating yourself and creating the future.

Use both hands.

THE HIGH PRIESTESS: THE POWER OF INNER CONSCIOUSNESS

Alternative Names: the Heretic,
the Knower, the Priestexx, Gnosis

Domains: mystery, inner knowledge, wisdom,
intuition, consciousness, the hidden

With the Magician, we learned to take action in our own becoming. With the High Priestess, we are introduced to the vital other side of that process: reflection. Where the Magician speeds about with their sleeves rolled up, creating and experimenting, juggling and performing, the Priestess teaches us how to sit still and listen. They show us how to tune in to the inner currents of the self, how to uncover previously hidden knowledge, and how to sit with mystery when that knowledge is not forthcoming. The Magician *creates* themself, but the Priestess *knows* themself.

For a card associated with secrecy, mysteries, and hidden knowledge, the Priestess has an appropriately arcane and murky past. The card is popularly known as the High Priestess today, but before the 20th century it was called *La Papesse*, "The Popess," a.k.a. the female pope. Far from the only card that's been rebranded over the years, the Popess is significant because it's *heresy*. There is no female pope—the Catholic Church is pretty strict about that. Though unnamed in the earliest decks, from the beginning this card clearly showed a woman with papal inclinations, wearing a nun's habit and a pope's triple-crowned hat, holding a closed book and a cross-topped staff. It's reasonable to assume that the card was likely known as The Popess even then, because the title appeared on cards soon after and remains in the Tarot de Marseille tradition to this day. So who was this Popess supposed to represent, and how did such a seemingly heretical card make it into the deck?

One popular theory is that the Popess represents the medieval legend of Pope Joan.[32] As the story goes, Joan was a wise and intelligent woman who disguised herself as a man to have the career and lifestyle she wanted. Living as a man, she became one of the greatest philosophy teachers in Rome and was eventually elected pope. Joan reigned as Pope John VIII until she became pregnant (apparently Joan was getting busy in the Vatican) and unexpectedly gave birth in the streets of Rome during a religious procession. The shocked crowd put two and two together, realized the pope wasn't supposed to perform *that* kind of miracle, and our brilliant and ambitious Joan met a violent end. Accounts vary, but our gender-transgressing popess either died on the spot in childbirth, was stoned to death by the crowd, or was killed in prison while the baby was shepherded away to become the antichrist.[*]

Historians today believe that Pope Joan was a folk legend or a fiction aimed to undermine or mock the papacy's power. But the fact remains that in the Middle Ages and much of the Renaissance, Pope Joan's tale was widely believed as fact. It's also known that the Visconti family, who commissioned the first tarot decks, were no fans of the Roman Catholic Church and had a long history of run-ins with papal power,[33] so it's possible that they would have enjoyed a cheekily subversive card such as this in their card game.

---

[*] In the latter version, the lover who fathered the child was said to be Satan himself, which I enjoy because of how ridiculously dramatic and pearl-clutching it is. Someone should immediately make this into a campy queer horror movie. I'm envisioning *Rosemary's Baby* meets *Saved!*, starring Moira Rose from *Schitt's Creek* in her pope costume.

Another theory for the Popess's genesis includes a Visconti ancestor, Sister Maifreda Visconti da Pirovano, who became an actual, real-life popess of a fringe Christian sect—until she too was executed for heresy. Maifreda was popess of the Guglielmites, who believed in equality of the sexes and salvation for Jews, Saracens (Muslims), pagans, and other non-Christians. If that wasn't heretical enough, the Guglielmites also believed their late founder, Guglielma, had been the female incarnation of the Holy Spirit and that humanity would only be saved through creating a new Christian church led by a female pope. Sister Maifreda was elected to be that pope, and she led the Guglielmites until she was convicted of heresy and burned at the stake in 1300.[34]

Tarot theorists disagree on whether the tarot's Popess was Pope Joan, Sister Maifreda, a completely tame reference to the church as personified by a woman in the same manner as classical virtues or seafaring vessels (ugh), or some other cultural reference lost to time. But whatever the card's origins, our takeaway for a radical tarot is informed by these radical holy women nonetheless. Besides, as I think the High Priestess would agree, a "provable" origin is beside the point here, since what counts as "proof" is usually defined by and in the interests of the establishment. Instead, we will follow the example of Muñoz's "queer evidence," which is "evidence that has been queered in relation to the laws of what counts as proof" and which listens to *ephemera*, or "[the] trace, the remains, the things that are left, hanging in the air like a rumor."[35]

What whispers can we glean from Joan and Maifreda if we dare to lean close? It's important to begin by clarifying that the Popess/High Priestess as an archetype *has no gender*, but the card's historical femininity is meaningful in that it highlights a marginalization. Aside from the fact that female popes weren't a thing, European women in the Middle Ages—and the Renaissance for that matter—could not hold any office in the church and had virtually no political power. Therefore, for a Popess to exist at all was a direct challenge not only to the church but to the nobility, landowners, and the entire socioeconomic power structure. In *Caliban and the Witch*, feminist activist and scholar Silvia Federici comments on the spreading popularity of heretical Christianity in the late Middle Ages (roughly 1100 to 1450),* explaining that heresy was more like a protest movement than a religious one, "the equivalent of a 'liberation theology' for the medieval proletariat." According to Federici, heretical groups challenged both religious and secular authorities by going over their heads to a higher truth, one that demanded a spiritually backed social justice without hierarchies or land ownership. Their "new, revolutionary conception of society," she explains, "redefined every aspect of daily life (work, property, sexual reproduction, and the position of women), posing the question of emancipation in truly universal terms."[36]

Heretic sects such as the Cathars, Waldenses, and the much shorter-lived Guglielmites were opposition movements as well as exercises in liberated world-building—ones that were characterized by equality of women, land and labor rights for the poor and working class, sexual liberation, and tolerance of or community with other faiths. I'm not saying their beliefs or societies were perfect by any means—it was medieval times, after all—but they were undeniably radical.

When we consider the tarot's High Priestess, perhaps we can consider the historical femininity of the card to indicate a certain antipatriarchal spirit, a kinship of the marginalized. Perhaps we might remember the religious and secular heretics across time and location who have found their own hidden pathways to spirituality, autonomy, and liberation despite persecution, who have cultivated their own self-sourced beliefs against the abuses of power. And perhaps we can listen.

The meanings associated with this card—autonomy and independence, wisdom and contemplation—are not of the sort handed down from the establishment. This is not the ordained and institutionalized wisdom of a pope, nor the authority and sovereignty of an Emperor, but a subversive power and authentic wisdom that stems from the *self* and the *margins*. This is a sacred knowledge that is forbidden because it threatens the status quo, hence the card's historical association with secrecy. This is a radical,

---

* It is important that the tarot came into being as the Middle Ages dissolved into the Renaissance. Federici also notes that the last of the heretic movements survived until 1533 (*Caliban*, 40), so it's reasonable that the figure of the Popess created c. 1420–1450 may have hinted at these heretic sects even while the card could be passed off as a personification of the church on the surface.

self-initiated, experiential theology, a system of belief discovered through listening, ruminating, and feeling, not through dictates and dogma. In challenging the papal authority, the Popess removes the middle person, kicks out the priest guarding the doors to salvation and, like the Guglielmites, makes it free to all who seek it. Like the neo-pagan High Priestess of the RWS deck, this card offers a first-person spirituality, a choose-your-own-theological-adventure, and an alternative to the established pathways of belief.

The Priestess initiates this process by reconnecting us to our own innate intuition, and by *intuition*, I mean all the senses we have been taught to devalue and ignore. This is the "gut knowing" and the tingle running down your spine, the message in a dream and the song on the radio. This is anytime you've had a feeling about something, good or bad, but you couldn't put your finger on why, and you turned out to be right anyway. These are all the inklings and inner knowings that patriarchal, logic-centered overculture has denigrated as illogical, irrational, and hysterical. Personal intuition is a threat to systemic control because when we listen to ourselves, we are not so easily controlled. Here in the High Priestess, we reclaim our intuition. We become our own priests, priestesses, priestexxes.

But intuition can be tricky. Intuition can feel like a sense of "knowing," but that feeling can too easily be conflated with learned conditioning, unconscious bias, and sociocultural pro-gramming. As Maria Minnis writes in her blog series *Antiracism with the Tarot*, "The love and light crowd tends to tell us to always trust our inner voices. Yet, how can we say everyone should always trust their feelings when people, with the deepest conviction, use their feelings to justify everything from microaggressions to gate-keeping to murder?"[37] When we begin listening to our intuition, we also must begin untangling and separating our enculturated bias and conditioning from it. We must get curious about what assumptions and prejudices we are mistaking for truth. All of us who have been raised or assimilated into white, Western soci-ety carry racism, ableism, misogyny, transphobia, homophobia, xenophobia, fatphobia, and more within us because those are the foundations and legacy of this culture. Becoming aware of how these function within us is the work of a lifetime, and it's work we can consciously begin as we search for our intuition.

Another word for this sense that the Priestess invites us to develop is *gnosis*, or personal spiritual knowledge and awareness.* Valentin Tomberg defines gnosis as "mysticism become conscious of itself," or "experience transformed into higher knowledge."[38] The Priestess, then, is the card of *becoming conscious*. Tomberg breaks the word down into its constituent parts and says, "*Con-sci-ousness* (con-science) is the result of two principles—the active, activating principle and the passive, reflecting principle."[39] Now, you know I'm not a fan of binaries. The active/passive binary is perhaps the most popular modern stand-in for the gender essentialist masculine/feminine binary, renaming it while maintaining most of the same problems. But what I want to highlight in Tomberg's line of thinking is his implication about *con-sciousness*. If we break it down, the word's Latin roots are *con-*, meaning "with, together," and *science,* meaning "knowledge."[40] To be conscious, then, is to have *knowledge-with*. Knowledge with *others* through listening and considering, knowledge with *ourselves* through intuition and reflection, and knowledge with *experience* through contemplative and lived personal gnosis.

This is where the Priestess meets us: at the doorway to wisdom. As we approach the threshold of their pillars, we step into the binary-spanning space of *con-sciousness*, of knowledge-with. We become *with ourselves*. In readings, the Priestess invites us to consider and reflect, feel and intuit, and gradually begin to wade through the mystery of our inner selves. The Priestess initiates us on the path of inner wandering, the path of mystery, where we begin to untangle our core selves from the snares of social conditioning and cultural programming.

This will be a long road of self-discovery—the work of the entire Major Arcana—but it all begins with opening to mystery. Because the most fertile ground for knowledge is acknowledging that we don't know it all.

---

* *Gnosis* is a Greek word that means "knowledge" or "awareness," and it's best known today for its use in Gnosticism, an offshoot of Judaism and early Christianity that believed personal spiritual knowledge and experience, or gnosis, was more important than religious authority or tradition. (Unsurprisingly, the Gnostics were condemned as heretics by the church. Are you catching a theme?)

THE EMPRESS: THE EROTIC FORCE OF CREATION

Alternative Names: the Erotic, the Creatrix, Generation, Nurture

Domains: creativity, growth, pleasure, emotion, nurturance, self-care, community care

The Empress is creativity and pleasure in full bloom. They are the poem that pours effortlessly from the pen, the song that moves the body and soul to dance, and the cuisine that draws a moan from the lips. They are the artist and the lover: generous, sensual, and enchanted with beauty at their fingertips. The Empress knows that nature is the most brilliant genius on Earth, and so they support us in connecting to the good, rich earth of our bodies that are part of nature, each one of our cells alive and thrumming with instinctual wisdom and intrinsic worth.

But this powerful and expansive archetype has not always been so liberating. In the earliest tarot decks of the 15th and 16th centuries, the Empress was painted as a well-dressed woman holding a shield emblazoned with the imperial eagle, a symbol that clearly designated her as the wife/consort of the Holy Roman Emperor.

This heraldic eagle also identified her as the heir-maker responsible for continuing the royal line and also, with the patriarchy's infinite flair for objectification, as a metaphor for the fertility of the Emperor's *land*.[41] Five hundred years later, things haven't gotten much better for the Empress. Today, the Empress is almost always illustrated with a pregnant belly or cheesecake curves—essentially, as mother or mistress, the patriarchy's two favorite roles for women. Empress entries in guidebooks feature keywords like *emotion, sexuality, gentleness, beauty*, and *motherhood*, all of which are worthy and excellent, but when conflated specifically with the female gender begin to resemble the old, tired stereotypes of women as emotion-ruled and irrational creatures only good for baby-making, housekeeping, and looking pretty. (As if raising children, running a home, and satisfying the patriarchy's beauty demands were *easy*.) Such equivalencies diminish the complexity of parenthood, situate domestic labor as easier and less important than work done outside of the home, and objectify women's bodies as either vehicles for procreation or male-centered pleasure.

The fact is that the ideas and qualities the Empress represents—emotion, connection, sensuality, pleasure—have nothing to do with gender. *Everyone* has emotions. *Everyone* can feel pleasure. But these capacities intrinsic to every human being have been denigrated by patriarchal and capitalist society to detach us all from a core source of wisdom, reserve pleasure and care only for the elite, and consolidate power. It is essential to assert that this card *is not inherently feminine*, because that only perpetuates the gender binary's disempowering grip on people of all genders.* At the same time, it is important to address how assigning these qualities a gender has historically robbed women and people assigned female at birth of their authority, robbed men and people assigned male at birth of their emotions, and robbed all of us regardless of gender of our power.

In short, the Empress isn't a card about women and femininity; it's a card about the human capacity for deep and powerful feeling as a source of self-knowledge, embodied wisdom, and

---

* For more on how removing the masculine/feminine binary from tarot helps and supports us all, see chap. 3 "No Bosses, No Binaries."

revolutionary connection. As tarot luminary Rachel Pollack puts it, the Empress "represent[s] something very grand. They signify the passionate approach to life. They give and take experience with uncontrolled feeling. . . . Only through passion, can we sense, from deep inside rather than through intellectual argument, the spirit that fills all existence."[42]

Audre Lorde writes about this kind of passionate depth of feeling in "Uses of the Erotic"—mandatory reading for this card, by the way. Here, the term *erotic* doesn't just mean sexual; it means so much more. Lorde writes that the erotic is "that power which rises from our deepest and nonrational knowledge," and "those physical, emotional, and psychic expressions of what is deepest and strongest and richest within each of us."[43] The erotic is what happens when we drop our guards of patriarchal intellectualism, release the learned shame around experiencing emotions and pleasure, and allow ourselves to deeply, *radically*, feel. Lorde tells us the erotic is revolutionary because "once we begin to feel deeply all the aspects of our lives, we begin to demand from ourselves and from our life-pursuits that they feel in accordance with that joy which we know ourselves to be capable of."[44] By reconnecting with our own feelings, with our capacity for pleasure and joy, and with what brings us to our internal sense of true satisfaction, we become more aware, less controllable, more authentic. We become reconnected to our internal knowledge and our agency to self-direct our lives in accordance with our highest joy and deepest pleasure. And we become irrevocably empowered to create the necessary changes in our own lives and in society at large, which better supports the availability of that joy for all.

This revolutionary power of feeling is precisely why capitalistic society denigrates emotion and pleasure as weakness and extols hard work and reason as strength. Activist and social psychologist Devon Price writes about the myth of virtuous productivity, which he calls the *laziness lie*: "The Laziness Lie tries to tell us that we must earn our right to be loved, or to even have a place in society, by putting our noses to the grindstone and doing a ton of hard work. The Lie also implies that our intuition cannot be trusted; our cravings must be ignored, our urges for pleasure, tenderness, and love must be written off as signs of weakness."[45] This lie keeps us busy, exhausted, and biddable while lining the pockets of the people in charge. It tricks us into delaying our pleasure and rest until some mythical quota of achievement is reached. It turns work and life into an endless sameness of desperation and drudgery, where we put up with abuses in the workplace because we should be "grateful" to have a job at all. Lorde calls this sort of work "a travesty of necessities, a duty by which we earn bread or oblivion."[46]

The Empress combats this travesty of necessities by reconnecting us to our intrinsic worth. They remind us that our worth isn't *earned*; it is *innate*. Our worth is not a measure that goes up and down depending on the length of our résumé, the number of our followers on social media, the shape or color of our bodies, or the grades we made in high school. A newborn baby is worthy of love and safety and care, are they not? And they haven't done anything to "earn" it other than *exist*. The same is true of you, and me, and all of us. Worth is not a score; it just *is*.

You may have heard the slogans "rest is revolutionary" or "self-care is a radical act," and it's true: every time you unapologetically take the time to walk in a park, go to a museum, have a nap, or enjoy couch time with your family, it's a tiny middle finger to the capitalist productivity machine. At the same time, we must be conscious that self-care has been co-opted by capitalism too, branded to sell bath bombs and facial kits made by factory workers who can't afford a nap, much less a bubble bath. The Empress celebrates pleasure, self-care, and indulgence, but not at the expense of another's well-being and not to the exclusion of community care. They ask us not only how we are tending to ourselves, but how we are tending to the health and prosperity of our interconnected human society, especially those who are marginalized, disenfranchised, and oppressed as well as to the Earth and its ecosystems—not just to our pedicures. The Empress knows that by caring for our communities, we also care for ourselves. Whether showing up for a friend in a time of need, picking up trash at the beach, or donating to a fund for refugees, we care for

the well-being and pleasure of all by nourishing systems of connection and support.

Lastly, the Empress connects us to bodily autonomy, body
positivity, and the revolutionary power of beauty. Not airbrushed
magazine beauty, not externally defined and socially dictated
beauty, but the wild diversity of self-sourced and wholly embodied
human beauty. The Empress puts no limits or conditions on beauty,
no constraints of gender, size, age, or ability. They love bikinis on
octogenarians and men in silk skirts. They adore soft rolls of skin
and a mustache above a fuchsia lip. They celebrate the smooth
sheen of scars and the pale tributaries of stretch marks. The Empress
liberates us from patriarchal and whitewashed beauty standards by
welcoming us into the joy of defining beauty for ourselves. This
means allowing ourselves the sensuality of self-discovery, of trying
something new, of wearing something to please ourselves instead
of others.

Body positivity means loving *all* bodies and *all* gender expressions, which also means having the bodily autonomy to do with
our bodies as we wish. From lip filler to hairy pits, natural hair to
wigs, press-on nails to drawn-on facial hair, the Empress's joy is
whatever makes you feel good. Instead of loving our bodies as they
are, this can also mean loving ourselves enough to change our
bodies. For some transgender, transsexual, nonbinary, and gen-
derqueer people, the most body-positive and self-loving thing we
can do may be starting hormone replacement therapy, wearing
a binder or shapewear, or having surgery to shift our bodies in
gender-affirming ways—or it might not be. All of these are radical
Empress acts of self-love.

The Empress also knows that loving our bodies isn't always
easy. Sometimes, the body-positivity movement's message to
love our bodies can feel like a commandment—we *must* love our
bodies *now!* For some of us, this can result in more feelings of
shame, but this time for not loving our bodies enough, not feeling
sexy or confident enough, not being liberated enough. When we
struggle to feel authentically jazzed about the bodies we're given,
the Empress can support us in working toward body neutrality

instead. Body neutrality focuses on acceptance and respect for our bodies as a part of us while acknowledging that bodies are not the *whole* of us. It takes the pressure off feeling beautiful and says that bodies don't *have* to be beautiful, because beauty does not define us or our worth.

The Empress does not only meet us in times of pleasure and euphoria; they are also with us when we're *not* confident, when we're *not* feeling cute, when our bodies are in pain, when our bodies are in transition, when we can't stay embodied for long due to dissociation or dysphoria, when our bodies don't feel like homes we want to live in. In these times, the Empress is a gentle reminder that we deserve love and care at all points, in every process, in every state of being, even when we don't feel like we do.

In a society where emotion has long been cast as inferior to the "rational" functions of logic and reason, where sensuality has been framed as base and primitive while restraint is pure and enlightened, where pleasure has become a luxury commodity affordable only by the elite few, the Empress's emphatic eroticism is truly radical. We have forgotten that the mind is *part* of the body. We have forgotten that emotion, sensation, and feeling are the voice of the body. We have forgotten that our bodies are part of the Earth. The Empress reminds us, reconnecting us to our emotions, to our bodies, and to each other through their mycelium web of empathy and care.

And that's how the Empress changes the world.

THE EMPEROR: THE CUSTODIAN OF CREATION

Alternative Names: the Custodian,
the Leader, the Steward

Domains: leadership, service, organizing,
power, systems, structure

To talk about the Emperor, we first have to talk about empire.

When we think of the word *empire*, we probably think of the sprawling Roman Empire that conquered the Indigenous peoples of Europe, North Africa, and the Middle East under its martial doctrine of continuous expansion. Or perhaps we think of the Holy Roman Empire that launched the Crusades and completed the assimilation of Europe's pagans into Christianity. Or maybe the more recent British Empire, which colonized more of the globe than any empire before it and annihilated whole cultures under its rule. Or the modern-day empires of multinational corporations, corporate globalism, and the good ol' U.S.A.

If we consider empires across history, we can identify a few common attributes: constant expansion, military might, social and economic control, and eradication or assimilation of Indigenous people and cultures into the culture of the empire. Historically, empires spread under a doctrine of superiority: the imperialist nation possesses either the so-called superior religion, society, military, or race. They declare themselves "the greatest society," "the greatest race," "the greatest culture," or "the greatest nation." (Sound familiar?) Today, empires don't tend to call themselves *empires*. The people caught on that empire doesn't usually work out well for them, so the empires rebranded. Now, empire is achieved under a guise of "unity" for the sake of peace. We must all agree, must join together under a homogenous banner, must become culturally whitewashed, must not rock the boat, must submit to the power of the one for the sake of peace for the many. Funny how many wars are waged for the sake of peace.

Whatever rationale an empire claims, whatever it calls itself, its roots are the same: the belief that they are intrinsically better, more advanced, more holy, more worthy than anyone and anything else. Supremacy.

That's what the tarot's Emperor card has historically been about. Keywords have included *authority, dominance, power, civilization,* and *war.* The earliest Emperor card showed the Holy Roman Emperor, designated by the heraldic Roman eagle on their crown, an eagle that moved to the Emperor's shield in Marseilles decks. In the RWS deck, the Emperor lost the eagle shield but maintained a militaristic zeal, plate armor visible under their robe. This image ratchets up the power-and-domination vibes higher than before, placing the Emperor on an unforgiving stone throne on a mountaintop, surrounded by a barren vista of craggy red rocks that screams the phrase "scorched earth." Tarot commentators have pointed out the Emperor's long, gray beard as a symbol of wisdom and experience, but all I can see is an older man on a hard throne, defensive and isolated, ruling over a kingdom of dust. Alone.

Something about this sad, lonely Emperor reminds me of the Fisher King of Holy Grail mythology, who carried a mysterious wound on his body that caused his lands to fall barren, his crops to fail, and his people to starve. Many scholars of literature and mythology have chalked up the king's cryptic wound to a metaphor for the king's infertility—he can't sire children, so the empire dies. But I've always thought the wound more metaphorical: a failure of leadership or service, a systemic wound in the foundations of government, a fatal flaw in the system caused by the system and which the system cannot heal. The king's poisonous wound is perhaps kingship itself. And the Emperor's wound? Empire.

This isn't the kind of Emperor we need because the last thing we need is an emperor. So what use does this card have in a radical tarot? Do we just throw it out of the deck? I don't think so, because kicking out the Emperor and its contexts and connotations won't remove them from our lives, our reality, or ourselves. As children of imperialism and colonization, as subjects of and participants in the present-day empires of nationalism, capitalism, and corporate globalism, empire and its voice of supremacy already lives inside us, and we must reckon with it.

Empire is the voice that demands perfection and compliance. It's the part of us that must be right always and apologize never, the part that is terrified of making mistakes or admitting weakness. Empire has taught us that anything less than perfection is shameful. Empire is the force of greed, entitlement, and competition within us, the part that believes it must take what it wants and hoard it because there's not enough to go around, ignoring the fact that its profit-obsessed systems of supply and demand are what create scarcity in the first place. Empire is the part of us that is afraid of difference—different ideas, faiths, skin tones, sexualities, languages, cultures—because difference is a threat to its superiority. Empire—which is white supremacy, patriarchy, cis-heterosexism, capitalism, ableism—has gotten into our brains and bones and convinced us that there's only one way to survive in this world that it created. We scramble to fit ourselves into that mold, and we shame ourselves and each other when we don't fit.

This card is an opportunity to confront that empire. It's an opportunity to figure out better models of leadership, community-building, and governance, ones that are sustainable, equitable, decentralized, and diverse. It's an opportunity to look for leadership in different places and with different approaches. Instead of shiny politicians and charismatic leaders, we can look to social justice organizers, Indigenous elders, queer visionaries, and environmental scientists. Instead of centralized, hierarchical power, we can explore decentralized leadership, systems of interconnectivity, mutual aid networks, and perspectives from the margins.

adrienne maree brown looks to the natural world for inspiration in social justice organizing and creating change. brown highlights the interdependence and decentralization of power in a flock of geese, in which each goose takes turns being at the front of the V: a place of service rather than prestige, taking on the extra drag of slicing through the air. They note the way ants share information about where to find food instead of hoarding it, because the more food they gather collectively, the better, and how oak trees survive hurricanes via interwoven roots.[47] "The idea of interdependence," brown writes, "is that we can meet each other's needs in a variety of ways, that we can truly lean on others and they can lean on us. It means we have to decentralize our idea of where solutions and decisions happen, where ideas come from."[48]

Academic, researcher, and member of the Apalech Clan in north Queensland, Australia, Tyson Yunkaporta writes about how Indigenous thinking can be applied to modern environmental, economic, and political crises to create a better world—or save this one. In *Sand Talk,* he suggests that to survive what's coming next, we need to think about creating "transitional ways of being," which require working with the land instead of against it, sharing knowledge while maintaining diversity, and returning to a custodial-based mindset that focuses on looking after each other and all living things. "Move with the land," Yunkaporta writes. "Maintain diverse languages, cultures, and systems that reflect the ecosystems of the shifting landscapes you inhabit over time. That is the blueprint."[49] And these aren't quick patches or easy solutions, Yunkaporta clarifies. Not tidy blurbs to put in your corporate diversity, equity, and inclusion report. Instead, they're a societal and spiritual shift that will change civilization as we know it—and that's exactly what we need.

Our way out of the crisis of empire is collectively. It's not an individual rebel leader who will save us, no Luke Skywalker flying an X-wing into the Death Star. Instead, it will require us to deeply and humbly question ourselves, our systems, and our leaders. It will require decentralizing power and decision-making structures and building interconnected and interdependent systems of sustenance, safety, communication, and support. It will require listening to marginal viewpoints even when they're uncomfortable to hear—*especially* when they're uncomfortable to hear. It will require lifting our voices and sharing our stories, admitting vulnerability and asking for help, sharing knowledge and seeking out learning, and radically changing our way of thinking from being the "masters of creation" to being the custodians of it. Yunkaporta says that in his Aboriginal cosmology, humans were put on the planet to be custodians: "Some new cultures keep asking, 'Why are we here?' It's easy. This is why we're here. We look after things on the earth and in the sky and the places in between."[50]

This is the work we must do with the Emperor.

Remember the Fisher King from earlier? The one whose wound rots the land? Here's the rest of the story: One day, a traveling knight named Perceval stumbled upon the Fisher King, who invited Perceval to stay the night at his castle. While there, young Perceval witnessed a strange procession of mystical objects being carried through the halls—a bleeding lance, two candelabra, the Holy Grail, and a silver dish.* The king gave no explanation for the procession, for the objects' significance, or for what the heck was going on, and Perceval had been taught good manners so was too polite to ask. He just assumed it served some purpose, shrugged, and went on with his evening. Later, after leaving the castle to continue his travels, Perceval learned from a maiden on the road that he could have healed the wounded king and returned life to the barren land. All he had to do was ask a certain question about the procession: "What do these objects mean, and whom do they serve?"

---

* Many people, most notably poet and Golden Dawn member William Butler Yeats, have pointed out the similarity of these four items in the grail procession to the four Minor suits of tarot: the lance could correspond to Swords, the candelabra to Wands, the Grail to Cups, and the dish to Pentacles (also called Discs).

Multiqueer witch and author Misha Magdalene suggests this question may hold keys to healing our relationship to *our* land, our leadership, and each other: "Let's avoid the well-intentioned mistake of Perceval. . . . Rather than accepting things as they are merely because they've always been that way or we don't want to rock the boat, let's ask *why* they are as they are, and who benefits by them being as they are. . . . In short, let us ask ourselves what these things mean, who they serve, and to what end."[51] In a suffering land of inept kings, in a pageant of artifacts that have lost their meaning, it is *we* who have the power and the imperative to ask the questions to start the healing. Only then can we discover the answers. Only then can we understand the grievously wounded systems working around us and within us. Only then can we collectively create better ones.

That's what the Emperor—*The Custodian* —needs us to do: ask the questions. Who or what are we serving? And why? Are we driven by fear, lack, competition, and ego? Or are we motivated by connection, responsibility, dignity, and service? Do we need to stand up to power, or are we the power that needs to step aside? Do we believe that we're better and more worthy than others, or do we believe we're lesser and undeserving? How does that impact our decision-making and the way we live and interact? Where did that messaging come from in the first place? What does it mean? And who does it serve?

THE HIEROPHANT: SHOWING WHAT'S HOLY

Alternative Names: the Teacher, the Elder, the Researcher, the Librarian

Domains: values, beliefs, religion, keeping and sharing knowledge, tradition, institutions

The Hierophant is a tough card for a lot of people. It's probably neck and neck with the Emperor for least popular card in the deck, a dubious honor having to do with its associations with dogma, tradition, institutions, and organized religion—all forces that have harmed and traumatized many of us who don't fit into the "traditional family values" mold. But that's precisely what makes this card essential to a radical tarot practice: It asks us to reckon with the traditions, institutions, and belief systems that we subscribe to, and underneath that, it asks us to confront *our* values. All traditions and institutions are based on values, after all, though sometimes we may not be aware of what those are until we start investigating. And it's only once we are in touch with those values that we can allow them to inform and guide our lives.

First, let's talk about tradition. Although a word that elicits shudders when wielded by a politician, tradition is not an inherently bad thing—or a good thing. Tradition just *is*. It's the practices, beliefs, value systems, and knowledge that came before us. Tradition connects us to our culture and our lineage: it's grandma's recipes, regional folk tales, and even how we celebrate birthdays. Tradition can be a part of our spirituality, whether we're into the Bible, Earth-based spirituality, or neo-pagan polytheism. It's also an intrinsic part of every profession, trade, and area of study: whether you're a philosopher, plumber, drag queen, or nurse practitioner, you have learned your trade from people who came before you. You have participated in, learned from, and likely built upon tradition. Maybe you've even helped initiate a new one.

Tradition isn't a static thing. It's a living body of practice and knowledge that grows and changes over time. Likewise, tradition and innovation aren't enemies. In fact, innovation has to start somewhere, and that somewhere is usually the current body of knowledge—a.k.a. tradition. It's true that sometimes traditions die, and sometimes starting from scratch is the best way forward, but usually we can't know that until we have first availed ourselves of the available traditional knowledge. It's the old adage, "to know where you're going, know where you've been." If we engage with tradition from this vantage, from a place of curiosity and critical thinking rather than rote learning and prescriptive dogma, then tradition opens a world of possibilities at our feet.

But when tradition becomes inert, it becomes toxic. When tradition becomes unassailable, it becomes dangerous. When tradition becomes compulsory, it becomes oppression.

Before this card was the Hierophant, it was called The Pope. It's no secret that the Catholic Church has committed grievous harms, from decimating Indigenous cultures and pagan religions and waging bloody wars in God's name, to demonizing women and LGBTQIA2S+ people and hiding child abuse by its clergy. Growing up in the American South, I saw firsthand how religion can be leveraged as an excuse for hatred, bigotry, supremacy, and an unwillingness to change. I was taught in Methodist Bible school that homosexuals, masturbators, and loose women went to hell. I was taught that by someone who had been taught by someone else, who had been taught that by someone else, and so on—a legacy of "gospel truth" laced in fear, a doctrine of consequences passed down and never questioned.

At the same time, I know Christians who are independent thinkers, who wrestle with the questions instead of claiming to know the answers. I know preachers who perform gay marriages in defiance of the church. I've known Christians who marched for gay marriage, trans rights, and the right to abortion, and Christians who are gay and trans themselves. My goal is not to evangelize—it's been a long time since I called myself a Christian, and I don't subscribe to any organized religion—but to suggest that religion *in and of itself* is not the problem with religion. It's more complex than that.

All institutions, religious or otherwise, bear responsibility for the consequences of their teachings, but so do the followers who wield those teachings to perpetuate harm instead of good. My mom used to say, "Don't let Christians stop you from being a Christian," which is perhaps a way of saying religion is what you make of it. In *Outside the Charmed Circle*, Misha Magdalene challenges the restrictive ideas of gender and sexuality still present in many neo-pagan and witchcraft traditions today. (Perhaps Magdalene would say not to let neo-pagans stop you from being a neo-pagan.) In it, they succinctly offer perhaps my favorite definition of religion: "Religion is about *finding or creating meaning* from what we observe. It can't model the physical universe worth a damn, but it can serve as a way of explaining to ourselves why we care, or why we should [emphasis added]."[52] The same is true of *any* system of values or beliefs and any knowledge tradition, whether spiritual or secular. The systems we look to for meaning matter, and it's in how we engage with these systems to define our values and guide our actions—in other words, in what we make of them—that all the grace and all the trouble lie.

The primary challenge of the Hierophant and what it represents is dogmatic thinking. There is comfort in surrendering independent thought to a higher power, whether that power is a god or a guru, a political leader or a social media influencer. Dogmatic thinking frees us of the responsibility of discerning what is right and wrong for ourselves. It releases us from the discomfort of living by our values when our values go against the traditions we were raised in or the popular bandwagon of the day. This is true on whatever side of the political aisle we sit and under whatever roof we worship: the most tantalizing thing that dogmatic thinking offers is answers to life's difficult questions—whether or not those answers are true—so we don't have to struggle with the answers ourselves. The drug of righteousness is a dangerous pill, indeed.

When we surrender our responsibility and disengage our critical thinking, we do ourselves, our society, and our beliefs a disservice. By *beliefs*, I mean spiritual or religious faith but also faith in whatever values, systems, and traditions we hold dear, whatever gives life meaning for us. Having faith does not mean unquestioning obedience to a doctrine or code. On the contrary, the things in which we place value to the degree of *belief* deserve an even higher rigor of engagement and inquiry than the things about which we are skeptical. But when our beliefs are challenged, most of us instead turn away from those challenges. We attempt to safeguard the purity of our belief within the stronghold of ignorance and denial. That's not putting much faith in our beliefs, is it, if we believe our faith to be so fragile?

Having faith does not mean abdicating responsibility. In fact, it means *taking* responsibility for our values and how we live in accordance with them—or don't. Octavia Butler put it best: "Belief initiates and guides action—or it does nothing."[53] If the values we profess to live by are not the values communicated by our actions, we might have different values than we think. If we hold beliefs but do not act on them in our lives, they may not be beliefs at all but instead convenient fictions. That's not faith; it's a shell of dogma haunted by the ghost of belief.

Audre Lorde wrote that the spiritual is political because both arise from the place of our deepest feeling and greatest understanding.[54] She also encouraged "the intimacy of scrutiny,"[55] a small but powerful phrase that suggests scrutiny as an act of love, an intimacy of rigorous awareness. The intimacy of scrutiny cultivates a love that is brave enough to examine itself, a love that knows itself through and through, an antidogmatic love, an unflinchingly thorough love. *This* is the kind of love we owe ourselves, our values, and our beliefs. This is the kind of knowledge that transcends the secular and stretches toward sacred.

Alice Sparkly Kat, in their rigorously researched *Postcolonial Astrology*, interrogates astrology's foundations in white supremacy, capitalism, and patriarchy and asks us to reckon with them from a place of accountability. Kat does this in an obvious act of love, one that bares astrology's toxic roots even as it reveres astrology as a community-made subculture and spiritual practice. They write that astrology is not inherently special or magical, but instead that the magic comes from the community that deconstructs, re-creates, and makes it their own: "[Astrology] works not because there is anything magical about the language itself but because the act of not believing readily, of believing where belief has been earned, of listening waywardly . . . *is* magic. Astrology is not magic. The community that recreates it in the contemporary era is."[56] We might say the same about tarot. And that phrase, *listening waywardly*, is another one to savor along with *intimacy of scrutiny*. Listening waywardly is listening past the loudest voices in the room, listening to the whispers and the mumbles and the traces of melody, and of following these traces to see where they lead. It suggests that belief—real belief, *earned* belief—is not arrived at through straight lines but winding paths, and that magic happens on the margins.

Faith, then, is believing in something enough that you can face its flaws and work to heal them. It's believing enough that you don't run from the challenge but meet it with inquiry, respect, and openness to change. It is not a pristine dogma trapped in amber, but a faith with blood and breath. If we can work with the Hierophant in this way, then our beliefs, spiritual or secular, can come alive.

That's the work of this card. The word *hierophant* comes from the ancient Greek words for "the holy" and "to show." Rather than showing the one and only path to salvation, as was suggested by the card's original title of The Pope, perhaps in a radical tarot we can take the Hierophant to show us the values that we hold holy, so we may forge our path according to them. Or perhaps we can take it a different way still, that *we* show—we demonstrate—the holy through our engagement and our actions, by living in alignment with our well-considered values, by cultivating an intimate scrutiny, by listening waywardly, and by having faith enough to change. The practices we form today will be the traditions of tomorrow, and even these words will one day soon need revision. Wisdom is knowing that knowledge changes, and faith is having belief enough to change.

THE LOVERS: DIFFERENCE AND CONNECTION

Alternative Names: Eros, the Mirror,
the Partner(s), the Friend(s)

Domains: love and self-love, relationships,
connection, mutuality, choice, commitment

The Lovers ask us to delve into our beliefs about love, what it means to love and be loved, and how we participate in loving in our lives. This card is often pigeonholed into romantic or sexual love only, so let's set it queer from the start: the Lovers is a card about *love*, and love is so much bigger, broader, and deeper than romantic or sexual love only. We share love with our friends, our families, our neighbors, our communities. We can extend love to ourselves, though too often we don't. Romantic or intimate love can be shared between two people or many people, can be monogamous or consensually nonmonogamous, can be asexual or sexual. True love, real love, is not a finite resource that must be hoarded, nor is it a hierarchical competition. It's not a prize that is awarded and owned, nor is it a commodity that remains static and unchanged over time. Instead, to quote queer feminist author and activist bell hooks, "Love is an action, a participatory emotion."[57] Love is something we *do*, something we *practice*, and something that through our shared engagement with it can radically and positively change the way we relate to others, to ourselves, and to the world.

Unfortunately, not many of us are familiar with this kind of love. In a society where dating apps operate on snap judgments and love is a TV competition on a tropical island with a cash prize, we absorb the messaging that we must be a certain way to earn love. Many of us were raised in home or community environments where love was conditional, doled out in return for good behavior or compliance, so we learned to mold ourselves in exchange for the scraps of approval that pass for love. Queer kids know this all too well. In *Cruising Utopia*, José Esteban Muñoz writes about being "a spy in the house of gender normativity," describing how he learned to study and replicate the movements of straight boys after being mocked for swaying his hips when he walked.[58] I have a similar memory of emulating the girls around me out of some feeling that I was doing femininity wrong, some instinctual fear that I had something to hide.

A concept frequently associated with the Lovers is *mirroring*, which in its best form is a reciprocal action of recognizing ourselves mirrored in another person, a mutuality of connection through a common bond. When we see ourselves mirrored in the world—in our peers, our media, our politics, our social apps—we are validated and connected, and we continue being who we are with scarcely a second thought. But when we *don't* find ourselves mirrored in the world around us—or we find ourselves only mirrored as wrong, ugly, inferior, or unnatural—we instead are invalidated and disconnected. It becomes painfully apparent that we are different, aberrant, that we do not belong. Consequently, we can become one-way mirrors, our true self constantly watching unseen from behind the glass while our crafted persona desperately performs for love, acceptance, or survival.

This is why representation matters, and representation is certainly Lovers work. That feeling of affirmation you get when you recognize your life experience in a character on TV? That's the

Lovers. That sensation of connection and "feeling seen" when someone uses your correct pronouns, when you get the queer-to-queer head nod walking down the street, when you hear a stranger speaking your language, when a friend acknowledges a part of you that rarely gets love and attention—that's the Lovers too. And so is being the person who mirrors that for someone else. For those of us who seldom experience the connective and affirmative side of mirroring, this can be literally lifesaving.

In her essential book on radical self-love, *The Body Is Not an Apology*, Sonya Renee Taylor posits that many of us first experience body shame when we become aware of our difference in childhood, and then we learn to disappear that difference for the sake of belonging. Taylor points out that every *-ism* there is—racism, sexism, cis-heterosexism, ableism, sizeism, ageism, classism, nationalism—can be boiled down to distrust of difference. But instead of facing difference, we try to erase it. We try to bury it via assimilation, masking, code-switching, diets, Instagram filters. We try to ignore it in others by claiming we're "color-blind" to race. We claim no issue with queer and trans folks "as long as they do it in private." According to Taylor, ignoring difference only perpetuates the problem: "Rendering difference invisible validates the notion that there are parts of us that should be ignored, hidden, or minimized, leaving in place the unspoken idea that difference is the problem and not our approach to dealing with difference."[59]

The Lovers ask us to face the way we deal with difference, starting by facing the difference in ourselves. They ask us to give ourselves the unconditional love that we have not received and that we deserve as our birthright. They welcome us to step up to the mirror and regard what we behold there not with judgment but with compassion. We need to partake of this radical work because we deserve nothing less than love, and because the practice of self-love is the sturdiest foundation for loving others. Audre Lorde's "intimacy of scrutiny" remains applicable here. In the speech in which she said those words, she implored her audience to turn the intimacy of scrutiny on their own differences, because "it is within our differences that we are both most powerful and most vulnerable."[60]

Take a moment to imagine what it would be like if you could love the ways in which you were different. What would that feel like? How would you move and behave? How would you carry yourself differently? How would your actions, choices, and out-look change? And now, what if you were able to love difference in others too? Even when it really challenged you? And what if they could love the same in you? What then?

It's hard work, learning to love difference. It requires some rewiring to stop perceiving all difference as a challenge or a competition with one winner and one loser. But if we can do it, if we can even just *try* to do it and land somewhere close, how much happier, smarter, fuller, safer, freer, more creative, more connected we would be.

Love does not mean that we never make mistakes, however. It doesn't mean we'll never hurt each other, never break hearts or have ours broken. It also doesn't mean that we are never moved to work on ourselves, to learn, to change. In fact, it means the opposite. The connections we make with people who are different from us may hold up a mirror that reveals a side of ourselves we don't enjoy looking at. We may discover, for example, that we're not as antiracist as we thought, or that the language we've been using is subtly transphobic, or that we haven't spared a thought to consider how people with a disability can access our space or work. All of these are unflattering but truthful mirrors that have been held up to me. It's painful, but necessary. And if we are then able to continue to treat ourselves with love—and loving ourselves when we have done wrong is one of the hardest times to do so—we will invariably discover that we are motivated to learn, to change, and to become better in those areas, because that too is an action of love.

The same is true in our love relationships with partners, friends, and family. Love is not a happily ever after, but a happily *sometimes* after. We cannot possibly always be in a state of loving bliss. Love has ups and downs, rage and grief, loss and sorrow. Love also has joy and strength and grit and humor. Love takes work, reflection, communication, and, yes, sometimes it takes change. Not change in the way that Muñoz had to change the way he walked, nor the way I had to perform femininity; not change in the way that so many of us misguidedly enter relationships hoping to change the other person, but a different kind of change.

When we love, we open ourselves to being fully seen and known by the other person or people, and in that process we come to see and know ourselves more fully. When we love, we dedicate ourselves to the happiness, support, and care of the people we love and they to ours, not as a form of ownership or obligation but because our joy is intertwined with theirs for as long as our love lasts. When we love, we do not mold ourselves for those we love, nor do we expect them to be molded by us, but through the alchemy of love connection we invariably find ourselves changed in deep and meaningful ways nonetheless. As bell hooks said, this is love as an action.

hooks continues: "This commitment to change is *chosen*. It happens by mutual agreement. . . . True love *is* unconditional, but to truly flourish it requires an ongoing commitment to constructive struggle and change."[61] This, too, is essential in our Lovers work: choice and consent.* Consent means that when we love a person, we do not act to control them against their will. We understand that we are not entitled to their bodies, energy, affection, or attention, though we may hope they decide to share these with us. The same is true in reverse: we do not have to bow to our loved ones' wishes, conform to their wants, or share ourselves with them in any way that we do not choose for ourselves. Choice means that all parties involved have the power of free will at any moment in time, including the option to change our minds. This is true even when we make commitments, and that only makes our commitments stronger. We choose to love each other, to share

---

* One of the enduring esoteric meanings of the Lovers card is choice, especially of a moral or ethical nature. This meaning arose from the Tarot de Marseille, which showed what appears to be a man choosing between two women, and was later underscored when the RWS changed the scene to Adam and Eve in the Garden of Eden, highlighting Eve's choice to eat the forbidden fruit of the Tree of Knowledge. Instead of framing Eve's choice as humanity's original sin, I've always been partial to reading her choice as humanity's first act of rebellion: choosing knowledge over ignorance, the first step toward self-actualization. I've recently learned that this interpretation is similar to one held by many in the Jewish faith that the point of the Eden myth was not to punish humanity for not following the rules, but to teach us the importance of always questioning authority.

ourselves, to connect, to listen, to engage in the "constructive struggle" even through change.

Maybe we don't choose who we love, but being an active participant in that love *is* a choice. Many people run from love when it beckons, afraid to be vulnerable, afraid to experience loss, afraid to commit or be rejected or be known or know themselves. Others must relearn how to love after a lifetime of bad role models and mistreatment in the name of love. A lot of us will love others unconditionally and still not be able to give that love to ourselves. Choosing love is choosing knowledge—the knowledge of our difference and our similarities, the knowledge of all the parts of ourselves, the knowledge of where we can grow and change for the better, the knowledge of loss and pain as well as joy and belonging.

When the Lovers appears, it asks us to make a choice. Between knowledge and ignorance, between connection and disconnection, between being ourselves or hiding ourselves—the choice is ours. And the answer is built right into the card: whatever you choose, choose with love.*

---

* Would you look at that? I talked about the Lovers without leaning on the masculine/feminine duality or using heteronormative sexual intercourse as a metaphor even once. The gender binary isn't so intrinsic to tarot after all.

THE CHARIOT: THE PACE OF PROGRESS

Alternative Names: the Journey,
the Way, Process, Pathfinding

Domains: movement, pacing, process,
the journey, determination, focus,
progress toward goals

Like the Magician, the Chariot is about intentionally directing the stream of time, energy, and cause-and-effect by taking action. But while the Magician is the ignition, the Chariot is the vehicle that gets us where we're going.

Chariots were originally machines of war in the Bronze and Iron Ages, and they remained a fixture in victory parades and ceremonial processions long after their martial use expired, so it's no wonder that the Chariot card has carried meanings of victory, success, achievement, and progress since the beginning. But while many read the Chariot as a sign to put the pedal to the metal because victory awaits just around the bend, in my experience the Chariot does not so much ensure victory as counsel pacing and process. The card is not about racing or bulldozing through obstacles, but about applying all our faculties—intelligence, wisdom, willpower, and intuition—to the journey. But first things first: we have to know where we're going.

To know where we're going, we have to talk about progress. Progress sounds like a good thing, right? Forward is usually a better direction than backward, no? Controversial opinion: not really. On the one hand, progress via productivity is how we earn our worth under capitalism. It's one of the things that makes us feel good and accomplished at the end of the day. Progress is also the bane of our existence, stressing us out, running us ragged, and keeping us up at night when we're not making enough of it. Progress is what so many of us fight and long for—progress in racial justice, trans rights, and disability justice, progress in cancer treatments, the HIV vaccine, clean energy. At the same time, progress is also the rallying cry of politicians, industrialists, corporate executives, and tech moguls racing to build billionaire hotels on Mars. The industrialization that is literally ending the world as we know it was once called progress. Westward expansion and the removal of Native Americans and Indigenous groups from their lands was progress. It was during the so-called Progressive Era of the United States that the government began forcibly sterilizing people with disabilities, the mentally ill, convicts, and Black and Latina women in order to "cleanse" the gene pool of perceived "defects" and curb the growth of the non-white population in the name of evolutionary racial progress.[62] Nazi Germany cited the same kind of progress to justify the genocide of six million Jews, along with Poles, Roma, Black Germans, disabled people, and homosexuals. The nuclear bomb, too, was progress.

What, exactly, is progress?

I'm not saying that progress is a blanket bad thing, or that we should go back to some romanticized ideal of the Stone Age, but I am saying that we need to be more specific about what we mean when we talk about progress. We hold the word up as a trophy or wave it around like a golden ticket to a brighter future, but by itself all the word means is headway toward a destination. Are we truly considering whether that destination is somewhere we want to go?

The original Chariot cards were likely not meant to represent a war chariot but a ceremonial chariot in a parade, like a modern-day float, often shown in art to be boxy and topped with a canopy like we see in the card. Rulers and triumphant generals would ride in these contraptions to show off and be fêted in the parades of the Middle Ages and Renaissance, giving the card a flavor of pomp and circumstance as well as pageantry. Another theory is that the Chariot is not a chariot at all but a pageant wagon of the sort used in traveling medieval plays.[63] Either way, this presents an image not of true victory but a performance of it (kind of like social media). Through this lens, we can glimpse the danger and downside of the Chariot: the temptation to follow the parade, to go through the motions, to perform a brand of success and happiness that we too often mistake for the real thing.

Society sets out a road map for life that many of us follow unquestioningly. We graduate from high school, go to college, choose a respectable career, find someone to marry, buy a house, have 1.94 kids. There's nothing intrinsically wrong with this life path if it's what we choose from a place of informed and liberated awareness, but so many of us start down it by default because it's sold to us as the golden ticket to happiness. We progress from milestone to milestone without fully considering what kind of life would make *us* happiest and most fulfilled. Even when we veer from this predetermined path to forge our own, we often still chase externally defined metrics of success that aren't authentic to us: artists turning themselves into content-creation factories, queer people chasing cis-heteronormative suburban security, and women climbing the corporate ladder by emulating the patriarchy and its abuses. It's true that many of us must go through these motions for safety and survival, but it's important to keep an eye on the difference between what we're choosing for ourselves and what we're accepting because we don't have a choice. That way, we can have the awareness and agency to choose in accordance with our inner compass whenever we can. As author and social worker Jessica Dore puts it in *Tarot for Change*, "The obstacle course of achievement under capitalism isn't built to teach pathfinding, it's built to teach compliance with a present path."[64] We need to learn some pathfinding skills.

One of the things I appreciate about Pamela Colman Smith's Chariot card is her incorporation of symbols referencing all the previous Major Arcana cards—a conceit I adopted in *Fifth Spirit Tarot*—providing a hint as to what some of those pathfinding skills may be. Creativity, self-knowledge, emotional intelligence, accountability, listening, awareness, reflection, love. What if, instead of chasing some external ideal of progress, we gathered the wisdom of all the cards so far and put it into practice to move with purpose down our self-determined path? This is not progress for progress's sake, but progress in alignment with authentic purpose. If we set our maps by these stars, we'll find where we need to go.

But the image of the Chariot has another piece of wisdom for us. Smith's chariot looks rather like a concrete box, and it seems to be drawn by a rather lazy set of sphinxes who aren't in a hurry to go anywhere. Similarly, in the Marseille pattern the chariot is pulled by a pair of horses, but the horses seem either curiously fused at the hips or missing their back halves. There are Platonic interpretations for the Marseille horses, stuffy esoteric reasons for the sphinxes, and a variety of interpretations for every symbol on this card, but I think the puzzling effect of the imagery makes a strong point all by itself. Though we may feel like masters of the universe riding high in our chariots, there is way more going on than we can possibly comprehend or control. We might, in fact, be spinning our fancy wheels and not going anywhere at all. In her analysis of the Chariot, Rachel Pollack brings up the sphinx's riddle from Greek legend: "What creature walks on four legs in the morning, two legs at noon, and three legs in the evening?" The answer, of course, is a human, who crawls as a baby, then walks, then leans on a cane later in life. According to the myth, the men who couldn't answer the riddle were eaten.[65] When we lack self-awareness of our strengths and limitations, when we lack humility and reflection, we become the instruments of our own destruction.

In its worst forms, the Chariot can be power-hungry and righteously destructive, or an attractive but hollow performance of a happy life. In its best form, the Chariot is a beacon of hopeful progress and attuned purpose, urging us onward with confidence and humility, willpower and restraint, intelligence and wisdom. When this card appears, our challenge and invitation is to harness these dualities in order to direct our progress on our chosen path, as the charioteer does their horses. In a radical tarot, we might align this card with what adrienne maree brown calls "intentional adaptation," which they specify is not the oft-destructive instinct of action and reaction, but instead is "the combination of adaptation with intention, wherein the orientation and movement towards life, towards longing, is made graceful in the act of adaptation. This is the process of changing while staying in touch with our deeper purpose and longing."[66]

Change is not a word that I've seen attached to the Chariot a lot. On the contrary, most interpretations seem to focus on aggressive progress in straight lines. But all roads curve at some point. Many are riddled with bumps, and most of us must take detours and rest stops along the way. The best route may be blazing straight ahead, or it may take a hard left turn, but if we are in touch with our longing and deeper purpose, if we act from the inside, then we can trust that we'll find our way.

STRENGTH: BEASTLY ENTANGLEMENT WITH LIFE

Alternative Names: Nature, the Wild Thing, the Heart's Creature

Domains: courage, facing fear, perseverance, self-compassion, powerful feelings, the beastly self, the more-than-human world

Strength.* Way more accessible a title than some of the other cards in this deck, am I right? Classically depicted as a femme person standing over a lion and placing their hands gently on its maw, the card seems to offer a version of strength that is notably different from the steely authority of the classic Emperor or the competitive ambition of the traditional Chariot. This is a strength that comes from compassion instead of control, gentleness rather than force,** and strength of character over brute strength. In some ways, the Strength card is exactly as obvious as it seems, counseling endurance through adversity and courage in the face

---

* Strength is number 11 in the Tarot de Marseille tradition and 8 in the Golden Dawn/RWS tradition, swapping places with Justice. People get quite militant about which is the "right" number. There are good reasons for each placement, but ultimately there is no "right" numbering, because it's all made up! Use whatever numbers you want!

** The traditional French name for the card is, in fact, La Force, but the word translates into English as "strength." Like the English *strength*, *la force* can mean brute force, physical strength, and power as well as figurative strength through challenges or as a positive personality characteristic.

of fear. In other ways, it becomes more complex, growing hair, teeth, roses, and rhizomes the longer you look at it. Fitting for a card that features a wild animal, the first appearance of wildness yet in the deck. (The horses in the Chariot, I'd argue, are thoroughly domesticated.) In this chapter we'll follow that shape, getting hairier and wilder and more unruly as we go.

Many modern readers interpret Strength from a psychoanalytical approach, situating the lion as the proverbial "beast within" that symbolizes our most powerful feelings, our demons, and/or our "shadow self." The *shadow* is a term from Jungian psychology that refers to the hidden or repressed parts of our personality, the ones we don't like to acknowledge but must be integrated for us to become fully self-actualized. I won't be using the term here because many brilliant activists and linguists have noted that using terms like *shadow*, *dark*, and *black* to describe bad or negative things contributes to racism and implicit bias.[67] Instead, I'll take a cue from the Strength card's imagery itself and employ the term *beastly self*. *Beastly* connotes something untamed that prowls the wildest fringes of ourselves, something with hot breath, long claws, and a beating heart, something frightening in its unknowability but not necessarily *bad*—just wild, different, unexamined. For our purposes, the beastly self encapsulates Jung's "shadow" and more: all our parts that scare us, our hidden shame and fear, our innermost struggles and desires, and all our deepest feelings that seem too powerful to feel lest they rip us apart with their exuberant teeth.

In many New Age arenas, these beastly qualities are treated as either "good" things that one can embrace, such as sexuality or kink, or "bad" things that one can overcome, like jealousy or vindictiveness. But these characteristics of our hidden or repressed selves, like most things, don't usually fit into such tidy binaries of good and bad. If we look to Strength's iconography as a model, the person's loose grip on the animal suggests that this is not a matter of overcoming, obliterating, or even subduing the beast. Instead, it seems more a process of acceptance, respect, and intentional participation. An exchange is happening between the creatures on this card. The person does not try to change the lion into something else, does not try to cage the lion or kill it for its strength like Hercules or the warriors of old. Likewise, the lion does not try to devour the person for lunch, such as one might fear from one's most hidden parts and powerful emotions. The lion does not even bite. Instead, the two come into contact with reciprocity: exchanging a gentle pet, a loving lick.

We put so much effort into subduing our emotions that when they finally break loose, they erupt from the pressure. We spend so much time denying the inconvenient parts of our personalities, urges, and secret desires that they fester inside us and turn into hate, which we direct inward at ourselves and outward at those we perceive to be too like our secret selves. We bury our beastly selves in so much shame that their unloved bodies pollute the water table. It does not have to be this way.

In the Empress chapter, we talked about the immense, revolutionary power of feeling our feelings. The same is true here; in fact, commentators on the RWS deck have noted that the Strength person resembles the Empress. But unlike the Empress, whose range envelops all feelings but most especially the pleasureful and empowering ones, Strength brings direct focus onto the feelings that are difficult, scary, ugly. And Strength reminds us that we need to feel them too.

Strength calls us to face the fearsome parts of ourselves with courage and compassion, to become what Sonya Renee Taylor calls *fear-facing*. "Fear-facingness is not the absence of fear," says Taylor, "but the interrogation of it."[68] Why do we feel afraid? What's scary here? What are we concerned will happen if we look these parts of ourselves in the eyes? Why do we think we're so beastly? "Courage" has long been a primary interpretation of the Strength card—it has even been the name of the card in some decks—and examining our most deeply buried parts is certainly courageous. "It is damn scary," Taylor writes, "to probe the depths of the thoughts, ideas, and subconscious principles governing our daily lives. To be fear-facing is to learn the distinction between fear and danger . . . and assess if we are truly in peril or if we are simply afraid of the unknown."[69]

When we stop denying our beastly parts and begin to figure out how to work with them with compassion, wisdom, and respect, we often find that there was nothing to be afraid of after all. But to get there, we first must decide to brave the fear and find out.

Real strength, however, is not only the strength to face our fears, our feelings, our beastly selves, but the strength to not look away from what we find. It is the strength to not abandon ourselves in our most vulnerable beastliness, our difference, our hurt, our shame. It is the strength to extend radical self-love to all the parts of ourselves and the strength to extend the fullness of that love to others too.

Many tarot readers, including myself, have interpreted this card as "taming" our beastly selves. But I'm not sure docility and domestication are the goal anymore. Is Strength a call to *un*-tame ourselves, re-wild ourselves, and embrace the delicious feral ferocity within? Is Strength the strength to *tame* the beast, or the strength to *be* the beast? Neither and both. Sallie Nichols suggests the title *Strength* references the two figures *together*, not one or the other.[70] Seen this way, the strength is not the person's or the lion's alone; it arises from their contact and mingling. It's all about that point of contact where the Strength person's hands touch the Strength animal's mouth. Strength asks us to open our inner beast's jaws when it is good and necessary to roar and bite and gnash some teeth, and close them when it is good and necessary to employ restraint and tact and composure.[71] Like the Magician, Strength uses both hands, but this time the contact is up close and personal, not commanded at a distance through a magic wand or a pointed finger. This is not a magus directing energy to their will, but a human being having a direct experience with emotion, with struggle, with desire, with *life*. Instead of wrestling the beast, the person caresses its jaw, the most dangerous and scary part of it. As anyone who has had the privilege to befriend a dog or cat knows, animals *allow* you to touch their muzzles—otherwise, you're gonna get bit. What we witness here is collaboration, mutual respect, coexistence. Not control.

But we're not done yet.

While writing this chapter, it occurred to me—I'm ashamed to say for the first time—that there's something amiss with the dominance of the human in the card, the way they lean over the lion, however gently. The fact that it's classically a lion, the king of the jungle, the apex predator at the top of the food chain, is no doubt meant to suggest the supremacy or elevation of humankind over all animal kin, even over nature itself. This is a dangerous mindset to have, seeing as it has led to the extractive human-wrought abuses that have put the planet and climate in such dire jeopardy.

It also reveals another false binary operating within dominant Western culture and tarot interpretation alike: man versus nature. As if nature is a monolithic entity instead of a tangled riot of variance and variety. As if humans are separate from nature instead of intimately entwined within its tangle. The man versus nature dualism situates humankind at the center of everything and the rest of all creation as the "other," which must be tamed, fought back, corralled, pinned down, used. This dichotomy also extends to how we popularly conceptualize our own psychology and inner workings, perceiving the mind and intellect as lofty, civilized, and supreme, and our emotions and instincts as base, wild, and animalistic. Emotions become misleading weaknesses that must be denied, and our urges monstrous beasts we must cage up and control in favor of the cold, hard "truth" of logic.

Sound familiar? This is the logic of toxic masculinity that says, "boys don't cry." This is the propaganda of patriarchy that snickers that women can't hold positions of power because *what if they get their period?* If we follow this line of thinking a few more disastrous steps down the poison path, it twists back and becomes the political rhetoric of what is "natural" and "unnatural" used to justify homophobia, transphobia, racism, misogyny, misogynoir,* ableism, antimiscegenation, and more.

One radical application of Strength is to reconsider our very conception of nature, our relationship to it, and our relationality within it; to consider that nature may not be a top-down thing,

---

* Misogynoir is a term coined by Moya Bailey in 2010 to describe the unique intersection of misogyny (the hatred of women) and racism that Black women, transgender and cisgender, experience.

not a hierarchical taxonomy with humankind at the zenith, but something interwoven, indefinable, and complex. If lions are the king of beasts, what of the bacteria that live in the lion's gut? What of the fleas and ticks that snack on its blood? We've all heard of the web of life, but philosopher and professor Timothy Morton suggests conceptualizing nature as a mesh: "a nontotalizable, open-ended concatenation of interrelations that blur and confound boundaries at practically any level: between species, between the living and the nonliving, between organism and environment."[72] Tarot commentators have noted that in the Marseille pattern, the lion appears to be fused with or emerging from the person's lower body. In the RWS deck, the person and lion seem to be wrapped in the same flowered garland—entwined, as it were, human with beast with plant with environment. Enmeshed.

Perhaps both ideas are present in Strength: the human propensity to separate, dominate, extract, force; and the human enmeshment with the nonhuman, the more-than-human, the wildness and aliveness of all things. However lofty and removed we think ourselves to be, however hard we scrub the dirt from our houses and from under our nails, however horribly we have mistreated the planet and each other and ourselves, Strength reminds us that we are not separate from nature, from the wild, from stream or spore or stranger. We are the wilderness too.

THE HERMIT: THE OUTLAW PHILOSOPHER

Alternative Names: the Wise One, the Seeker, the Philosopher

Domains: contemplation, solitude, truth-seeking, soul-searching, the unconventional path

Historically, hermits were religious individuals who lived lives of seclusion and asceticism, often retreating into the wilderness to devote themselves to contemplation, meditation, prayer, and closeness to their god. Today, hermits have moved into the secular sphere as eccentric and often antisocial recluses; think *Grey Gardens* or Maine's North Pond Hermit, or sage figures like Yoda or Baba Yaga. The tarot's classic image of the cloaked, staff-wielding, white-bearded Hermit is prototypical Gandalf, Dumbledore, and every wizard you've ever seen on the cover of an '80s metal album. Perhaps our radical Hermit is somewhere in between: eccentric, wise, holy, unorthodox, and more than a little bit magical. A card for the original thinkers, social weirdos, and unconventional souls of the world, the Hermit invites us to depart the well-trodden paths in life and be brave enough, faithful enough, and strange enough to enter the wilderness and carve out our own.

While there are many archetypal wise, old men with beards to whom we could trace this card, my favorite is ancient Greek ascetic philosopher Diogenes the Cynic, contemporary of Plato and one of the founders of Cynicism. Cynicism the philosophy is not to be confused with cynicism, the modern attitude of distrusting other people's motives, though it is not completely dissimilar. Instead, philosophical Cynics prioritized living one's life in accordance with nature and with what is natural to each individual, often leading them to deride popular culture and society. This was certainly the case for Diogenes, who famously renounced all his material wealth and lived inside a barrel in the marketplace in Athens, where he would flout and mock social conventions in often humorous public displays designed to critique what he viewed as corrupt and immoral social norms. One of his favorite stunts was to walk through the crowded marketplace in broad daylight carrying a lit lantern or candle in front of him. When asked why, he would reply, "I'm looking for an honest man," the implication being that none present were honest or virtuous people.[73] This story has been captured frequently in art, where Diogenes is nearly always rendered as a hunched, cloaked, bearded man leaning on a staff and holding a lantern before his face—the very image of the tarot's Hermit.

Perhaps, then, the Hermit does not only counsel self-reflection and solitude, as the most popular interpretations say, but turning a critical eye on social norms and conventions, cultivating one's own ethics outside the influence of popular opinion, and generally not giving a damn what anyone thinks about it. This Hermit possesses a rebellious, nonconformist spirit, not for the sake of show or attention, but for the sake of living honestly. The only way to live a truly authentic, moral, and happy life, the Hermit tells us, is to live it your own way and not sweat the haters. With Diogenes as a guide, we can also see the virtue of having a sense of humor, because living an unconventional life often comes with struggles. It's easy to live your own way until someone comes along with their opinions and disapproval, and few of us are impervious to ridicule. But we do have a better shot at peace and happiness the more thoroughly we know our own mind and heart, and that is the point of the Hermit's journey.

The lantern-bearing philosopher was not the original prototype for the Hermit, however. The earliest decks show the figure of an old man, often leaning on crutches, holding up not a lantern but an hourglass. Names for this version included The Old Man and Time, and the card is thought to have represented exactly that: old age and the swift and unstoppable passage of time.[74] The card came to be associated with Saturn/Kronos, god of time and limits. In at least one deck, the 16th-century Leber Tarot, the card was named *Rerum Edax* or "Devourer of Things,"[75] a reference to Kronos, who famously ate his children, and to Time, which devours all in the end. This version of the ninth card is a smidge dourer than the truth-seeking spiritual recluse or the philosophical public menace, but it does make clear the stakes. What's the point of amassing immense wealth, societal status, and power when, as they say, you can't take it with you? So much of human endeavor is focused on chasing immortality through fame and influence, when even that will fade with time, or through the fountain of youth, when no creams or diets or fillers will cheat death in the end.

But we haven't reached the Death card yet. Here in the Hermit, we are engaged with that eternal struggle spurred by the looming figure of Death, that age-old question: Why are we here, and what does this mean? Whether we carry the hourglass and ponder time with the wisdom of old age, or we carry the lantern to search for authentic truth and how to live as an honest human, in the Hermit we are engaged in the pursuit of meaning.

The Hermit, then, offers a third path to spiritual knowledge.[76] We were introduced to the first by the High Priestess, who invited us into the mysteries of the subconscious and subjective spiritual experience: the inner path of intuition and personal gnosis. We encountered the second in the Hierophant, who offered us the established teachings of the ages for our learning and study: the outer path of tradition and external knowledge. With the Hermit we arrive at the head of the third path, where outer meets inner, where gnosis meets knowledge, where we leave the temple of the subjective self as well as the walls of civilization and embark on a wild and solitary adventure to seek self-defined meaning. We might call this the path of philosophy.

On the Hermit's path of philosophy, we are not searching for personal inner truth, nor for objective outer truth, but for a synthesis of the two, or maybe for a third thing altogether. Robert M. Place connects the Hermit to old woodcarvings of philosophers searching for the *Anima Mundi*, the "World Soul," the life force that vivifies creation and the essence that connects all beings.[77] In these woodcarvings, the Anima Mundi is personified as a woman holding flowers and sometimes a six-pointed star, as the Hermit does in the RWS Tarot, walking into the wilderness while bearded philosophers with their lanterns and walking sticks follow searchingly behind. "The Anima Mundi is invisible," Place writes, "but in his wisdom the Hermit knows he can find her by the evidence that she leaves. Although she leads him away from the town, the crowd, or from popular opinion, the Hermit follows his invisible guide."[78] This is not only Hermit as philosopher but as a kind of spiritual detective, resolutely investigating every clue to discover some greater truth.

Choosing the untraveled path is no small task in a society that rewards conformity and adherence to its straight-and-narrow (or broad and eight-lane) highways. Hermits are often people whose values or perspectives do not line up with the dominant society, making the Hermit a wonderful ally card for those who feel like outcasts and misfits. The Hermit can also show up as an ally for neurodivergent folks, reminding us that our brains are as natural as anyone else's and we do not need to conform, mask, or perform neurotypical behaviors if we don't want to. Hermits tend to be unconventional souls whose choices are sometimes met with confusion or disapproval from others. This was and still is the case for many LGBTQIA2S+ people who face discrimination at work, in housing, and from their families and communities, and who may decide to remain in the safety of the closet in parts of their lives. In these cases, the Hermit can be a powerful card for preserving, nurturing, and following our own light even when we cannot share it. The Hermit reminds us that our light is *our* light, our path is *our* path, and we get to traverse it in our own way, whatever that may be.

The Hermit can also appear for us even when we *do* have a supportive community, because some things just need to be worked out on our own. This was the case when I was figuring out my gender, for example. I mulled over it in private for months before I ever mentioned it to my partner, and for many months more before I brought it up to him again, and for more than a year after that before I first said it to a friend: "I think I'm nonbinary." I was surrounded by queer, trans, and nonbinary friends and supportive loved ones, but still I had to walk that part of my journey on my own. I needed to explore it and define it entirely *by* myself, *for* myself, so I could know it was wholly and deeply mine. So many clients of mine are distressed to see the Hermit in readings because they think it means they will be alone. And, yes, Hermit experiences can be lonely, but loneliness is not the point. The point is having the solitude to arrive at our own fully self-defined and deeply felt truth. Even if we experience some loneliness along the way, the strength of that self-knowledge is worth it in the end.

The Hermit's wilderness can be found in the barren deserts of the early Christian hermits, on the snowy mountaintop of the RWS, on a walk in the park, or in the living room of a city apartment, because this wilderness is not a location but a mindset. We began this work in the Strength card, where we grappled with our inner beasts and met their wildness with compassion, and now here in the Hermit we can walk through our wild and lonely places with courage and peace. The card does not require that we give away all our material belongings and take a vow of silence on a mountaintop, but it might suggest withdrawing from the world in a less dramatic way, such as moderating our 24-hour news intake, removing ourselves from a group dynamic that is confusing our values, tuning out the unsolicited opinions of others, or taking a social media break. If we've been raptly following a leader, movement, or belief system, the Hermit can show up to say it's time to locate our own, authentic path before we get too in the weeds following Hierophants. Group conformity in this way may afford community, but sometimes it is at the expense of individuality and honest introspection. Writers and artists frequently pursue mini-hermitages in the form of residencies, retreats, or the proverbial "writing cave" where one isolates to concentrate exclusively on a project. (Hello from the writing cave!)

This time of deep contemplation and soul-searching can be carried out in total solitude or in company, as long as we can maintain the mental space to mull over our thoughts independently of outside influence. Like the hermits of old, in the Hermit we turn our back on the distractions and opinions of the wider world to seek the untraveled path of our own original thought, because at the end of that path lies our truth, our meaning, our peace.

THE WHEEL OF FORTUNE: SHIT HAPPENS

Alternative Names: Change, the Cycle, the Middle

Domains: chance, change, forces outside of one's control, cycles, the simultaneity of opposites

As you may have sussed from the title of this chapter, the Wheel of Fortune is about all the things in life that are outside our control. This is the card of chance, luck, and purely random events, and the card of synchronicity, serendipity, and destiny. It's flat tires and meet-cutes, lotto numbers and late flights. It's rain on your wedding day and the rest of the Alanis Morissette song "Ironic," none of which is actually *ironic* but instead is chance, life, and the weather, but is still a very good song. It's all the seemingly insignificant movements that make up the grand design of a life, and it's all the larger forces that shape our lives but are outside of our individual control. In other words, the Wheel of Fortune represents the neutral and natural fact that shit happens and everything changes.

In the Middle Ages, the Wheel of Fortune, or *Rota Fortunae*, was a popular theme that illustrated the folly of chasing fortune and worldly power, which can be ripped away in a crank of fortune's whimsy. The motif appeared extremely often in medieval artwork and was almost always rendered the same way: Lady Fortuna, Roman goddess of luck, turning a large wheel to which multiple people clung. Typically, a king sat on top of the wheel and a beggar or old man was crushed below it, while on one side of the wheel a person rose to prominence and on the other a poor soul sunk to misfortune. These four figures were often accompanied by scrolls that, like medieval speech bubbles, bore the slogans *Regnabo, Regno, Regnavi, Sum Sine Regno,* or "I will reign," "I reign," "I have reigned," "I am without reign." Turning the wheel, Lady Fortuna frequently wore a blindfold, symbolizing her impartiality to whom she favors . . . or her indifference and mercilessness in regard to human plans and ambitions. (What's that old Yiddish proverb? *Der mentsh trakht, un Gott lakht.* Humans plan and God laughs.)

There's a dual implication here. First, that those in power will be brought low in the end, and those on the bottom may rise to the top. And second, that anyone who believes themself safe in fortune's favor is dead wrong. Some versions of the *Rota Fortunae,* including those in the earliest Wheel of Fortune tarot cards, gave the person on top of the wheel the long ears of a donkey, the rising person budding donkey ears, and the declining person a donkey's tail. Only the person on the bottom remained fully human. The point: only asses depend on fortune's whims. Or maybe: misfortune makes us human.

This card isn't only about misfortune, however. The Wheel brings good things too—windfalls, surprise opportunities, happy accidents—just as easily as bad. It also brings neutral things, the weird and random stuff that makes life interesting. Nonetheless, a lot of people have a hard time with this card—including me, a person with anxiety, complex PTSD (C-PTSD), and um, shall we say *light* control issues. When I'd pull this card in readings, I would look over my shoulder all week, waiting for the *Rota Fortunae* to come careening down the road to flatten me like the giant boulder from *Raiders of the Lost Ark.* Because listen: uncertainty sucks and change is hard. Especially when we don't choose it.

Perhaps ironically, it was the COVID-19 pandemic that changed my relationship with the Wheel of Fortune. That, along with two straight years of civil unrest, financial roller coasters, climate apocalypse, three family deaths, political attacks on my bodily autonomy as a trans person and a uterus-haver, and reality generally tearing apart at the seams. It seems counterintuitive, but it took being crushed by the Wheel to finally start figuring out how to ride the damn thing. (And therapy didn't hurt. Thanks, Charmagne!) The process will look different for everyone, but in case it helps, here's what has worked for me (or *is working*, because the Wheel never stops). I found it helps to acknowledge my anxiety, my fear, and my spiraling doomsday thoughts for what they are—*thoughts*, not realities—and say, "Yep, those scary, awful things might happen. And they might not." When I feel emotional pain, grief, horror, or sadness, instead of running from these feelings, I try to support myself in feeling them to the extent that I can while reminding myself that the feelings are not permanent. On the flip side, when *good* things have happened, when celebrations have arisen—and many have, even in these dreadful times—I am figuring out how to fully feel, appreciate, love, and enjoy them, even though I know they may slip away on another turn of fortune's fickle wheel.

I'm not saying that I'm cured—quite the opposite. I'm saying that I'm learning how to have anxiety, C-PTSD, the general stress and worry of living, *and* be happy sometimes. *And* find peace sometimes. *And* experience joy when it visits and appreciate it after it leaves.

Underneath the arcane symbols on most Wheel of Fortune cards, this arcanum is about the simultaneity of opposites. If we freeze the Wheel in time, it appears to have an up and a down, but if we let it roll we find that there is no permanent up or permanent down. Everything moves, and every point is always necessary and present. Many tarot readers have likened the card to the Wheel of the Year, which shows the cycle of time through the seasons: sometimes we are in winter and sometimes in summer; though they sit at opposite sides of the Wheel, both are necessary for the continuance of life. Summer in the Southern Hemisphere is winter in the Northern; both extremes exist simultaneously on the global wheel.

We can also apply this to our emotions and to the various happenings of life. There is no world populated by only good things. There is no humanity composed of only happy emotions. As hard as we might try, we cannot fully embrace our happy emotions if we cannot also accept the sad ones. Instead of enjoying the good times, we will constantly be on the lookout for the proverbial other shoe to drop, experiencing only a half-happiness in anticipation of a disappointment that has not arrived. But by accepting them both, by embracing the reality that shit happens and everything changes, we can enjoy the good times from a place of peace and gratitude *and* find resilience and perspective to pull through the bad times.

We might liken this to seeking the center of the Wheel. Comparative mythologist Joseph Campbell has this observation about the medieval *Rota Fortunae*: "If you are attached to the rim of the wheel of fortune, you will be either above going down or at the bottom coming up. But if you are at the hub, you are in the same place all the time."[79] Echoing this *Rota Fortunae* wisdom, tarot teacher Lindsay Mack says the tarot's Wheel is all about finding our center in the present moment. As Mack teaches, instead of bumping up and down in the tire of the Wheel, instead of being slung around into hurts of the past or fears of the future, we can try to find our center in the here and now.[80] From this center of radical acceptance, we can take on whatever good or bad may come.

Speaking of centers, the Wheel of Fortune is the center of the Major Arcana. It, along with Justice, marks the exact middle of the 22-card fifth suit, and indeed this card finds us in the messy middle of things. Here at the center of the Wheel, at the axle of the Major Arcana's turning, halfway to the journey to the World, we encounter the vastness of the process we are caught up in, the whirring number of its spokes, the swift perimeter of its outer rim, the steadily revolving center. We meet for the first time in the tarot all the things we cannot control in the wide, wide scope of life, in the immensity of everything. If you ask me, that's why later

Wheel cards, like the RWS's, look so damn arcane and confusing, because this card is to some extent about realizing that not only can we not *control* everything, we cannot even *understand* it all. Maybe things happen for a reason, and maybe they don't. Maybe there's no grand design, or maybe there is, but either way we can't possibly comprehend it. *And that's okay.* When we're at the top of the wheel, it is easy to mistake ourselves for gods. When we're at the bottom, we remember we are human.

The Wheel's radical acceptance should not be taken as an excuse to give up, however. Acceptance and living in the present do not mean we stop trying, stop caring, stop being responsible and prudent when we can be. Writing about the binary thinking that so many of us fall into, where every single thing is either a victory or a failure with no room in between, I think of what author and activist Rebecca Solnit says is missing: "An ability to recognize a situation in which you are traveling and have not arrived, in which you have cause both to celebrate and fight, in which the world is always being made and is never finished."[81] Of this world-in-becoming, ecological poet-philosopher Bayo Akomolafe says, "Everything begins in the middle. . . . The middle isn't the space between things; it is the world in its ongoing practices of worlding itself."[82]

This continuous traveling, this worlding, this place of middles is the essence of the Wheel of Fortune. This is its core lesson, that change never stops, that everything is always mysteriously becoming and unbecoming. Here, in the unfinished center, in the ever-moving middle, is where everything happens. Here is also where we always are—in the present, in the act, in the worlding, in the becoming—at least until we pass from this life. And who knows, maybe even then. As Sallie Nichols says of the Wheel, "Everything is becoming and everything is dying—not sequentially in time, but all at once."[83]

When the bad things *do* happen, when we fail, when change smacks us in the face, when chance bankrupts our plans, let us take the circumstances as they are, even while we work for better. We feel the pain, the disappointment, the rage, the grief, and we respond in the best way we can. We feel the good wholeheartedly and without fear, even in times of desperation. We may pause, but we don't stop. We are in the middle. We find our center. The world keeps worlding. We keep becoming. The Wheel rolls on.

JUSTICE: BALANCE DOES NOT EXIST

Alternative Names: the Activist, Accountability

Domains: morality, accountability, balanced decisions, discernment, honesty, creating change

If the Wheel of Fortune is about accepting change, Justice is about *making* it. When we read the card's title and see the sword-and-scales iconography that graces so many courthouse lawns, our minds probably go directly to the legal system: to cops, judges, and lawyers, to the people who enforce, make, and argue about the law. But Justice has little to do with the legal system; or more accurately, our legal system has little to do with justice. Rather, the American so-called justice system is an engine of *in*justice, one that disproportionately targets people of color, oppresses women and transgender people by stripping their rights to bodily autonomy, incarcerates individuals to turn a profit, privileges the white and wealthy in its courtrooms, suppresses the vote of actual humans while it declares that corporations are people, and literally gets away with the murders of Black and Brown people by police every single year.

So no, Justice bears little resemblance to the justice system. Instead, the tarot's Justice invokes something much larger yet more personal than the law, something that has nothing to do with police batons and parking tickets and everything to do with morality and action.

Morality is not a sexy concept. It smacks of Sunday school teachers, children's stories where horrible things happen to kids who don't follow the rules, and Puritans named "Abstinence," "Sorry-for-sin," and "If-Christ-had-not-died-for-thee-thou-hadst-been-damned."[84] (All actual Puritan names.) But that is not morality; that is fear-mongering and compulsory obedience, and that is exactly why in a radical tarot we need to take a closer look at our collective and individual moral foundations. It is standard to attach words like *fairness* and *impartiality* to the Justice card, but how do we judge fairness if not by the scales of our morality, by the balance of what we consider to be right and wrong? One could argue that fairness must be arrived at through *impartial* judgment. But how do we achieve the objectivity required to be impartial from inside our extremely subjective and inescapably partial human brains?

Scholar and author Tyson Yunkaporta, writing about applying Aboriginal cosmology to environmental sustainability solutions, calls objectivity "an illusion of omniscience," and "an impossible and god-like (greater-than) position that floats in empty space and observes the field while not being part of it."[85] Everything we observe can *be* observed only because we are in some sort of relationship to it. Every thought we think is passed around in our brains via neural networks that have been mapped by our life experiences, by our particular nexus of privilege and oppression, by the people we love, by the media we consume. True objectivity would require getting out of our very brains, which is not very likely. Yunkaporta suggests that instead of clamoring for an unattainable God's-eye view, we could simply accept that we are a subjective and enmeshed part of the field. From there, maybe we could start figuring out some real, sustainable solutions to our problems together, by listening and integrating multiple, flexible viewpoints instead of insisting upon a mythical, overruling omniscience.

If we apply Yunkaporta's line of thinking toward Justice, if we can mark the traces of our belongingness, our presence, our impact, our subjectivity, then perhaps we can begin to work toward a less "perfect" but more alive kind of fairness. Perhaps by revealing the subjectivity of objectivity, we can strive toward a justice that is not judged by a disembodied and illusory objectivity—one that is usually codified by the state and the status quo, might I add—but by an embodied and examined morality. Not by a floating God-mind but by a beating heart.

When I talk about morality, I am talking about the seed of respect, love, and care that has always existed in humans. I am talking about the invisible gravity of goodness within every person, regardless of creed or faith, that leads us to be kind to one another and help each other, even when it does not benefit us, even when no one's watching. I'm talking about how we strive to do right in the world, even though we will inevitably mess up, hurt each other, and cause harm despite our best intentions—but still we try. I'm talking about the bone-deep imperative that leads us to grapple with uncomfortable questions, to depart from the ideology of our religions, to stand up to power despite personal consequence, to get arrested for civil disobedience, to risk our safety to help a stranger. I am talking about the pulse of social justice movements, the drum beat of protests, the slow but steady tempo of meaningful social change.

The Justice card—and justice at large—demands that we never settle for a static and externally defined morality, but always weigh it against new perspectives and experiences to determine if our moral codes require adjustment. As author and civil rights activist James Baldwin wrote in 1962, "morality, if it is to remain or become morality, must be perpetually examined, cracked, changed, made new."[86] This moral retooling is why Christians can wear poly fibers and gay couples can get married, though not always in church. This is why we have the 13th, 15th, and 19th amendments to the U.S. Constitution, which abolished slavery, prohibited voting discrimination on the basis of race, and gave women the right to vote—though the majority of Black women and men did not truly have voting rights until the Voting Rights Act of 1965, and their votes are still suppressed today via processes like gerrymandering. This is also why we must acknowledge that the struggle for civil and human rights is *far from over* domestically and globally, and we must not let those moral scales complacently rest as we sit idly by.

Justice calls on us to read that record, and not only the versions of it that make us feel comfortable and good. In writing about the tarot card, Rachel Pollack says that "the psychic laws of Justice, by which we advance according to our ability to understand the past, depends on seeing the truth about ourselves and about life."[87] This is why tarot's Justice wears no blindfold, she says, in contrast to the blindfolded courthouse version. Justice requires us to interrogate our passively accepted morality, building on our values work from the Hierophant. As a people, Justice asks us to stare bare-eyed into our past and reckon with how we have been complicit, with the consequences of our actions or inaction, with what injustices we still profit from. As Baldwin and Yunkaporta both advised in different contexts, from opposite sides of the globe and half a century apart, we must listen to multiple viewpoints rather than hiding within illusory objectivity and (im)moral righteousness. We must, as Baldwin wrote, "[attempt] to tell as much of the truth as one can bear, and then a little more."[88]

In our personal lives, Justice calls on us to do the same, to reflect with unflinchingly honesty on our actions and behaviors, be accountable where we bear responsibility, and try to do better. Justice shows up when we are on the fulcrum of its scales and can make a meaningful change. As Pollack says, "We are formed by the actions we have taken in the past; we form our future selves by the actions we take now."[89] Here, we have an opportunity to tip the scales. Here, we can choose to learn from the past and act in the present to change our future.

A tarot student of mine who was also a dancer once said to me that balance is not a static state, but a series of constant, small muscle adjustments. This word—*balance*—is another term constantly attributed to Justice, but balance does not exist in the way we think it does, as some stable and constant point of harmony. Neither does Justice. Justice's balance is like the dancer's that my wise student described. It is an unceasing process of change, adjustment, and adaptability. It is deeply imperfect, and sometimes we will overcorrect or make mistakes. But Justice does not require perfection because perfection doesn't exist. What Justice does require is *action*. It requires *trying*. It requires becoming accountable for our actions, stepping into our responsibility, and imperfectly but earnestly trying to make positive change in our lives and the world. It requires fighting our complacency and examining our morality.

Justice is not a statue of equality forever in static balance, because balance requires movement. Justice moves.

THE HANGED ONE: BECOMING SHAMELESS

Alternative Names: the Dangling One, the Other, Sacrifice

Domains: waiting, sacrifice, surrender, being misunderstood or othered, nonconformity

The Hanged One is the card of the in-between, the liminal space of waiting, and the deep unfathomable waters of the unknown. Hanging upside down, they reflect a period of feeling stuck or powerless, but they can also mark a change or reversal in perspective that leads to greater insight, wisdom, and liberation. The Hanged One is not afraid to be different or go against the crowd, and they learn to weather the knocks and hardships this can bring with resilience and grace. They are the outsider, the Other, and the misunderstood, shunned for their differences and beliefs, for who they are or who they love. Though this experience can be a painful one, the Hanged One ultimately teaches us to not abandon ourselves for the approval of others, but instead to sit with the discomfort of being ostracized or misunderstood. Being liked is no replacement for being respected, and fitting in is no path to belonging.

From the earliest tarot decks, the Hanged One's iconography has always been nearly the same: a person hung upside down by the ankle from a tree or gallows. This style of upside-down hanging was called *baffling* and was originally a form of torture, punishment, or humiliation reserved for traitors, heretics, and those with unconventional beliefs, including Christians during the Roman Empire, Jews and Muslims in Christian Spain,[90] and those accused of witchcraft.[91] In other words, those who held beliefs that were considered a threat to the state-sanctioned ones. In Renaissance Italy, public portraits of people being "baffled," called *pittura infamante* or "shame paintings," were a popular form of character assassination and were likely the inspiration for this card; in fact, one of the Italian names for the card is *Il Traditore*, "The Traitor," and the Visconti-Sforza family just so happened to have a long history of traitorous ancestors.[92]

By the time Antoine Court de Gébelin, the first occultist to imagine tarot's mystical and unfounded ancient Egyptian origins, got his hands on a pack of cards in the 18th century, shame paintings were almost entirely forgotten. Puzzled by the upside-down positioning, he assumed it was a printer's error, turned the card around, saw a man treading on a serpent instead of hanging by his foot from a rope, and declared the card the Cardinal Virtue of Prudence—ironic, considering.[93] Others have connected the upside-down position to St. Peter, who asked to be crucified upside down to humble himself for denying Jesus,[94] or, in versions where the figure appears to be holding bags of money, as Judas Iscariot, who betrayed Jesus for 30 pieces of silver.[95]

Not counting Court de Gébelin's error, the connecting thread between these origins of the Hanged One is the same: shame.

Shame is not radical or liberatory. In fact, shame and humiliation are tools of oppression and control. Shame is wielded by the powers that be to keep people in line, punish those who wander, and enforce the status quo. Shame teaches us to hate our bodies, distrust our desires, and demonize our differences. It keeps us small, disempowered, and afraid, or it suffocates us with defensive and destructive rage and perpetuates the cycle of shame and abuse.

It's important to note here that *shame* is not the same as *guilt*. As shame researcher Brené Brown has noted, guilt is behavior-focused, while shame is self-focused. Guilt says, "I'm sorry. I made a mistake," while shame says, "I'm sorry. I *am* a mistake."[96] Guilt is feeling responsibility or remorse for having caused harm, which can be a good thing. As Audre Lorde wrote, "If [guilt] leads to change then it can be useful, since it is then no longer guilt but the beginning of knowledge."[97] Shame, however, is the enemy of knowledge. It sucks us into a self-perpetuating cycle of self-loathing, rejection, and fear. When we're in a constant state of agony and desperation instead of curiosity and connection, when we're focused on shoring up safety or seeking approval, when we're shutting down to protect ourselves, we can't access the openness required for learning, growth, and change—and the status quo is upheld.

Shame at its core has nothing to do with guilt or wrongdoing. Instead, shame is something we learn from a young age: when adults comment on our weight, when we're bullied for the clothes we wear, when we're chastised for being too loud, too wimpy, too brash, too soft. We then grow up to punish ourselves and others for failure to adhere to a mythical norm, which in American society tends to be white, thin, able-bodied, cisgender, heterosexual, and middle-to-upper class. As we've discussed before, this fear of being different is what leaks self-hatred into our bodies, what traps us into gender roles, what enforces archaic morality codes, and what underlies racism, sexism, homophobia, transphobia, ableism, and more.

What does this mean for the Hanged One? In a radical and liberatory tarot, we must unlearn shame. We must become shame-*less*, which means becoming unafraid of difference—both our own difference and others. When we become unafraid of difference, we become unafraid of defying group norms when the norms are harmful, unafraid of disrupting the status quo when the status quo is oppressive. In other words, we become unafraid of being a traitor to the systems of oppression and injustice that run on shame and run the world.

This willingness to stand against the crowd is not without risk. Our difference can be wielded against us. It can get us ousted, maligned, targeted. It can mean family and loved ones turn their backs on us.

This card asks us to sacrifice a certain amount of comfort, safety, and societal acceptance in order to strive for something better. When we link arms at a protest, we are each becoming The Hanged One. When we speak up to a co-worker when they make a racist or transphobic comment, we are becoming The Hanged One. When we unionize, we are becoming The Hanged One. When we come out to our family, we are becoming The Hanged One.

The Hanged One is an uncomfortable card, to be sure: dangling upside down by an ankle, arms behind their back, alone, exposed, vulnerable. Yet if we look closer, most tarot decks, including the Visconti-Sforza and some Marseilles decks, show a figure who is not thrashing or crying but hanging calmly. In other decks, most notably the RWS, the person appears suspended pendulously in a state of peace and near-bliss, a halo behind their head to symbol-ize enlightenment and divine grace. Not the vibe of your standard "shame painting."

With arms behind their back, our Hanged One's chest and heart are open, a position of both vulnerability and connection. Their crossed legs are reminiscent of the World, which is transcen-dence and completion. Like the Norse god Odin, who was called the Hanged God because he willingly hung from the World Tree for nine days to gain the wisdom of the runes, the Hanged One is suspended with a purpose. This isn't shame and punishment; it's a sacrifice for something better. It's a trial through which a deeper wisdom, a greater peace, a transformed and expanded sense of self emerges.

The Hanged One can reflect uncomfortable periods of waiting when it feels like our hands are tied, but it counsels us to find com-fort in the discomfort. The wait will be worth it, this Hanged One says. For trans, nonbinary, and gender-nonconforming people, this card can speak to the transition experience, whether medi-cal, social, or psychological, when it can feel like we're hanging in limbo, waiting for some future time when we'll feel comfortable, accepted, and/or correctly perceived. (It has been my steady companion through my own transition.) The card can connect to situations familiar to many marginalized groups, such as having a clear and justified perspective that is invalidated, sidelined, or gaslit by dominant social and power structures. When we are in a position of privilege, the Hanged One asks that we use it to help those who are more marginalized, to subvert the power systems that oppress them, and to take the heat when the establishment doesn't like it. Alternately, it can mean that our power to control the situation is limited, but that we can find solutions with resilience, imagination, and perhaps a shift in perspective.

An end to shame, an embrace of difference, a willingness to sacrifice comfort and privilege and risk rejection—none of this is easy, but all of it is necessary. To borrow a phrase from Audre Lorde, the Hanged One asks you "to feel the consequences of who you wish to be."[98] Will you be your authentic and vibrant self, allow yourself to be vulnerable, wait through discomfort, and take risks for what your heart knows is good and true? Or will you abandon yourself for the false security of conformity and acceptance into the status quo? Neither is without its consequences, but only one leads to your full and liberated self. Only one leads to a more equitable, compassionate, connected, flourishing, liberated world.

DEATH: EVERYTHING ENDS

Alternative Names: Endings,
Disintegration, Compost

Domains: endings, letting go, releasing,
unmaking, mourning, composting, transition

Death: the thing so feared that for centuries the tarot card bore no title, only the number 13, lest the very word draw death near. Since the birth of tarot, Death's image has been the human skeleton, pictured ready to reap souls with their scythe or astride the pale horse of the apocalypse à la the book of Revelation. The first tarot decks were created on the heels of the Black Death, the plague that decimated half the European population in the 14th century and was still rearing its sickly head in outbreaks during the tarot's creation in the 15th century. Tarot historians connect the imagery of the card to the danse macabre, a medieval allegory born of the Black Death in which Death personified as a skeleton whisks fine ladies and beggars alike into the mortal dance of death—a grisly message that death does not discriminate based on class, wealth, status, power, or even age.[99] This undoubtedly influenced the card's presence and appearance in the first tarots: a literal reminder that Death comes for us all.

In the New Age tarot of the past 50-odd years, Death has been stripped of its wicked scythe and sanitized into a comfier message of *transformation*. The icky dying part has been glossed over in favor of a beeline to rebirth. Butterfly metaphors abound. But this does us all a disservice by skipping the hardest part of the transformation process: the fear, the grief, the mourning of letting go. Death is a card of endings, of rupture, of dissolution and decay. Its skeletal visage refuses to release us from the haunting knowledge of these bones beneath our skin, of these bodies stitched from temporary blood and meat, of what will be left when our lives are through. When it appears in a reading, the Death card does not herald an actual physical death—the first thing all readers assure their clients when this card hits the table—but I do not think we should attempt to slip from its bony claws so easily. To understand the Death card, to really *get it*, we have to look Death in the hollow-eyed face. We have to join the dance, because we're already in it, whether we like it or not. So let us rip off the caterpillar-to-butterfly Band-Aid and dig into the meaty, broken heart of things, the thing we try to evade with metaphors of metamorphosis: the unavoidable, universal truth that *everything ends*.

Death is natural. Nothing could be more natural. We live it every year with the cycling of the seasons, in the death of fall and the grave of winter that precedes the rebirth of every spring. The food we eat was once living, and it died so our life could continue. Every moment we are alive, we are also dying. The cells in our bodies are constantly dying and replacing themselves (with less and less efficiency), so that every seven years we do not share a cell in common with our body from seven years before. Today, 36-year-old me is very literally not the same person who said "I do" to my ex-husband at age 26. This brings me comfort. At the same time, today-me does not live in the same skin that was last hugged by my late grandma in 2014. This brings me sorrow. In nature, dead matter is broken down by bacteria, insects, animals, roots, fungi. It becomes the compost that nourishes the soil so new life can grow. The energy of bodies becomes the energy of dirt becomes the energy of plants, and maybe one day some vestige of us will transform sunlight in a leaf, will breathe carbon dioxide into oxygen, will become food for another creature and nourish it for a day. There is happiness and sadness to death, but mostly there is necessity. There is nature. There is truth.

Indeed, the Death card has close ties with nature and the land. Though Death is popularly associated with the sign of Scorpio and the planets Mars or Pluto today, Death's iconic scythe is a symbol of agriculture classically associated with Saturn.[100] Before Saturn was known in modern astrology as the boss daddy of labor and limits, he was an agricultural god associated with the land, the harvest, and the fickleness of nature, which can give aplenty as well as take away on a whim.

It's not hard to see how Saturn and his scythe became associated with death and time. This throwback to agrarian Saturn also reveals a contrast to how we treat nature and agriculture—and death—today. Instead of doing the best we can and then letting nature do its thing, we cling and grasp and control. We develop weed killers and pesticides that cause cancer and poison our water. We tinker with plant DNA to make larger, more fruitful, more pest-resilient crops that cannot reproduce, so we patent them for a profit. We siphon the fluids from our dead and pump their bodies full of chemicals to delay decomposition, embalming them in a poisonous rictus of false life. We industrialize farming and death and everything else in between.

Alice Sparkly Kat reminds us that Saturn is "a wrathful god and one whose consequences become more and more dire the more they are delayed. By refusing to gamble with the agricultural god and seeking to pathologize him as that which needs to be controlled, we have only postponed payment for our ever-increasing gamble with nature."[101] Saturn's payment perhaps is climate change, is the extinction of species, is world hunger, is the continuously growing and vacuous disconnect between humans and the earth that birthed us and to which we will all return in the end. Éliphas Lévi's description of the tarot card is apt: "Death, reaping crowned heads in a meadow where men are growing."[102]

When we avoid the specter of Death or try to control it, what we are really avoiding is the reality of suffering. But, as we covered in the Wheel of Fortune, avoiding the hard things in life means avoiding the good things too. Who reading this has ever been in love and not also been gripped by fear of losing that love? Who here has achieved a dream and not been terrified of it ending? To love is to accept that we will one day grieve, and to grieve is to accept love's longing. Bayo Akomolafe calls for a new approach to life's pain: "Suffering needs a new onto-epistemology—not one that rules it out for eventual fixing, but one that recognizes its entanglement with well-being. Grieving must be part of [our] lives for happiness to become meaningful."[103] Suffering, sadness, mourning—these are treated as things that require solutions, require control, require *fixing* as if they are broken. But what if they aren't broken? What if we accept the pain of endings as a necessary part of the process of loving and living? Grief is as necessary to love, suffering as necessary to life, as dying is necessary to birth.

If we can face our deaths and endings in this way, then we might find that pain, loss, and grief can also be generative. bell hooks writes, "The place of suffering—the place where we are broken in spirit, when accepted and embraced, is also a place of peace and possibility. Our sufferings do not magically end; instead we are able to wisely alchemically recycle them. They become the abundant waste that we use to make new growth possible."[104] Our suffering becomes compost, but like compost, we must turn it. We cannot ignore it, defer it, lock it in a box or a concrete tomb sealed six feet under, or it will never become nourishment. It will only become rot. But if we *do* tend to our suffering, if we grab it with both hands as mourners do in traditions across the globe, pulling our hair and ripping our clothes and wailing in grief, then it becomes something else entirely. On the transformation of the Death card, Nichols writes, "Between the pruning away of the old and the maturation of the new lies a period of black mourning. In referring to this stage of the journey to self-knowledge, the alchemists used the term *mortificatio. Blessed are they that mourn* [emphasis in original]."[105] Maybe this is what Oscar Wilde meant when he wrote from his prison cell, "Where there is sorrow there is holy ground."[106] The ground of loss, the ground of sorrow, that is the ground from which creation springs.

Now we can talk about transformation. Tarot's Death appears when something is ending. Sometimes, this is an external thing—a relationship, a job, a season of our lives. Many times, it is an internal ending—a part of the self, an identity, a mask of the ego. The Death card often appears when we are struggling to let our endings happen, when we are cleaving to parts that are naturally trying to die. But if we refuse death, nothing can be born. In the end, death will come whether we accept it or not, but like the danse macabre from which the tarot's 13th card was born, Death invites us to look at it, to dance with it, to accept its reality and necessity, to mourn. It asks us to embrace our endings so we may let them go. Life starts with birth and ends with death, and the two are not so dissimilar. Death is painful and frightening and life-changing and sometimes it asks us to push, to accept what is ending and participate in its release, to be the doula of our next becoming.

If there's a part of the caterpillar/butterfly transformation cliché that is worth repeating, it is this: in the chrysalis the caterpillar dissolves itself. It releases enzymes and digests itself into a protein-rich goo, which then fuels the cell division that becomes wings, eyes, proboscis, exoskeleton. It unmakes itself completely, becomes its own compost, so it can then become anew. This is what Death asks of us: that we too digest the carapace of our former selves, become unmade, become liquid, become unrecognizable so that we may birth ourselves into our next stage, whatever that may be. Nichols writes of the Marseille card's scattering of human heads, hands, and feet, that Death is a dismemberment: "Death pictures that moment when one feels 'all in pieces'—scattered—the old personality and ways so mutilated as to be almost unrecognizable."[107] In Death times, we feel like we are falling apart, because we are. We are coming apart so we can come together in a new form, resurrected or reborn. Like the caterpillar, first we crawl, then we become goo, then we grow wings. As Akomolafe says, "A good journey is about dismemberment, not arrival."[108]

I said at the beginning of this chapter that in order to understand Death we must face it. But in facing it, we discover that understanding isn't the point. To live with Death, we must relinquish the fearful ego-driven desire to understand it. We must let go of knowing what happens next, and of defining a point or a meaning to the exercise. Accepting Death isn't about understanding it at all, but about letting go of the need to.

When Death appears, there are no guarantees that life gets better. There are no promises that the compost becomes good soil, that the crops don't fail, that our next self is better than the last one. There never were. But we can plant our seeds and cast our dice. We can let our deaths dissolve us and remake us. We can plant the bones and see what grows.

TEMPERANCE: THE HEALING IN BETWEEN

Alternative Names: Synthesis, the Healer

Domains: healing, patience, synthesis, fluidity, "wise mind," rebirth, combination, moderation

Of all the cards in the tarot, Temperance is certainly one of the queerest. We can observe this in the imagery: two cups, between which a gravity-defying stream of liquid flows, and in the angel's feet, one resting on water and one on land, straddling the boundary and the meeting place of two worlds. Temperance thrives in the liminal space between here and there, on the fringes of the known and the unknown, and in the center where the confluence of seeming opposites meets. They are the border-walker, the bridge, the angel of the in between and the spirit of fluidity. Temperance is nonbinary. A. E. Waite said of the angel, "I speak of him in the masculine sense, but the figure is neither male nor female."[109] Their cups symbolize the labels and categories in which we try to place people and things so they stay put and behave, so they become quantifiable and understandable, but Temperance shows us that nothing in this life is so tidy and docile. The liquid leaps unruly from its vessels, defying categorization and the laws of physics, bridging the space between supposed binaries, intermingling in a graceful riot. Life refuses to be artificially contained.

The work of the previous card, Death, is essential to Temperance's magical synthesis—and by magical I mean rule-breaking and seemingly impossible—because we cannot embrace life's truly nonbinary nature until we are able to face life's endings and sorrows. The nonbinarity of all things should not be unfamiliar by this point in our pursuit of a radical tarot; we have worked toward it in nearly every Major Arcana card, but especially the Lovers, Strength, the Wheel, and Death, unraveling our preconceived notions and rigid categories a strand at a time. Nonbinary is not just a gender identity; it is a way of thinking beyond artificial divisions and reductive categories, a growing awareness of our ecological, social, and spiritual interconnectedness, and an embracing of life's inherent fluidity and diversity. Coming on the heels of Death, the penultimate card in the Major Arcana's underworld line of unlearning, the rebirth of Temperance is a rebirth into a nonbinary sensibility.

The word *temperance* may seem an unlikely moniker for a card about the category-defying fluidity of existence. But, as ever, there is more than one way to understand a word. Temperance comes from the Latin *temperantia*, "self-control, moderation, restraint,"[110] which in turn is derived from the verb *temperāre*: "to exercise moderation, restrain oneself, moderate, *bring to a proper strength or consistency by mixing*, maintain in a state of balance [emphasis added]."[111] Temperance is all about the mixing, the combining, the synthesis of supposed opposites into a harmony, exchange, and flow. It is connected to the process of *tempering*, by which steel is heated to an extreme temperature to decrease its brittleness, resulting in a tougher steel that will not break as easily. Steel is usually tempered after it has been *quenched*, a process in which the metal is rapidly cooled to an extreme temperature to increase its hardness, demonstrating how opposite extremes can work together to achieve the best combination of hardness and flexibility.

In the card from *Fifth Spirit Tarot*, this quenching and tempering can be seen in the hot red/orange and cooling blue of the liquid arching between the angel's cups. The image of Temperance exchanging liquid between vessels is not unique to tarot; in fact, it is a very old representation of the Platonic classical virtue and Christian cardinal virtue of Temperance, who was typically depicted mixing water between two pitchers or pouring liquid from a pitcher into a basin. This iconography may reflect the practice of tempering wine, wherein water is added to wine to dilute its strength so it can be enjoyed while remaining sober.[112] Today we may consider this ruining a perfectly good glass of vino, but this practice of tempering arises from an ethos of moderation in which life's pleasures can—and should be—enjoyed, just not to excess or detriment. Instead of rigid self-restraint or abstinence, with which the word has come to be associated thanks to the anti-alcohol temperance movement, temperance is perhaps better understood as the heightened pleasure of experiencing all things in the right measure.

Robert M. Place describes Temperance as "the virtue that leads to balance, health, and harmony. . . . She does not represent the denial of desires but the satisfaction of desires in a way that is healthy and beautiful."[113] The word *healthy* is a battleground of many opinions, so perhaps instead of *healthy* we might substitute the word *enough*. In her book *Pleasure Activism*, adrienne maree brown writes about the liberatory power of pleasure as an engine and a goal for creating anti-oppressive social change. In a section entitled "Pleasure Principles," brown says, "*Moderation is key*. The idea is not to be in a heady state of ecstasy at all times, but rather to learn how to *sense* when something is good for you, to be able to feel what enough is [emphasis in original]."[114] I adore this idea and this feeling of *enough* in relation to Temperance. This brings the card out of the too-easily-righteous arena of portion sizes and calorie counting and into the realm of being *satiated*.

Temperance does not only deal with physical pleasures but also with the spiritual, emotional, and mental realms. Temperance is taking a 20-minute cooldown when you're becoming too angry to be respectful to your partner. It's getting outside to feel the sun when you're feeling depressed. It's the ability to put yourself in someone else's shoes and consider their perspective instead of doubling down on your own. Temperance knows how to feel their own balance, how to sense themself body and soul and intuit when they need a tempering force to restore harmony.

These days, however, it seems that we've forgotten the art of temperance. The modern world swings us wildly between extremes. We work until burnout, then recuperate vegetatively on the couch so we can work till burnout again. The "work hard, play hard" lifestyle is a rapid pendulum between stress and escapism. Emotionally, we plunge between feverish happiness and destitute despair, with little to no middle ground other than a numb kind of boredom that we cultivate so we can go to work, do the chores, and get through the grind of life. Moderation is forgotten in a landscape of crash diets and food deserts, tent cities and luxury housing developments, where the terrain between the lower and upper class is not an incline but a cliff. There is none of the mixing and combination of Temperance in the modern political arena, in which extremism and fanaticism reign and partisans dig themselves ever deeper into their trenches, exchanging only blame and explosive rhetoric lobbed like grenades. As a rather radical leftist myself, I do not mean to suggest that the politics of so-called moderates are the solution, as they only tend to uphold the privileged status quo, but instead to point out that the political system and way of life in the United States and many other Western nations in the early part of the 21st century has become hard and brittle to the point of failure. When steel is wrongly tempered, it will break.

There are more problems in the world than temperance can remedy, but Temperance's call to mixing, combination, and fluidity is a place to start. Temperance asks us to look for the sites of connection and confluence instead of separation and division, offering opportunities for dialogue, understanding, and mediation. They remind us, to paraphrase Audre Lorde, that our differences can be used as bridges instead of barriers. They invite us to, as brown says, "relinquish [our] own longing for excess and to stay mindful of [our] relationship to enough,"[115] which may help balance Western society's endless hunger to consume, extract, own, and sprawl, and replace it with a satiated abundance of sharing and enoughness. They break the false vessels of gender norms, racial stereotypes, international borders, and all the artificial categorizations of our dissociated Western society, and they let the fluid truth pour out.

As an alchemist, Temperance is also a healer. Temperance has been associated with the medieval notion of balancing the humors (blood, yellow bile, black bile, and phlegm) to achieve peak health and good temperament, which was considered to be one's mood or disposition and that was dictated by varying combinations of humors.[116] In the psychoanalytical view of tarot, Temperance can be considered to heal the psyche by balancing the inner self and outer persona or by opening the flow between the subconscious and the conscious minds.[117] In modern DBT we might liken Temperance to the concept of "wise mind," in which, according to my DBT therapist, the emotional mind and the rational mind meet and overlap to become wisdom. Social worker and tarot reader Jessica Dore aligns Temperance with another skill of DBT, that of "think[ing] in a way that can synthesize opposites rather than exacerbate stark divisions" and accepting that many seemingly opposing realities can be true at once.[118] As for opposites, poet and ecological mythologist Sophie Strand makes this powerful observation: "The opposite of patriarchy is not matriarchy. . . . The opposite of a human is not an animal or a rock or a blade of grass. The opposite of our current predicament—climate collapse, social unrest, extinction, mass migrations, solastalgia, genocide—is, in fact, the disintegration of opposites altogether."[119] In mixing their cups, Temperance doesn't just bridge opposites; they dissolve them into a queer and multiplicitous awareness, entangled and simultaneous, divergent and wise. Maybe Temperance's nonbinary consciousness and marginal magic is exactly the healing we need.

In nearly every deck there is, Temperance is pictured with wings, yet it keeps one foot in water and one on the ground. May we keep this in mind as we seek natural harmony in a human-made world of extremes, as we dance in the in between and revel in our unruly queer diversity. May we release our stranglehold on "either/or" and ease into the hammock of "both/and," rocking gently between the forest's trees. May we return nourishment to the earth and each other. May we eat when we're hungry, drink water when we're hot, wrap a blanket around our friend's shoulders when they're cold, offer our surplus garden harvest to neighbors and leave some for the birds, drink just enough wine, smoke just enough weed, cool off in the rain, feel our contradictory emotions, exist as more than one thing at once, carry the earthworms from the sidewalk to the grass. May we have wings but not forget the ground.

THE DEVIL: THE OPPRESSOR AND THE LIBERATOR

Alternative Names: Oppression,
Kyriarchy, Liberation

Domains: controlling/being controlled,
manipulation, oppression, addiction, compulsion,
avoidance, denial—or liberation from all the above

The Devil almost scared me away from tarot. I was in my teenage bedroom, door closed, probably listening to the theme song from *Charmed*, dealing my brand-new tarot deck onto my bedspread in front of me. It was perhaps only the third spread I'd ever done, and lo and behold, right in the middle: the Devil. My stomach dropped straight to H-E-double-hockey-sticks.

Being raised Christian in the Deep South, I knew tarot was supposedly "the devil's work"—along with sex, drugs, most mainstream music, and every other belief system besides Christianity—and, being a disaffected queer teen, that's half of what attracted me to the Devil's picture book (a.k.a. tarot) in the first place. But the image of Pamela Colman Smith's hairy Baphomet, goat-headed and bat-winged with an inverted pentagram on its forehead, leering over two rather-too-chill-looking naked humans in chains, was enough to break me out in a cold sweat. I didn't believe in Satan or Hell and had been strongly skeptical about God since the fourth grade, but I half expected the boogeyman to jump out of my closet and drag me down to the Pit. *I actually looked over my shoulder.*

Weeks would pass before I mustered the courage to read the cards again. My deep religious programming had done exactly what it was designed to do: scare me back into line.

That's the Devil. Not shaggy Baphomet, nor the pitch-fork-wielding Halloween devil. Not the Stranger at the crossroads, nor the smooth-talking Mephistopheles, nor the lusty Lucifer of the Witches' Sabbath. The real Devil is whatever controls, manip-ulates, represses, or oppresses us, and it doesn't live in a tarot deck but in our statehouses, boardrooms, and purity camps—and in us too. The Devil is the cultural earworm that whispers you're too big or too small or too loud or too weak. It's the corporation that runs you ragged for a paltry paycheck because if you don't like it, you can be replaced. And it's the capitalist system that calls that "good business." The Devil is the substance that was once your escape and is now your compulsion, and it's whatever drove you to need escape in the first place. The Devil is racism, homophobia, trans-exclusionary radical feminism, gender essentialism, misog-yny, nationalism, and any ideology that teaches us to hate those who are different from us or hate ourselves. When the Devil card rears its ugly head, it is not because the Devil is coming to get you—it's because the Devil is already here.

In a radical tarot, we can work with the Devil to identify what's pulling our strings—hence the puppet-master card for *Fifth Spirit Tarot*—and snip them. The real invitation of the card is awareness for the purpose of liberation. Because to learn how to be free, we have to know what's controlling us.

In most tarot decks from the 17th century to today, the Devil is portrayed as a part-human, part-animal beast standing or perched on a pedestal to which two people are chained. In Mar-seille decks, the two people, along with the Devil, are given the bestial qualities of antlers, animal ears, and tails. Some tarotists have pointed out that the three figures appear to be wearing skull-caps or helmets to which the horns and ears may be attached,[120] suggesting an illusion or a game of dress-up. Tarot scholar Paul Huson connects the Major Arcana sequence to medieval mystery plays, which were stacked with infernal sets and actors dressed up in elaborate devil garb. These plays, Huson notes, were begun as a means of converting remaining European pagans to Christianity, and later became useful tools of ecclesiastical instruction to the masses—a good way to keep peasants in line is to terrify them with specters of damnation in the form of entertainment, apparently.[121] The fearsome specter of the Devil was later leveraged to great (according to the witch-hunters) and terrible (according to everyone else) effect in the European witch hunts of the 16th and 17th centuries.

I lay this all out because it seems that the Devil has only ever existed as an instrument of control via fear and persecution by association. Underneath the Devil's costume, there's just a human—or humans—with too much power, pulling all our strings.

In her groundbreaking book *Caliban and the Witch*, Silvia Federici reveals in stark detail the role medieval witch hunts (which, by the way, barely had to do with witches) played in the transition to capitalism, functioning to put down rebels and dissenters who challenged the landowners and the state, to scare the general populace into submission, and to denigrate the humanity of the people capitalism exploits—namely women, colonized people, enslaved Africans, and immigrants.[122] According to Federici, the church and state used the idea of the devil, along with taboo sexuality and proximity to animals, to denigrate women and "other" them by association. Witch-hunters claimed witches copulated with the goat-headed, talon-footed devil and raised a variety of animal familiars, which they nursed like babies. Federici notes that "the surplus of animal presences in the witches' lives also suggests that women were at a (slippery) crossroad between men and animals, and that not only female sexuality, but femininity as such, was akin to animality."[123] The demonization of women and female sexuality in the witch hunts then dovetailed neatly into new criminal codes that outlawed nonprocreative sexual activity, including homosexuality, sex work, use of contraception, adultery, sex between ages and classes, and birth out of wedlock.[124]

Women weren't the only ones persecuted in the witch hunts. Gay men, who had been accepted earlier in the Renaissance, were now considered unproductive for the purposes of capital accumulation via reproduction, and therefore evil. They were sometimes burned with the kindling beneath a witch's stake. Accusations of devil worship were also leveled at the Indigenous peoples of the so-called New World, providing justification for their colonization and extermination in the eyes of the European colonizers,[125] and at enslaved Africans, justifying their kidnapping and enslavement for the economic benefit of the white American colonies. By the 17th century, "the Devil was portrayed as a black man and black people were increasingly treated like devils."[126] According to Federici, all of this—the oversexualization and animalization of Blackness and femaleness via fabricated association with a fabricated devil—provided the grounds for making their exploitation and subservience natural and obvious.[127] And that's how modernity in the West was born.

None of that was fun to read, I know. But that's the ugly work of the Devil card. The Devil asks us to use it as a mirror, to see ourselves dressed in our own devil costumes, relaxed and unbothered as the humans in the card appear to be, complicit in our own destruction. It begs us to wake up to the injustices of the systems we live under, to the oppressive control of capitalism and white cis-heteropatriarchy that have sexism, racism, heterosexism, and colonialism as their foundation and their continuation. An alternate name for the Devil might be *kyriarchy*, a term feminist theologian Elisabeth Schüssler Fiorenza coined in 1992, which refers to the combined power structure of numerous interwoven and interlocking structural discriminations and oppressions.[128] Another key concept that must be named is *intersectionality*, coined by leading critical race theory scholar Kimberlé Crenshaw in 1989, which highlights the nuanced ways that structural and political inequalities overlap to form different modes of privilege and oppression.[129] For example, queerphobia and transphobia affect me as a white, queer, and nonbinary person differently than they will affect a Black trans woman, who will additionally have to deal with racism, misogyny, misogynoir, and the overlapping ways all these tangle together. So often, the supposed "success" of a social movement is measured according to the white and/or cisgender members of its constituency, ignoring the continued oppression of its more marginalized members—for example, in the erroneous perception that gender equality has been achieved because there are (mostly white and cisgender) women in positions of power, while women of color and trans women are still suffering.* The Devil calls our attention to the intersectional and tangled ways we are each diversely chained to the same pedestal of the kyriarchy so that we may come together to fight for our mutual liberation.

In the RWS deck—and one could argue the Marseille decks as well, though more subtly—the Devil shows a visual subversion of the Lovers card. Instead of two people coming together with an angel overhead, we now see two people chained to a demon overhead. As we have seen, the Lovers is a card about relationships of mutual respect, love, and choice. In the Devil, perhaps our collective work is to become aware of the ways we have *broken* that compact of respect and love for our fellow humans, the ways we have *revoked* choice, or the ways we have been complicit in this, so we can begin the work of healing our relationship and working toward liberation together.

The *Meditations on the Tarot* provides another perspective on the Devil's imagery. Instead of two people enslaved to a demon, it suggests instead that the pair have *created* the demon: "It is they who are the parents of the demon and who have become enslaved by their own creation."[130] The author calls upon the occult concept of the *egregore*, a noncorporeal spirit that arises from the collective thoughts or beliefs of a group of people. An egregore is what happens when groupthink gains a life of its own—if enough people believe a thing, they can make it true.

---

* These versions of feminism are commonly known as white feminism and trans-exclusionary radical feminism (TERF), respectively.

Whether you believe egregores are an actual *thing* or a handy concept for the mutual mind of a collective, when the Devil card comes up, we are likely engaged with a harmful egregore or one run amok. The election denialism that culminated in the January 6, 2021, attack on the U.S. Capitol is an example of a harmful egregore, one intentionally created to spread lies and manipulate people's wills. Moral panics such as the Lavender Scare of the mid-20th century and the Satanic Panic of the 1980s could be considered destructive egregores that stoked irrational fears and prejudicial accusations among colleagues, neighbors, and family members. But these destructive thought-forms can be much more subtle and seemingly benign: some New Age "love and light" philosophies, for instance, offer their believers a passport to avoid dealing with conflict, difficult emotions, and social issues such as racism, cultural appropriation, and economic inequality. Also known as spiritual bypassing, it effectively renders their adherents complicit in upholding the kyriarchy.

Whether it's a malignant thought-form, structural discrimination, or something more individual like a toxic workplace, an emotionally abusive spouse or parent, or an addiction or dependency, the Devil ultimately shows up for our liberation. Perhaps this is why many modern readers have begun seeing the *good* in the Devil, interpreting it as sexual liberation, consensual BDSM,[*] defiance of social norms, breaking taboos, or creative release after a stifling situation.[131] According to Arthur Rosengarten, these may number among the Devil's "more adaptive aspects," which include "risk-taking, experimentation, sexual exploration, shadow awareness, paradox, playfulness, disinhibition, and even humor."[132] All of these involve breaking past the barriers of repression instilled by sociocultural codes of propriety—liberating oneself—and are the domain of the queered and radical Devil.

Maybe, then, when the Devil comes up, we might all take a page from the Witches' Sabbath, the midnight rite à la the imagination of the Inquisitors, where witches flew to the woods and the mountaintops to dance naked around bonfires and cavort with the Devil. Federici says that "class revolt, together with sexual

---

[*] BDSM is a portmanteau abbreviation for erotic play involving bondage and discipline, dominance and submission, and/or sadism and masochism.

transgression, was a central element in the descriptions of the Sabbat, which was portrayed both as a monstrous sexual orgy and as a subversive political gathering," one that ended with "the devil instructing the witches to rebel against their masters."[133] Sounds like a good time. That's what the burgeoning power structures of modern oppression were most afraid of and sought to exterminate. So maybe, then, we can reverse the Devil. By embracing our power, our solidarity, our sexuality, our defiance, our shaggy and bat-winged and rebellious liberatory spirit, we *can* resist. We can become the oppressor's nightmare—and the liberation's dream.

Gather your brooms. We fly at midnight.

THE TOWER: WHEN THINGS FALL APART

Alternative Names: Destruction, Cataclysm

Domains: destruction, deconstruction, catastrophe, chaos, sudden disruption or change, epiphany

Skyscrapers. Fortresses. Prison towers. Cathedral spires. Towers come in many varieties and many purposes, but one thing they all have in common is that they're man-made. Achievements of human engineering, towers are built for glory or protection, for vanity or office space, to keep people and things out or keep them in. We also build psychological towers of ego, defense mechanisms, comfortable ideologies, and belief systems designed to shore up our safety and keep out uncertainty, danger, and pain. Towers can take years to build—but only moments to fall. This is the card of upheaval, destruction, and chaos. This is when it all comes tumbling down.

In its traditional imagery, the Tower shows a tall stone tower with a crenelated top being blasted off by a lightning strike and two people leaping from its flaming ramparts. Tarot commentators frequently connect the card to the Tower of Babel, the legendary ziggurat built so high that it offended God, suggesting an edifice of pride destined for destruction. Robert M. Place links the entire last seven-card sequence (the Devil through the World) to the apocalyptic events of the book of Revelation,[134] with the Tower depicting the cleansing of the Earth in a rain of "hail and fire mingled with blood,"[135] promising apocalypse but ultimately salvation. Paul Huson compares the card to the popular medieval mystery play *The Harrowing of Hell*, which depicted the story of Jesus traveling into Hell after his crucifixion to liberate the souls in Limbo so that they could ascend to Heaven. According to Huson, in the set designs Limbo was typically a prison tower with flames shooting out of its top.[136] (Sound familiar?)

The destruction of the tower of Limbo was not a triumph of evil, then, but of good, not a punishment but a mercy. Observed in this light, the tarot's Tower becomes not a senseless destruction, not a bad thing, but a release, a catharsis, a freedom from confinement.

That said, the action of the Tower is never pleasant. Often, the Tower's lightning strike functions as epiphany, a sudden and powerful realization that we want something different for ourselves: a different career, a different spouse, a different life. While this self-knowledge is ultimately a blessing, the life changes that it may demand can be difficult, destabilizing, and even heartbreaking. Alternately, this epiphany can bring new information that reveals an entirely different truth beneath the reality we thought we knew: an unfaithful partner, a beloved teacher discovered to be corrupt, a reality check to our inflated ego, a secret come to light. This one can be especially tough, as it can undermine our trust in others or in our own judgment.

When our psychological towers come down, the resulting instability and anguish can be devastating. The lightning's flash of truth can be too bright to handle. Some people respond by building taller and stronger psychological towers and sealing themselves in with padlocks of denial—a plan that's about as solid as building on quicksand. We must face the reality that the Tower exposes, including all the anxiety and fear that comes with it, in order to figure out how to move forward in our new, lightning-blasted landscape.

When the Tower appears, there's no going back to the way things were before, but we might just be able to build a better world in the old one's ashes. But that's the territory of the next card, the Star, and we're not done with the Tower yet.

I've often seen it repeated that the Tower only tears down what already had a shaky foundation to begin with—heck, I've repeated it myself—but I think it's important to clarify that *that isn't always true*. The Tower represents any upheaval that leaves reality as you knew it stripped to ribbons, and that can be the destruction of ego towers and the revelation of hidden desires and unknown truths—faulty towers that were bound to fall—but it can also include tragic events like illnesses, deaths, and natural disasters. Sometimes bad things happen for no reason. Trying to pretend otherwise is only more tower-building, more erecting of comforting untruths instead of dealing with the heartbreaking reality that sometimes awful things happen. Period.

Let me demonstrate with a personal example. When my little brother was diagnosed with schizoaffective disorder as a teenager, it was certainly a Tower event for him and for my family. It meant his life would be harder than most. He would never go to college or have a traditional career, would probably never live independently. He'd never have what most would call a "normal" life. If my parents didn't have the resources to get him care, he would likely be unhoused. That was no benevolent lightning strike. My brother was not a tower that needed to fall.

As a Tower event, it did what Towers do: shredded my family's reality. It also pulled that secondary trick of the Tower's infernal magic and made us stronger and better people—more aware, more compassionate, more involved in mental health-care advocacy, disability justice, and social justice in general. But that does not provide a justification, does not provide a *reason* for my brother's disability. That's simply what we made from the rubble of our reality afterward.

If you have experienced similarly unnecessary tragedies, you will know what I mean when I say that *not everything happens for a reason*. Sometimes, bad things happen and we don't deserve them.

Sometimes, no personal development story arc will ever come close to making it "worth it." Sometimes, the wrecking ball comes and we never recover. If we are to use the tarot to reflect on the experience of living, then the tarot must be able to converse with these most difficult of subjects, with senseless loss and brutal devastation, with cruel injustice and unmerciful calamity, because this, too, is the stuff of life.

And that brings us to the Tower's studs. One of humankind's biggest struggles is with meaninglessness. We want everything to have a meaning. We want it all to be explained and codified so we can sleep easily in our Towers at night. We love a good theory of everything. But not everything has a meaning, and that's one of the lessons of the Tower too. Sometimes, the structures that burn are the houses we've lovingly built for meaning to live in, the temples we've erected to worship belief. When an event so surprising and brutal slams into us like lightning, we may survey what's left in the flickering light, our eyes still glowing with retinal burn, and find that we have lost our faith, our identity, our grasp on the future, our entire framework for understanding ourselves and the world in the blast. The scaffolding of reality turned to dust, we are left on our knees in a ruin of chaos.

But chaos is the birthplace of all creation. In Greek mythology, Chaos was the name of the primordial void from which the Earth was born. The *Merriam-Webster Dictionary*, with a surprisingly poetic bent, defines *chaos* as "the inherent unpredictability in the behavior of a complex natural system (such as the atmosphere, boiling water, or the beating heart)."[137] In science and mathematics, chaos theory deals with the behavior of seemingly random systems from which patterns nonetheless arise. We often forget that randomness is part of creation, that destruction clears the way for creation to come through. The Tower, with its four walls and orderly corners, is an archetypal example of humankind's attempts to impose rigid order on unruly nature. While order has its place, when it is unsustainable or too contrary to the wild emergent creation of nature, it will inevitably fail. We see it all around us: global warming, the energy crisis, industrial collapse, late-stage capitalism. The bad news is that it's all coming down, and it's going to suck while it's happening. The good news is that when the Tower has fallen, when we're standing in the ashes, we can trust that new life, new patterns, new creation will emerge.

In old decks, the Tower is named both "The House of God" and "The House of the Devil."[138] Maybe it's both. The Devil card showed us the chains so we could identify what controlled us, and now the Tower shows us the mechanism of our divine liberation. How? It reveals cracks and stirs our discontent. It shows us that this reality is not the only one there is, nor even the best or most stable one. So often when world-shaking events or epiphanies strike, we still attempt to cling to the decimated world with which we're familiar. We are afraid to throw ourselves into something bold and wholly new, afraid to take another Fool's leap of faith after our fall from the Tower. But the House of the Devil doesn't need some surface remodel—it requires a gut job. We cannot continue living in the house that abuse built, the house that lies and violence built. We cannot continue living in a house on fire. When the Tower appears, when we feel its discontented rumblings, it's time to make our exit—and maybe throw another match on our way out. Then, we can brush the ashes from our feet and follow our longing, our homesickness, our hope toward a better home under the silvered light of a new Star.

And for the Towers that didn't need to fall, for the calamities that happened for no good reason, I'll leave you with this: Sometimes things don't happen for a reason. Instead, things happen and we *give* them a reason as a way to soothe our grief. We make the reason, create the meaning, and then sometimes, as we continue living and breathing, hoping and trying, as we continue creating the future, we make it true.

THE STAR: HOPE HURTS

Alternative Names: Hope

Domains: hope, openness, fluidity, peace, acceptance, imagination, guidance, idealism

Ever since the first human gazed at the night sky and wove a story about what they saw there, the stars have been the playground of the human imagination. The stars are the home of the Gods, the vault of Heaven, the map of myth, and the atlas of omen and prophecy. Venus, the Morning Star, heralds the dawn. The star of Bethlehem led three magi to the manger. The North Star guides lost travelers. Stars are beacons to navigate our lives by and, with the help of astrology, might even cast glimmers of what's to come. After the Tower's destruction, the Star appears as a twinkle through the smoke: not a promise of success, not a guarantee of safety, but a glimmer of that uplifting and heart-wrenching and resilient thing called hope.

The Star introduces a trio of cards named after celestial bodies: the Star, the Moon, and the Sun. In ascending order of brightness as seen from Earth, these three cards pave the way to the Major Arcana's final destination, which, according to many tarot commentators and esotericists, is enlightenment—*en-lighten-ment*, meaning "into the light." In our radical tarot, our destination will defer from the classic Age of Reason brand of enlightenment in favor of a different, more entangled and emergent kind of wisdom, but the Star is still our celestial launchpad.

In the early decks, the Star came in a variety of designs. The earliest Stars showed a woman in blue, who probably represented a personification of astrology, holding up a star in her hand. Other versions depicted either one or two people holding astronomical instruments and gazing up at a star overhead, perhaps divining predictions from the astrological weather. One woodblock printed version showed just the star, front and center. The card's most enduring imagery, however, is its most fantastical: a naked person kneeling by a pool in a peaceful landscape, pouring liquid from two pitchers while eight stars shine brightly overhead. Like Temperance, the Star person straddles the boundary of earth and water, one knee resting on dry ground and the opposite foot in the pool. But unlike Temperance, who exchanges liquid between two vessels, the Star pours their vessels out freely, emptying one onto earth and the other into water.

Symbolically, this marks a breakthrough in overcoming dualism, moving from Temperance's synthesis of opposites to something much more expansive and fluid in the Star. The Star's liquid is no longer confined between two vessels but returned to the sea and the earth, reunified with the wild. This is a homecoming. No longer held within the binary prison tower of Cartesian dualism that fractured the world into mind versus matter, the Star returns us to ourselves, mind to matter, spirit to earth. The Star person's body forms a circuit along with their out-pouring vessels, a circuit that bridges elemental, physical, and spiritual borders, connecting earth and water and air, flesh and blood and breath, with the fiery stars burning overhead. These connections are catalyzed through another fire: the magical fire of *action*. In the card, this is modeled for us by the pouring out of their vessels—the action of *becoming open and fluid*. And that is the deceptively complex and wildly liberatory secret to the Star's teachings of peace, acceptance, imagination, and hope.

Hope is like water. It adapts to obstacles and flows past despair. When a person takes a bold action of hope, it ripples. Hope is an openness so wide open that, like the Star's overturned pitchers, it pours itself out even as it is replenished. This is a radical openness, an openness to all possibilities, good and bad, because hope is not the assurance that nothing bad will happen; rather, it is the knowledge that danger and tragedy are everywhere and the determination to act on hope nonetheless. The famed philosopher of hope Ernst Bloch wrote that hope is inextricably entwined with its defeat as a condition of its existence: "[Hope] too can be, and will be, disappointed; indeed, it must be so, as a matter of honor, or *else it would not be hope* [emphasis in original]."[139] In other words, hope is not hope if it's a sure thing. Hope is not hope unless it can be failed, wrenched away, disappointed. Hope does not exist *despite* defeat, devastation, or heartbreak, but *because of it*. Hope carries the reality of these outcomes in its heart. It is a paradox, a both/and, a nonbinarity of epic proportions. We might say that hope, then, is a fullness and an emptiness at the same time. Hope is a vessel that is unafraid of emptiness, so it pours itself out and thereby becomes full.

But hope comes hard for some of us. When the heart has been broken too much, when relief seems impossible, when trauma's wounds are not yet closed, the present can be too painful to open ourselves to hope's future dreaming. Some of us were taught from a young age that hope is foolish in this brutal world. Some of us find safer comfort in expecting the worst than in hoping for the best. Some may be too frightened or too weary to act on hope's bold imperatives. Hope hurts. And for us, the Star is bitter medicine that is nonetheless deeply needed. If this is you, the Star counsels healing, rest, and patience. This is a time for stitching wounds, relearning trust, and slowly—because it *will* be slow—discovering how to hope again. Hope's hurt is not fatal; its pain is like blood returning to a sleeping limb. We need to let the feeling return, as unpleasant as it may be, and then we'll find that we can move again.

But still, in a world like ours, hope can be hard. In the despair after 9/11 and during the Iraq War, Rebecca Solnit wrote an entire book, *Hope in the Dark,* on the necessity of hope in an increasingly bleak world. "To hope is to gamble," Solnit writes. "It's to bet on the future, on your desires, on the possibility that an open heart and uncertainty is better than gloom and safety. To hope is dangerous, and yet it is the opposite of fear, for to live is to risk."[140] Solnit pushes back against the overwhelming cynicism that traps people into powerlessness. She highlights numerous examples of activist victories that are small but substantive and that build to a transformative sea-change over time, noting that meaningful change is rarely instantaneous. Revisiting her work in the foreword to the third edition in 2015, 11 difficult years after its first publication, Solnit had this to add: "It's important to say what hope is not: it is not the belief that everything was, is, or will be fine. . . . It's also not a sunny-everything-is-getting-better narrative, though it may be a counter to the everything-is-getting-worse narrative. You could call it an account of complexities and uncertainties, with openings."[141]

There's that word again: *open*. Open like the Star person's body language. Open like their vessels. Open like the opposite of the Tower's high stone walls. Open like the fissures of a broken heart. Open like the depths of longing. Open like the smallest of holes that water will find to free itself from any vessel. Hope requires radical acceptance of what is, what was, and what might come, and hope drives us to fight for better. This is the Star's openness, their hope, and their wisdom.

Hope, then, is staying open despite agonizing uncertainty. It is striving for better even when you know things will probably get worse. It's positive action in the face of horrifying devastation. Hope is what resilience is made of. Hope is digging yourself out of the rubble with your fingernails and then helping the person next to you. Hope is refusing the easy lullaby of giving up. Hope dreams despite relentless disappointment, tries despite overwhelming odds. Hope is exhausting. Hope keeps us waiting. And yet, hope is the only thing that will save us.

Many assume hope is a naive thing, a thing of childhood and innocence that is gradually crushed out by the cynicism of experience and the grind of the day-to-day. But these people mistake hope for naivete. Hope is also not a product of victories and good fortune; that's confidence or privilege. Hope is instead born of failure, suffering, discontent, and the searing desire for a better reality than this one. It requires that we extend ourselves out from the present and into some imaginary future that does not yet exist, as Audre Lorde called for in her visionary queer Black feminism, as José Esteban Muñoz envisioned in his queer utopian philosophy when he declared, "The here and now is a prison house. We must strive, in the face of the here and now's totalizing rendering of reality, to think and feel a *then and there* [emphasis in original]."[142]

This is a hope that casts a star map of the future in wild, electric colors. This is a hope that refuses the constraints of the status quo's cold reality, even while the realists shout that hope is silly! Idealistic! Not pragmatic! But tell me this: if the dreamers, the visionaries, and the activists of the world were pragmatic and realistic, if they were not bold and fantastical and, yes, idealistic, if they did not *demand the impossible until it is possible*, then where would we be? (Who gets to decide what's "pragmatic" and "realistic," anyway? The status quo, that's who.) "Some will say that all we have are the pleasures of this moment," Muñoz wrote, "but we must never settle for that minimal transport; we must dream and enact new and better pleasures, other ways of being in the world, and ultimately new worlds."[143] The future always belongs to those who are bold enough to dream it into being.

So what radical new worlds are waiting in your dreams? What bold actions will you take, what desires will you chase, what new selves will you bare naked under the light of this new star? There is reason to hope, the Star tells us, and that reason is hope itself. The Star comes after the Tower because hope is not a gift we are born with, though for some it does come easier than others. Instead, hope is revealed through the ashes of experience. Hope is a seed that only germinates in fire. Hope is the defiant riot of life that grows in the ashes of destruction, that grows despite the knowledge that it may burn again—or that it *must* burn again, one day, inevitably, for the next world to sprout. And sprout it will, despite the sickle, despite the stomping feet, despite the drought and the flood. Hope is a rooted thing, and it grows toward stars.

THE MOON: STRANGE STRANGERS

Alternative Names: the Unknown

Domains: the unknown, the strange, fantasy, confusion, fear, illusions, feeling haunted

The Moon rules the nighttime and all its sly creatures: dreams and illusions, fantasies and fears. Beneath its silvery light, shapes lose their edges and morph into phantoms and fearsome things: a pile of clothes becomes a waiting man, a shrub, a hulking demon. The moon presides over the subterranean realms of the mind that we wander nightly in dreamtime and over privacy and all the things that go on behind closed doors. The sun usually gets all the credit for its life-giving rays, but the moon and its invisible gravity creates the tides and stabilizes the Earth's wobble, playing a significant part to make life on this planet possible. The moon's waxing and waning is the ancient timekeeper of the heavens, telling farmers when to plant and harvest, aquatic life when to reproduce, and birds when to migrate.

The Moon has long been associated with femininity, connected by the roughly 28-day cycle of menstruation, but instead of being a super cool thing that demonstrates the human body's link to the rhythms of nature, "rational" patriarchal society rebranded this as a negative and frightful thing. Prior to the Scientific Revolution and the Enlightenment, the moon was perhaps the most influential celestial body in astrology. One Renaissance friar who condemned magic and divination said it would be irresponsible to practice medicine without consulting the phases of the moon.[144] But around the time of the Enlightenment, anything the solar citadel of patriarchal intellect didn't understand was relegated to the lunar domain, including women's bodies and women's labor, humankind's animal nature, the wilderness beyond the cities, "lunatics" or people whose brains work in ways not privileged by society, and nearly anything considered strange, aberrant, or "other." Waite sums up this patriarchal attitude nicely when he describes the classic imagery of the Moon card: "The intellectual light is a reflection and beyond it is the unknown mystery which it cannot shew forth. It illuminates our animal nature, types of which are represented below—the dog, the wolf and that which comes up out of the deeps, the nameless and hideous tendency which is lower than the savage beast."[145] The "intellectual light" to which he refers is the light of the sun, which the poor, dull moon, being female, can only reflect. In the card imagery, the fearsome beast of the deeps of which Waite is so afraid is . . . a lobster. Enlightened, indeed.

The Moon has no gender (it's a rock), but like the High Priestess (who is also associated with the moon) and Empress, its designation as feminine by Western patriarchy situates the Moon as "other" and makes it a worthy ally for a radical tarot. The Moon is uncertainty, confusion, the magical, the uncanny. It travels in spirals and cycles instead of straight lines. It is emotion and intuition, instinct and impulse, the sub- and unconscious realms where logic fears to tread. It is the psychedelic dreamscape and the void of the eternal sleep from which the ego wakes screaming. It is difference and contradiction and the wild, queer diversity that proves sameness a lie. The Moon is anything and everything the rational mind cannot contain, categorize, own, or explain. These are what the rational lights of the human intellect fear most: the encroaching twilight of the unknown, the nocturnal world of doubts and dangers, the horror of the unexplainable.

Traditional versions of the Moon card show a giant crawfish or lobster (Waite's "hideous tendency") crawling from a pool of water in the foreground, from which a path rises. The path winds between a dog and a wolf in the middle ground before meandering toward the horizon, where it is flanked by two distant towers standing ominously under a huge moon in eclipse. There are no humans in the card, except for those suggested by the artificial towers. I will admit that once upon a time the presence of the towers puzzled me—hadn't we knocked these down two cards ago?—until I realized that I was thinking of this card too logically. The phrase *entre chien et loup*, "between dog and wolf," is a French expression for twilight,[146] and indeed the Moon requires a twilight mode of thinking. We see not one but two towers in the card, recalling again the dualism that has been our challenge for the entire Major Arcana, but they appear far off and almost haunted, like an artifact of memory appearing in a dream. Our viewpoint in the card is not focused on the towers, but on the water, the strange animals, and the middle path that weaves between them. Perhaps the towers are a reminder that most people hide inside the walled safety of the known world—but not us. Not at this point in our radical tarot journey. Rather, we are in the moonlit landscape with the creatures and beasts. We have left our Towers, and we know how to navigate by our Stars. Having made the acquaintance of our beastly selves in Strength, we are unafraid to swim in deep waters and howl at the moon. The Moon, then, is the experience of what goes on *outside* the towers of human rationalization and civilization, because there is so, so much else out there, and what a huge, strange world it is.

The Moon is an invitation to wander, to wade into strange waters, to stray from the straight-and-narrow path of society's supposedly linear progress. "Radical possibilities for transformation dwell in the unsure path," writes Bayo Akomolafe, "in the obstructed path—not the one cleared solely by human hands, bound to repeat the same oppressive timeline heading for the same apocalyptic Future."[147] In order to do anything differently, in order to create a future where life on this planet survives, we need to get a little bit wild. Indeed, a suggestion of the Chariot and its highway of progress is present in that curious lobster crawling from the depths and onto the winding path—the crab is the symbol of Cancer, which corresponds to the Chariot in esoteric tarot. But the Moon troubles the Chariot's momentum by turning the wheels backward. We can imagine the charioteer devolving in rewind from a fancy person in armor back into a crab, a creature that moves not forward but sideways, a creature that knows land but also depths, a creature that wears its skeleton on the outside and keeps softness and secrets under its shell. Like the pairing of domesticated dog and feral wolf, the crustacean reminds us of our primordial past when all life crawled from the ocean on its belly. It reminds us of how close we still are to the growling tangles of animal nature, a coat of fur waiting just beneath our skins.

This chapter takes its subheading from a queer ecology term coined by Timothy Morton. *Strange stranger*, a spin on philosopher Jacques Derrida's *arrivant*,* is a queered way of thinking of and perhaps relating to animals and other nonhuman lifeforms that humankind has thoroughly disparaged sheerly by virtue of their being not human. (Note again Waite's weirdly strong disdain for the lobster.) Noting that "Ecological critique has argued that speciesism underlies sexism and racism,"[148] Morton suggests swapping the oft-pejorative word *animal* with *strange stranger* instead: "Strange strangers are uncanny, familiar and strange simultaneously. Their familiarity is strange, their strangeness familiar. . . . Yet their uniqueness is not such that they are independent. They are composites of other strange strangers. Every life-form is familiar, since we are related to it."[149] Strange strangers highlights the relationality of our sameness and difference and exposes the weirdness of how we're all—human and insect and beast—spun from the same base pairs of DNA. "How things exist is both utterly unmysterious," Morton writes, "and unspeakably miraculous." We have far more in

---

* Derrida's *arrivant*, French for "a person or thing who is arriving," is a way of relating to the unknown, unexpected, or "other," from a stance of welcome and hospitality.

common with the dog, the wolf, and the lobster than we do with the stone towers. So why, then, do we identify so strongly with artificial civilization? Why do we hold nature at such distance?

Perhaps because of the long-standing human fear of the unknown. The High Priestess introduced us to mystery, and at this point in our radical tarot journey, we know that not all mysteries need to be solved. But Western society tends to perceive mystery as a problem, as something that needs to be cracked, solved, tamed. If we can't tame a thing, it's dangerous. We must exterminate it or put it in a cage. If we can't prove a thing, it doesn't exist—not God, not ghosts, not magic, not "irrational" and untraceable ways of alternative knowing—although science has repeatedly shown the limits of its own empirical knowledge by routinely blowing itself up with wild, strange, impossible discoveries. In her discussion of the Moon, Jessica Dore observes this paradox of knowledge: "Knowledge can expand what we see as possible, but it can also be like a box we settle into where we unconsciously defend against our own growth."[150] The more we know (or think we know), the more closed off we can become to the discoveries and creative currents of the unknown. Think back to the last time you encountered something that confused you. Did you become curious? Did you step outside the comfort of the known to try to understand it? Or did you shut down, close off, and retreat into your sanctum of certainty?

The Moon pushes us out of our box and into uncertainty because no creativity, no innovation, no discovery was ever found on certain ground. Here in the Moon we arrive once again in the place of knowledge's ending and are faced with the truth that there are simply some things we cannot know to the modern intellect's satisfaction—and that's okay. Dore writes, "To be in a state of not knowing creates openings, illuminates new pathways, and is thus ripe with potential, even as what we can't grasp yet may scare us." The Moon's seemingly irrational and dangerous openness is in fact fertile ground for new understandings, queer epiphanies, and unexpected liberations.

But for all its wonder-filled creative power, the Moon can also be truly scary. Aligned with the subconscious, it can dredge up things long buried that we may not like to revisit. The Moon is the realm of things that cannot be tamed or vanquished by logic, after all, and that includes repressed emotions, phobias, obsessions, and psychological difficulties. As a person with C-PTSD, the Moon has shown up for me to represent triggers, past traumas, psychological wounds, and all the "irrational" thoughts and feelings that crop up sometimes because of it. These are things that can't be easily put to bed with well-meaning rational lullabies of "it's over now," "it's not your fault," or even "you're safe." The Moon holds wounds that require a sideways approach, a deeper, slower, nonlinear healing. Here, the Moon's path between dog and wolf holds another kind of wisdom, recommending a path that stays in touch with both the wild and the tame so we can attend to our depths while not becoming completely lost to them, so we can find our way back to ourselves. Though we may wish the things the Moon dredges up stayed buried, their appearance does give us the opportunity to journey further in that healing. I say "journey" because healing is not a destination but a process, and when the Moon is involved, this process can happen in surprising and indirect ways. The Moon may bring challenges that transpire only in our emotional, psychological, or dream landscapes, which never break through to the surface of waking life but are no less transformative because of it.

The Moon confronts us with all the things we've been taught to fear, with the wild and the irrational, with the murky terrain of our own minds, with the glittering void of the unknown. But the message of this card is not to run for the hills, not to pinch ourselves and wake up, not to drown our fears or to shove the uncanny in a cage of preordained and tidy meaning. Writing on the obstacles we meet on the unknown path, Akomolafe says, "The challenge is not to go 'through' them and come out unscathed on the other side. The invitation is to know them, to stop for a drink, to resist unsheathing a sword, to be grateful for a wound, and to share a joke with shadows."[151] The Moon's challenge is not to fix these strange strangers, not to tame them, not necessarily even to know them in a codified and categorized way. The challenge is to be *with* them. To let go of expectations and experience the uncertainty and complexity of this strange, wild life. To grow and shrink to invisible rhythms. To taste the dream on your tongue. To let out a howl and wander toward the dawn. To realize we need not be afraid of the dark, because we are a part of it.

THE SUN: EVERYDAY JOY

Alternative Names: Joy, Illumination, Bliss

Domains: joy, happiness, visibility, freedom, authenticity, radical self-love

If the Moon rules the nighttime spaces of the unknown, the Sun rules the illumination of the known. The card follows the Moon not only because its illumination is brighter in the ascending celestial sequence of the Star-Moon-Sun, but because we must first pass through the realms of not knowing before we can reach any authentic knowledge. The knowledge revealed by the Sun is not the same knowledge bequeathed by the Hierophant and handed down as fact, but knowledge authentically gained through direct lived experience. In other words, the Sun is the wisdom that is only gained through trials and challenges, through integrating the Moon's dark nights of the soul, and through embracing the wild uncertainty and complexity of living this life. When the Sun card appears, it can mean clarity, joy, happiness, success, and good and promising tidings, but the real lesson of the Sun is not to invest our happiness in external things—achievements, material possessions, life milestones—and instead live our joy in the day-to-day.

Symbolically, the Sun provides light and warmth to the beings of the planet. It's the source of life and the center of the solar system. We literally revolve around it. But as we know by now, no tarot card is all good or bad, and the Sun can burn and blister as well as warm. The sun is the symbol of the Enlightenment, representing the dominance of reason over emotion and science above superstition, and the emblem of patriarchy. The sun has a long history of association with all-powerful gods, most especially monotheistic ones that burn out the "darkness" of polytheistic paganism. One theory of the placement of Jesus Christ's birthday on December 25th is to coincide with and absorb the feast of Sol Invictus, the "Unconquerable Sun" god of Rome. Through its illuminating properties, the sun is metaphorically associated with sight and visibility, and therefore with the all-seeing omnipotence of God and the state. The sun is a powerful and therefore politicized symbol. And, as Alice Sparkly Kat so aptly points out, light does not come without its shadows: "If the Sun's job is to illuminate the world, then it also creates an order of visibility and representation. The visual culture promoted by the Enlightenment encouraged some ways of seeing—inspecting, sanitizing, and seeing in [a] way that is oriented toward the capital—while discouraging others."[152]

When we talk about the Sun in a radical tarot, we also have to talk about the function of this selective illumination and its power dynamics in our society. In the Western world, our most visible and celebrated bodies are white, young, thin, and conventionally attractive according to the gender binary's beauty standards. Any bodies that fall outside those lines—Black and Brown bodies, trans and gender-nonconforming bodies, older bodies, disabled bodies, fat bodies—are rendered invisible and/or seen as a threat and subjected to violence. The illumination of cis-heteronormative whiteness spreads backward across history and into our education curricula with the banning of anti-racist accounts of history and books that dare to mention sexual and gender diversity. This selective illumination dictates the literal direction of our gaze: we look away from people in need who sit outside grocery stores and hold signs on street corners. We call the police to clear the "unsightly" camps of people experiencing homelessness in our neighborhoods. We pretend we don't see the person having a mental health crisis in a coffee shop. *We quite literally avert our eyes from realities we don't want to see.* If we want to talk about being enlightened, if we want to talk about transcendence and spiritual ascension, which is supposedly the goal of esoteric tarot, this selective illumination is not it.

In a radical tarot, therefore, working with the Sun means intentionally shining the light of awareness into all our cobwebbed corners and neglected places. It means facing the things that make us feel uncomfortable, because those things need our attention most. It means uplifting the voices and interests of the marginalized and giving up power that is held in corrupt and oppressive systems. One of the classic meanings of the Sun card is *freedom*, and as Ray Charles and Solomon Burke sang, none of us are free if one of us is chained. Truly living in the Sun means breaking the cycle of gaining power by oppressing others and instead seeding our power into community, interconnectivity, mutuality, and healing. It means not looking away, even when it's hard, because no problem was ever solved by ignoring it.

Leave it up to me to make the Sun a downer, right? But this radical work can be done with *joy.* Everywhere I look these days, joy is bursting through the cracks of adversity and creating phenomenal and positive change. adrienne maree brown is centering joy and pleasure in her activism in order "to reclaim our whole, happy, and satisfiable selves from the impacts, delusions, and limitations of oppression and/or supremacy."[153] Sonya Renee Taylor is leading the way to "expand and unleash the full power of radical self-love as a tool for social change."[154] Gender-nonconforming writer and performance artist Alok Vaid-Menon, who styles their name ALOK, is embodying freedom and joy in their fashion and public speaking because "trans people can actually teach the world transition is possible, not just between genders, but between paradigms."[155] In these times of injustice, grief, fear, and turmoil, the people who are changing the world in truly transformative ways are doing it through unapologetic pleasure, self-expression, creativity, love, and joy—through radical reimaginings and queer embodiments of the very attributes of the Sun.

In a radical tarot, the Sun also means bringing *our* full selves into the light, because coming into ourselves is a joyful act. In *Beyond the Gender Binary*, ALOK describes how they felt the first time they wore a dress in public: "I was twenty years old, but I had never felt more giddy and carefree when I walked out of my front door. . . . It felt like a reunification of my mind, my body, and my spirit—for the first time in a long time, I was able to be completely present with myself and the world."[156] *That's* the Sun. That joy, presence, and sense of rightness in body, mind, and spirit. That reunification of self. That giddy feeling of being *you* and being *seen*. At the same time, being seen is not without its dangers for some of us. A vocal advocate for LGBTQIA2S+ rights, ALOK speaks frequently about the street harassment they receive for dressing and moving through the world as themself, but they keep going because they know the transformative power of authenticity: "That's what the healing is going to take in this world, is if we stop living in someone else's fantasy of who we should be and we actually get intimate with who we actually are."[157]

If we're ready, the Sun calls on us to be ourselves *out loud*. Many times, I've seen the Sun come up for clients to reference coming out, even in situations where their disclosure was not met with welcome, because coming out is a Sun-aligned act of visibility and radical self-love. Dressing how you want to dress, loving who you want to love, asserting your pronouns, changing your name, getting that butch haircut, letting yourself flame—all of these are beautiful and celebratory commitments to our self-defined truth, no matter the world's resistance. Whenever we exist in our authenticity instead of folding ourselves into an externally defined mold, we are choosing joy over conformity and love over conditional approval. We are choosing the Sun. This is true for all of us, for *you* reading this, whether you're trans or cis or queer or straight, Black or Brown or white, skinny or curvy or disabled or abled. The Sun welcomes you into the full knowledge and love of yourself, mind and body and spirit, unified and shining and beautiful and whole.

In many versions of the Sun, including the Tarot de Marseille and some older decks, the card shows a luminous sun shining down on two children or, in the case of the RWS, a single, naked child riding a horse. Children have long symbolized innocence and renewal in the human mind. They are unselfconscious, open, and free. They are curious about difference instead of afraid of it. They have not yet learned shame. Nearing the end of the Major Arcana, we ironically discover that the secret to the happiness and prosperity we've been seeking has been behind us all along. It is in *un*learning and *un*doing the artificial binaries, the controlling categories, the oppressive machinations of modern Western society that our greatest joy lies.

The Sun, then, is *a return to ourselves*. In unlearning our shame and "shoulds," we relearn what it means to be free. However, like all returns, we never return unchanged. We can't erase the knowledge and trauma of the intervening years in which we learned to be self-hating and other-hating, shameful and ashamed. But that's what makes the Sun all the more radical—it invites us to be shameless, joyful, playful, and naked in a world that tries so hard to keep us closeted, anguished, despairing, and ashamed. We too often think that joy has a long list of requirements that must be satisfied before it can be attained. We think happiness is the top of Maslow's hierarchy of needs, attainable only when security is secured, power consolidated, and capital accumulated, and so we scrape, fight, and oppress each other to claw our way up that pyramid.

But the thing about hierarchies and pyramids is that the top is hard and pointy, with no place to rest. And the radical thing about the Sun is in realizing that joy, pleasure, beauty, and happiness are not acquired commodities but *lived experiences*. Happiness is not a promotion or a prize, but a feeling you share when you're with people you love. Joy is not a hermetically sealed bubble; it can coexist with pain and is all the brighter for it. Contentment is not earned through a paycheck or bought on a credit card, but lived through laughter, through dance, through a stimulating conversation, through helping a friend, through stepping outside in your favorite outfit and feeling good. The radical work of the Sun is in learning to let joy saturate our existence every day, even when grief and struggle are knocking down our door. "Resistance is the secret of joy," Alice Walker wrote.[158] And joy is the secret of resistance.

If we don't figure out how to experience joy and happiness in the process of living, with all the complexity and messiness and strife life involves, then we're never going to find it. There is no final destination of perpetual joy, at least not one in this lifetime. So don't wait for the pieces to fall into place, don't hang your happiness on some distant future event, don't delay your joy for an insistence on perfection. The Sun calls on you to live your joy *today*.

JUDGMENT: REVOLUTION AND TRANS-CENDENCE

Alternative Names: Revolution, Awakening, the Trumpet

Domains: revolution, awakening, transcending, transformation, higher callings

Here we are at the penultimate card in the Major Arcana. In a movie or a musical score, this would be the climax of the action, where the music swells to euphoric and portentous heights and the plot crests on a wave of triumph or tragedy, depending on what kind of story we're telling. The card's traditional iconography depicts the scene of the Last Judgment, the ultimate day of reckoning in the Bible, when the dead will be resurrected and held accountable for their deeds in life before God, ascending to paradise or being damned to Hell, accordingly.

But good news: the world doesn't end every time you pull Judgment. Instead, Judgment can be interpreted as a card of accountability and consequences, when the deeds of the past catch up to us and we have to deal with them, for better or for worse. Modern tarot tends to take a softer view, one that is focused more on

155

the angel's clarion call to awaken rather than the next step—to be judged. In my experience, Judgment is a combination of both. It's a time when the forces we have put into motion in our lives come to a head and we hear the proverbial call to make a significant change. There is a gravitational pull to the Judgment card, an inevitability, as if all the moments of our life have led to this one—because, technically speaking, they have. In Judgment, our actions, behaviors, and longings coalesce into something larger than us, an intersection with something like divine providence, a life-defining juncture where the choice we make has the power to rewrite our stars.

This card connotes big decisions, but they don't have to be *hard* ones. When Judgment appears, it usually comes with a magnetic pull to transformation that rubs up against our fearful clinging to the known. If that sounds familiar, it's because in Judgment we circle back to the cliffside territory of the Fool, divided between the reckless utopian leap and the limiting entrenchment of the status quo. Indeed, some tarotists have placed the historically numberless Fool after Judgment and before the World instead of at the beginning of the Major Arcana. Perhaps the impetuous leap into beginnings is not so different from the inspirited lunge toward the end. Judgment incorporates this Fool energy into its faithful and exultant rising up—or, we might say, *uprising.*

Judgment is a call to transcend and a call to action, a call to rise above the systems that have contained and controlled us and into a greater awareness and vision. In the card's most common imagery, an angel blows their trumpet from the clouds, calling the dead below to rise from their graves and be judged. The resting places from which they rise, naked and equal and rejoicing, are represented as rectangular stone tombs, and we can read these tombs as the boxes of binaries, dualisms, and confining categories that we've been sleeping in for so long—self/other, male/female, human/nature, mind/body, good/bad—the list goes on and on. It is an awakening and a rising into the multitudinous possibilities beyond the roles, norms, and structures we've been conditioned to believe are our only options.

The judgment implied in this card is not so much based on our pasts—though it certainly can be—but more predicated on *what we decide to do now*. The cross on the angel's flag can be understood as representing a crossroads as well as a meeting point, a point of confluence and divergence where we have the opportunity to choose tremendous change—or stick with more of the same old, same old. This is a momentous juncture, and heeding Judgment's call is also a great act of faith, because leaving our boxes behind requires believing that other ways of being are possible, even though these ways may not exist yet, or may exist only as a glimmer of trumpet sound on the wind.

On the collective level, Judgment has another, very pressing meaning in our time. Judgment Day, it must be said, is synonymous with the apocalypse in Christian eschatology. It's called the *Last* Judgment because it occurs at the end of the world. While it's probably true that the people of every age have thought the apocalypse was upon them, in the 21st century we find ourselves in apocalyptic times indeed. Wildfires rage in the Amazon rainforest and the Pacific Northwest, and in Australia, France, and rainy England. Floodwaters drown the hollers of Kentucky, drought-parched California, and a third of Pakistan's land. Rivers and lakes dry up and exhume our past, revealing sunken Nazi warships in the Danube, a prehistoric stone circle in a Spanish reservoir, bodies in Lake Mead, dinosaur tracks in Texas.* Human-made climate change is here and is already reshaping the planet and altering (and ending) life as we know it. "This apocalypse is real," Tyson Yunkaporta writes in *Sand Talk: How Indigenous Thinking Can Save the World*. "On the upside, apocalypses have proven to be survivable in the past, although on the downside it usually means that your culture and society will never be the same again."[159]

To survive what's coming, according to Yunkaporta and climate scientists, *we have to change*. We can't go on as we have been. And small, comfy change is not enough. As transgender studies scholar, documentary filmmaker, and queer theorist Susan Stryker put it in a 2019 interview, "If we live in an anthropogenically

---

* Every one of these extreme weather events occurred in 2022 alone. With the exception of the wildfires, which now occur with unprecedented devastation in the Amazon, Australia, and the American West nearly every year.

changing climate, one way to address that is to change what it means to be human. And so [we can] imagine a human subject that desires differently, that imagines its relationship to the environment differently, that imagines sociality to be different, has a different relationship to technology and embodiment."[160] Judgment meets us at this moment of radical transformation, calling on us to imagine new and emergent ways of relating to ourselves, each other, and the more-than-human world, to enact different ways of consuming, working, living, and to embody what Yunkaporta calls "transitional ways of being"[161]—something that trans and gender-nonconforming people like Stryker have some experience in. "These are the things that we're talking about with trans," she says. "To make that gender transition, you confront the possibilities and potentials and terrors and dangers of what it means to radically transform."[162] Judgment asks us to do the same in our own ways both personally and collectively, to face our fears of the unknown on the other side of transformation and embrace the unknown as a matrix of fantastic possibility. To devote ourselves to the transition. The future demands transformation.

On the individual level, Judgment appears when we "hear the call" of a new purpose, prefacing personal transformations, career changes, or new focuses in life. It can show up during big life transitions—divorces and breakups, marriages and commitments, major moves, becoming a parent or an empty nester, retirement—because these are threshold moments where we hold massive potential to reinvent our lives. Often, the changes for which Judgment calls are ones that the people around us don't understand—gender transition, nontraditional career choices, nonmonogamous relationship styles—leaving us feeling quite literally *judged*. Sometimes, Judgment's call defies common sense. I pulled Judgment constantly when I quit my job, gave away everything that wouldn't fit in my compact car, and embarked on a cross-country road trip to start a new life on the West Coast with no employment or apartment lined up, and all while I was going through a divorce. Everyone thought I'd lost my mind. But despite the cacophony of unsolicited opinions and well-meaning concern, the decision felt *right* in that rare cosmic way that happens rarely in life, so I followed that feeling instead of succumbing to fear. Now, five years later, I can absolutely confirm that the move was the right choice, one that radically changed my life for the better and launched me into revelation after revelation about who I am, what I can do, and how I want to live my life.

Judgment's call wouldn't be momentous, after all, if it was safe and easy. Judgment asks us to choose something new and bold enough to scare us, to choose risk over safety and possibility over predetermination. Judgment calls on *you* to make the choice about what is right for your life, regardless of the rules on "how it's done" and the opinions on "how it's always been." Creating a new world always requires departure from the paradigms of the old one— otherwise it's just the same old house with a new coat of paint.

Judgment is similar to Justice in that it involves reckoning and choice, but where Justice emphasizes morality, discernment, and personal accountability in taking incremental action for change, Judgment emphasizes a call to something greater. Judgment shifts realities, shakes us awake, and invites us into radical transformations and world-altering change. In this way, Judgment can feel like a combination of Justice's accountability with the Tower's regime-toppling seismic epiphany, but in the Tower the cataclysm is not chosen, while in Judgment the upheaval is consciously risen to and claimed. Judgment is a *revolution*. It incorporates the binary-transcending magic of Temperance and the soul-rightness of the Sun, along with a healthy dose of the Star's utopian visionary dreaming. Judgment calls us to liberate ourselves (the Devil) from our constructed boxes (or Towers) and rise with hope (the Star) into the unknown (the Moon) in pursuit of our joy (the Sun). Truly, Judgment marks a culmination of all the preceding cards, a moment of critical mass where reality ruptures and a new, transformative World breaks through.

But we're not in the World yet. We are still in the midst of the action, surfing on the tension of the moment of change. We can choose to refuse Judgment's call, and maybe it will come again when we are more ready—or maybe it won't. Or, we can rise to meet a different destiny. The choice is ours.

"The time has come," human rights and environmental activist and author Arundhati Roy famously wrote. "Another world is not only possible, she's on her way. Maybe many of us won't be here to greet her, but on a quiet day, if I listen very carefully, I can hear her breathing."[163]

The trumpet sounds. Do you hear it?

THE WORLD: BECOMING UTOPIA

Alternative Names: Utopia

Domains: journeys, completions, closure, enactment, embodiment, actualization, end of one chapter and the beginning of the next

Here we are at the end of the journey. The final card in the Major Arcana is called The World, ironically naming the place we've been all along. The title could refer to the planet, to the Earth as a being or organism, or to the wider world outside our fences. It could allude to the nature of existence and reality, to the universe or the macrocosm, or to a new vision of the world after the awakenings and transformations of the previous card, Judgment. The oldest recorded divinatory meaning of the card, from a Bolognese manuscript dated before 1750, gives the World's meaning, somewhat prosaically, as a "long journey."[164] The World's meaning as *journey* or *travel* has stuck around, and while it might seem rather uninspired on the surface, what have we been doing this whole time if not taking a journey through the Major Arcana, also known as The Fool's Journey?

A journey is no trip to the grocery store; it's something much bigger—a quest, an expedition, an odyssey wherein our movement is much more than locational. Bayo Akomolafe reminds us, "Journeys are not the tame servants that bear you from one point to another. Journeys are how things become different."[165] As the final card in the Major Arcana, the World suggests conclusions, completions, a journey completed. But, having been through the Wheel, Death, the Tower, and Judgment, we know well that endings never stay still but wriggle with new life emerging. So here, in the World, we consider how we've been changed, how we've become different, and we look forward to what we might still change, what our world might still become.

The most prevalent version of the World is the one from the Tarot de Marseille and later the RWS Tarot. This version shows a nude person who appears to be dancing in midair, surrounded by a laurel wreath and watched over by four creatures—a lion, a bull, an eagle, and a person—one in each corner of the card. The card design, like so much of the tarot's symbolism, has Christian roots, this time in a standard Christian icon known as Christ in Majesty. Modeled after descriptions from the revelation of Christ enthroned in Heaven, Jesus is pictured seated in the center of the frame, surrounded by a pointed oval or almond shape called a *mandorla,* and flanked by a man, lion, bull, and eagle in the four corners. These four beings are the "four living creatures" of Ezekiel that hold up the throne of God, and in Christian symbolism are also aligned with the four evangelists of the Gospels, corresponding to Matthew, Mark, Luke, and John, respectively. In modern tarot, the four creatures are most often attributed to the four classical elements and the four fixed signs of the zodiac: Aquarius as the man and air, Leo as the lion and fire, Taurus as the bull and earth, and Scorpio as the eagle and water.*

Robert M. Place points out that this arrangement of the four elements around a central figure is an old pattern predating Christianity called a *quincunx*, in which figures representing the fourfold physical world surround a fifth sacred figure in the middle.[166]

---

* The eagle is considered to be a higher version of Scorpio's scorpion in astrology and esotericism.

He connects the quincunx pattern to Buddhist mandalas, representations of the Orphic creation myth of Phanes, and images of the alchemical Anima Mundi, which was discussed in the Hermit chapter as the World Soul, the animating essence of all life and creation. The World Soul is also called the *quintessence* or the "fifth essence," from which *Fifth Spirit Tarot* got its name.

This version of the World card, with its nude dancer supported by the four elements of the Earth and the four fixed constellations of the heavens, shows us a slyly subversive vision of the sacred, one that replaces the male Jesus with a female-presenting figure* dancing on his throne, symbolically ousting the patriarchal judgment of Christ in favor of the transcendent and joyous soul liberated from binaries and in harmony with all creation. We have seen this pattern before in the RWS Wheel of Fortune, which features the four creatures or four elements in its corners, and so the World calls us back to the Wheel's cycles of change. Here in the World, it is not that change has *finished*—it never will—but that we are in tune with its rhythms, dancing to its beat. The dancer is the World Soul and is *us*, risen from our boxes in Judgment and twirling in our newfound freedom, aligned with our inner truth and outer purpose, changed and changing, creating new worlds.

There's another version of the World card worth talking about in a radical tarot. In many of the earliest 15th- and 16th-century decks, well before the World as dancer came onto the scene, the World was depicted as a walled city inside a globe, held up by two cherubs or presided over by a woman or angel. Its position following Judgment provides a key clue to the city's identification: it is the City of God, also called New Jerusalem, that will descend from Heaven onto the new Earth after the apocalypse and Last Judgment. (No big deal.) This "kingdom come," to quote the Lord's Prayer that I grew up on, is paradise renewed, Heaven on Earth, salvation.

---

* In the Marseille and RWS decks, the World dancer is depicted as having long hair and breasts, with their genitals hidden by a floating scarf. In esoteric tarot, the dancer was often said to be a hermaphrodite, or a person having male and female sexual characteristics, to represent the unification and transcending of all opposites as symbolized by the masculine/feminine binary. It's problematic to use gender or sex traits to represent abstract ideals—this is the entire issue with gender norms—and to objectify marginalized groups such as intersex people into archetypes. That said, some intersex, transgender, nonbinary, and gender-nonconforming people celebrate the idea of a gender-transgressing World dancer as a representation of transcendence, while others consider it just more objectification and fetishization of marginalized gender and sexual minorities by the cis-heteronormative status quo.

Unfortunately, we aren't whisked away to eternal paradise every time we pull this card. Instead, we find ourselves living in the regular, old imperfect world, with all its suffering, injustice, and pain. Rebecca Solnit outlines the problem with paradise: "Paradise is imagined as a static place, as a place before or after history, after strife and eventfulness and change: the premise is that once perfection has arrived change is no longer necessary."[167]

In a living world, insisting on a utopia of perfection is not only unlikely, but it can also prevent us from enacting better, though imperfect, potentialities. In a radical tarot, we employ paradise as an orientation toward the *possible* instead of the perfect, with the goal of enacting better worlds right here in this one, in the flawed and living world we have. José Esteban Muñoz, the quintessential theorist of queer utopia, has said that the viability or pragmatism of utopia isn't the point; the striving toward it is: "I do not wish to render a picture of utopia that is prescriptive. I want instead to connote an ideality—a desire for a thing, or a way, that is not here but is nonetheless desirable, something worth striving for."[168] In Muñoz's approach, utopia is not a destination or an end point for our future arrival, but a "horizon of possibility,"[169] a direction to continuously travel, never arriving, without end. Utopia is not a place but a creative way of being that is geared toward embodying and enacting the worlds we want to create, bringing their existence closer to reality by living toward them in our daily lives. "I attempt to inhabit a queer practice," wrote Muñoz, "a mode of being in the world that is also inventing the world."[170]

This is akin to the notion of "politics of prefiguration," which Solnit explains is "the idea that if you embody what you aspire to, you have already succeeded. That is to say, if your activism is already democratic, peaceful, creative, then in one small corner of the world these things have triumphed."[171] This is the message of the World: an invitation into world creation via lived embodiment. If you want to live in a kinder, more accepting world, then treat yourself and others with kindness and acceptance. If you want to live in an equal world, then educate yourself on anti-racism, transgender rights, disability justice, and other intersectional justice movements and fight for them with your votes, your voice, and your wallet. If you want to live in an anticapitalist world where workers have rights, then prioritize spending your money at businesses that share those values, join a mutual aid network, and practice wealth redistribution in what ways you can. Utopia and paradise are not walled gardens or distant future societies that exist only in religion or philosophy but actual potentials that we can prefigure by our participation, worlds we can build by the enactment of our principles in our individual lives and communities, even in seemingly small ways.

This is another iteration of the Magician's principle of "as above, so below," the well-established metaphysical idea that the macrocosm and the microcosm are essentially connected and reflective of one another. The world that we create in our individual lives also creates the world at large, just as the world at large also creates the world of our individual lives. Living the world we want into existence is not only a *practical* solution, but a *magical one*. And so the World circles back to the Magician's directive to create the world with both hands. But now, having been through the journey, we don't only create with our intellect, our art, and our actions—we create with our *embodiment*. The World card's dancer is not standing behind a Magician's table but is *dancing*, moving, out in the open, in the middle of life. This is not creation as the beginning of life, not creation as the big bang or the seventh day, but creation as *life itself in the process of living*. This is that process of *worlding* that we discussed in the Wheel, but this time, we are consciously involved in the worlding, in the creation, in the closings and openings of building the reality we want and need.

Utopia is impossible. Paradise will never exist in this world. But that's not what matters; the *journey toward it* does. Journeys, remember, are how things become different. Journeys are how we change. The goal of revolution, Solnit tells us, "is not so much to go on and create the world as to live in that time of creation."[172] Even at the supposed end of the journey, even in the final trump of the World, change is ongoing. When something is completed, we do not remain in some euphoric stasis of completion for long;

we have a celebration or a wake or another ritual of completion, and then, in the morning, we begin the next stage. We start anew. The World connotes closure, conclusions, actualization, even success, but it does not suggest permanence. Nothing does, in this life at least. The World may be the kingdom of God, but Octavia Butler said, "God is Change."[173] Endings are not endings alone; they are kingdoms of change. They're pivot points on which we may dance and twirl. They are portals where the circle of closure becomes the zero of possibility, where we slip from the World into the Fool, stepping off cliffs toward the next horizon.

The World invites you into your next world, your living world, your personal revolution.

Welcome home.

PART 3

THE MINOR ARCANA

THE WANDS THAT SPARK CREATION

Domains: energy, action, passion,
motivation, desire, purpose

Wands, the suit of fire, tell the story of the energetic realm of life. When these cards show up, they bring up the things that excite us, get us up in the morning, or get us fired up. Maybe it's our career, our art, or our family, or maybe it's our activism, a cause, or a meaningful project. The Wands are the suit of what we feel most passionately about. In a radical tarot, we can look to the Wands to connect with our purpose, ignite our creativity, and channel our passion into meaningful positive change. Wands are the action suit, a powerhouse for daring moves and electric ideas that can inspire innovations, rally movements, and change the world. However, anything that burns so hot risks burning out. A flame can warm and illuminate, but it can also rage out of control and become all-consuming. So the Wands teach us to cultivate self-worth instead of ego, to collaborate rather than compete, to learn how to say no, and to enjoy the process of chasing our passions. When we really care about something, when it lights up our fire for living, that's a spark worth stoking with attention and care.

ACE OF WANDS

The Ace of Wands is the pure, essential element of fire, representing a new burst of energy, motivation, or inspiration. Aces can reference beginnings and opportunities, so this is a great time to explore our passions and pursue what excites us. The Ace of Wands can also represent a time of high energy, motivation, creativity, or sex drive, urging us to get out there and live our lives to the fullest. If the Ace shows up when we're feeling blah and uninspired, it encourages us to reconnect with our reasons for doing what we're doing in the first place. We might need to rekindle the fire, so to speak, so consider branching out, getting creative, or trying something new to get the energy flowing again. Like all Aces, the Ace of Wands represents a potentiality, not a sure thing. Just as the hand on the Ace reaches out to grasp the wand, we must grab our own fiery potential. Harness that fire to make your passions manifest.

TWO OF WANDS

The Two of Wands meets us in a place of envisioning, longing, and desire. The card often shows a person standing on the wall of a castle with a globe in their hand, gazing out over the landscape at the horizon. The implication is that we've got the world in the palm of our hand, so why are we still sitting at home? This is a card of wanderlust, arising when we feel restless and are itching for a change. It can feel like an internal battery is charging up without a place to discharge, so the Two of Wands invites us to funnel all that energy into exploring, visualizing, and planning our next adventure. This card can also accompany an ambiguous sense of dissatisfaction or a lack of direction. If that's the case, it's time to identify the gulf between our present discontent and our sense of purpose and close that gap. This card isn't so much about indecision (that's the Two of Swords' domain) as *hesitation*. Usually, we know deep down what we want to do, but we're afraid of the risk, the change, or the consequences. We are caught once again in the age-old battle between the known and the unknown. This card's gift is *vision*: let yourself imagine what else life might hold, flirt with the possibilities, and plan your departure. At the end of the day, you'll have to choose to stay or go, but the decision will be clearer with a plan.

THREE OF WANDS

A card of expansion, ignition, and movement, the Three of Wands is where we launch our plans into action. If you're starting something new, this card says it's time to make your move. If you're in the process of an existing journey, this card encourages you to expand your horizons, step outside your comfort zone, or put yourself out there in new or bigger ways. Threes have to do with growth, so this can be an invitation to survey the territory for where you can supportively expand. But beware: the RWS card shows a person who may be a merchant or a soldier overlooking a body of water in which ships are heading out to sea, hinting at a dangerous side of this card. The colonialist mindset of Western imperialist culture can fool us into thinking we need to dominate, be the absolute best, or possess everything. Not only is that untrue, it's a destructive and unattainable recipe for misery. When growth becomes appropriation and domination, we'll end up in the sweaty and oppressive Five and Ten of Wands real quick. So let the Three of Wands be about curiosity rather than conquest, stretching rather than stampeding, and you'll set yourself on a sustainable path toward future growth.

FOUR OF WANDS

The Four of Wands is a card of steady, stable fire. We've put in the work and have arrived at a place of comfort, warmth, and joy. This card says to let ourselves enjoy it! We may not have achieved our goals quite yet, but we've reached a place of success that is worthy of celebration. This is sometimes called the card of "domestic bliss," so it can bring up home life and relationships. If things are in a good place, this card invites us to fully appreciate the people that warm up our lives. If things are not so great, this card reminds us that relationships, like fires, take maintenance and tending to keep them alight. Make sure you're not taking the people who love you for granted and spend some time nurturing your bonds. Lastly, this card brings up our sense of belonging. Many of us struggle with feeling at home in our families, our workplaces, our bodies, or the world at large, and this can make the Four of Wands a tough card. When it shows up, it invites us to lean in to the places and people that make us feel at home, even if—*especially* if—they are unconventional. Sometimes, the bonds that we forge with our chosen family shine even brighter and hotter than the ones we were born with. Ultimately, this card says that you *do* belong. Home isn't the place you're born; it's the place you build.

FIVE OF WANDS

All fives are cards of challenge, and the Five of Wands portends a battle. This card brings up anger and conflict, ego showdowns, and power struggles, with an overall vibe of chaos and disarray. When this card rears its ugly head, the fighting is usually unnecessary, and we duke it out for no better reason than competition. In other words, the real battle is not with others but with our own feelings of *inferiority*. Western society turns everything into a competition—promotions and paychecks, likes and favorites, steps walked and books read—pitting us against each other in a capitalist game where everyone loses. We can start regarding colleagues, friends, and even family as obstacles instead of people, and start regarding ourselves as works in progress or commodities rather than living, breathing human beings.

This dehumanizing perspective is rooted in the capitalist belief that our worth is contingent on external metrics of success, productivity, and appearance rather than innate to all living things, a belief that divides us, makes us easier to exploit by keeping us insecure, and robs the joy from life. Competition may be a very real thing under capitalism, but the lesson of the Five of Wands is that it's also very much a mindset, and we have a say in how much competition controls us. By prioritizing process instead of product and collaboration instead of competition, we can cultivate more fulfilling and joyful lives.

SIX OF WANDS

The Six of Wands shows up to say we have something to be proud of, whether that's a big achievement or a baby step toward a goal. The card often depicts a parade with a person riding high on a horse and draped in laurel wreaths, a symbol of victory. The implication is one of success, accomplishment, and recognition. So, congratulations! You did the thing! Let's celebrate! This may seem like a surface-y or simplistic reading of the card, but many of us don't spend nearly enough time relishing our successes in this life. We're socialized to immediately turn our sights to the next step, the next big thing, instead of enjoying the moment and—goddexx forbid—resting for a bit. If you tend to undercut your own successes with self-criticism, overfocus on the flaws, or insist on perfection, this card is for you. What you've done is awesome! Take the compliment and enjoy the parade.

If the mere idea of basking in your success makes you nervous, read on. Building on the work of the Five of Wands, the Six can also bring up the topic of "impostor syndrome," or doubting our abilities despite evidence to the contrary. This phenomenon particularly affects women and people from marginalized groups, but the problem isn't us; it's the institutionalized power structures that prop up a narrow vision of white, patriarchal worth to the detriment of everyone else. The usual "fix" for this is to teach people to be "more confident," counseling us to "lean in," "fake it till you make it," and demonstrate "leadership qualities"—but this only molds us into tiny CEOs, reinforcing the systems of patriarchy and toxic masculinity that created the problem in the first place. There's a difference between confidence and competence, as evidenced by the sheer number of bumbling, overconfident white men in the world, and the Six of Wands invites us to explore what confidence, leadership, and success can look like outside those models. Reflect on your proven competence and your well-earned accomplishments, big and small, and feel good about yourself—not because you're perfect, not because you're the best (even if you are), but because you're learning, trying, and growing, and you're doing a great job. *That's something to be proud of.*

SEVEN OF WANDS

The Seven of Wands brings up the scorching territory of anger. This card can reference very real situations of having to fight for ourselves—for our rights, our safety, our people, our livelihood, our environment—situations in which justified anger at being wronged can be a superpower that fuels our fight for what's right. This is the energy of protests, picket lines, polemics, and speeches that move the energy of a populace to stand up for change. This is the energy of the Stonewall riots and the silent, stubborn insistence of sit-ins, reminding us that there are many avenues to channel our anger for change. When this card shows up in times of adversity, it supports us in standing our ground and fighting for what we believe in.

Anger, however, is often shouted down by those on the receiving end of it. "Don't use that tone with me" is wielded as a weapon to silence those fighting to be heard, and "feeling attacked" becomes a smoke screen to avoid engaging with the content of what has been said. This is the other, antiproductive side of anger: defensiveness. We get defensive when we're afraid of being wrong, or because we can't yet hold the difficult feelings of being accountable for causing harm, so we redirect our own anger back at the aggrieved party, refuse to engage in conversation by claiming a faulty "moral high ground," or frame ourselves as the real victim.

The tricky part of the Seven of Wands is knowing which one is which: when are we rightfully standing up for ourselves, and when are we avoiding accountability with a shield of defensive anger? In cases of defensiveness, our avoidance usually comes from a very human and very tender place of feeling shame, which, as we discussed in the Hanged One, comes from a place of feeling unworthy of love. When we're afraid of being wrong, we fear that our error will render us less likable, less lovable, less worthy. When we evade accountability, we avoid being exposed as imperfect, as fallible, as *human*. But flawlessness leaves no room for forgiveness or for growth. We must let go of perfection and embrace the human fact of fallibility before we can meet confrontations with the desire to understand, learn, and grow, rather than attack, annihilate, and defend.

EIGHT OF WANDS

The Eight of Wands is interpreted by many as a card of swift movement and rapid progress. Referencing the RWS imagery that shows eight wands soaring through a clear sky, my friend, magician, and tarot reader Erik Arneson, calls the Eight of Wands the "Hooray, Free Wands!" card.[174] To him, it signals an unexpected windfall, a sudden blessing of opportunities, energy, or other good stuff. To me, however, those soaring wands don't look like a blessing but a threat. The first time I ever laid eyes on the card, I thought they looked like javelins flying or bombs falling. Instead of "yay, wands!" I thought, "take cover!" This may say more about Erik and me as people than it does about the card (Erik, a generally jolly and good-natured guy; me, a suspicious person by default with anxiety and control issues), but I think our differing takes on the card can show the two main manifestations of the Eight of Wands, which mostly depend on how we approach its volatile but powerful energy.

Like the Wheel of Fortune, this card is essentially neutral: it simply means stuff is happening, perhaps quickly. Those of us who have learned to distrust good things or have a hard time with unplanned changes may approach this card with so much suspicion that we miss the free ride. On the other hand, the speed of this card is such that we might get quickly overwhelmed or veer wildly off course if we don't stay in control of ourselves—which is often the extent of our control in this uncontrollable card. Perhaps a good approach to the Eight of Wands is somewhere between Erik's free wands and my duck and cover: an approach that is spontaneous enough to take advantage of a good thing, flexible enough to adapt to quickly changing circumstances, and circumspect enough to stay in possession of ourselves along the way. The Eight of Wands asks us to step up to the limits of our power and work with what the universe throws at us for the rest. In this way, the card is one of co-creation, and its lesson is in knowing how to ride the ebbs and flows of energy and adjust as necessary.

NINE OF WANDS

The Nine of Wands shows up when we're tired, worn out, exhausted, and can't handle one more thing going wrong—and then it does. This card recognizes our weariness and exasperation, but it also says it would be a damn shame to give up now. The positive side of this card is that it uncovers a new and deeper well of resilience within us, showing us that we're even stronger than we thought. The downside is the fact that such resilience is necessary at all. It's exhausting to be strong all the time. It's unfair to have to keep persisting despite oppression, discrimination, illness, injury, injustice, and the plain fact that the universe sometimes doles out undeserved misfortune after misfortune onto some of us for no good reason. Yet that's the reality sometimes.

This card has shown up for me in times when I felt judged and marginalized because of my gender and my choices surrounding my body and transition. During one particularly frustrating stretch of time, it showed up time and time again while I struggled to explain myself to people in my life. I wanted to be understood and taken seriously, and the Nine of Wands told me that I would be one day, but that day was not today. In such cases, this card can be a reminder that our *mere existence* is revolutionary. We don't have to change anyone's mind, no matter how much we'd like to. We can live our fullest lives and seek our own joy even though life is hard and unfair, even though others may ridicule us or try to keep us small and quiet, and that's a radical act of resistance all on its own. Whatever's happening in your life right now that's making you want to call it quits—don't. You may need to adjust your boundaries to preserve your energy and well-being, shore up your resources for support, or call in reinforcements, but you *can* make it through this. You and what you choose to fight for are worth every bit of the effort.

TEN OF WANDS

If you've been paying attention, you may have noticed that the primary challenge of the suit of Wands has been around sense of self and self-worth. The fire suit is about passion, purpose, desire, and ambition, but these things above all else require *knowing who we are and what we want.* If we don't know who we are and what lights us up, we won't know where to put our energy. Furthermore, we need a healthy sense of self-worth and awareness of our own energetic limits in order to go forth and light our proverbial fires. Otherwise, it's too easy to get taken advantage of, sacrifice ourselves to please others, or burn ourselves out in the pursuit of shiny-but-empty goals that were never our own to begin with. It's okay to know what's too much and what's just enough, what's not for us and what is—in fact, it's vital.

That's where the Ten of Wands comes in. As the culmination of the Wands suit, this card is where we meet the spoils of our success, whether that's comfortable achievement or crushing responsibility, a pleasant blaze or total burnout. If you're on the ashes-and-embers end of the equation, the good news is that the Ten of Wands is not forever. The tarot always moves and recycles, and the culmination of the Tens is only a moment in time. We can decide to make a change for a better future outcome, and with the Ten of Wands that change is usually around the life goals we pursue and the power of saying yes or no.

When this card appears, we might be saying yes too often and for the wrong reasons. Taking on responsibilities out of a sense of obligation, guilt, or the desire to please rather than because we truly want to take them on is a sure-fire road to burnout town. Likewise, saying yes out of a sense of scarcity—i.e., the belief that we have to hoard every opportunity because there's not enough to go around, or the fear that if we refuse then no opportunities will come around ever again—is a great way to waste our precious energy on scattered projects and tasks that our heart isn't in, to the detriment of the thing that gets our passion smoldering.

When we put energy into things we truly love, they may demand hard work and long hours, but those things will feed us right back with energy, purpose, and joy. When we pour energy into things we don't, they become black holes that won't stop sucking. You'll probably have to ax some of your other projects and responsibilities to make room for your passion, and this card says "don't hesitate." If you pay attention to how each makes you feel, you'll know what to cut and what to cultivate.

ACE of CUPS

THE CUPS THAT HOLD
THE DEPTHS

Domains: emotion, intuition, imagination, love,
connection, satisfaction, fulfillment

The suit of water, the Cups tell the story of the emotional realm of life. Emotions are a huge part of our daily realities. They color our perceptions and experiences and, along with thoughts, make up much of the terrain of our inner worlds. Even when our physical needs are met, unhappiness can make life unbearable. Likewise, emotional fulfillment can turn even the most dismal circumstances into a paradise. Emotions flow like water, fluid and constantly changing. They can be bright and shallow as a trickling stream, calm and soothing as a warm bath, turbulent and powerful as a monsoon, or deep and mysterious as an ocean. Cups speak to us about our emotions and our lives under the surface of everyday consciousness: the realm of dreams, memories, intuition, repressions, and all the murky waters of the subconscious. In a world where emotions are denigrated as weakness and intuition is scoffed at as irrational, the Cups suit offers us a pathway to feeling our emotions and reclaiming our intuition as a radical act.* Because when we are tapped into our inner currents, we are connected to a powerful source of information and self-knowledge. We discover deeper wells of empathy, connection, love, and awareness, and can unlock whole new worlds of joy and fulfillment for ourselves and communities.

ACE OF CUPS

Like all Aces, the Ace of Cups signals something new in the watery realm of its suit. This may be the beginning of a new emotional journey, a new relationship or way of relating to ourselves or others, or a new spring of intuition or creativity. The Wands' creativity is of the fiery, will-driven sort, but the Cups' creativity bubbles up from the subterranean realm of dreams and emotions, gushing from previously unknown reservoirs of imagination and feeling. As the raw element of water, the Ace of Cups can reference a wellspring of strong emotion or a powerful emotional experience. It can quite literally mean a lot of tears, but they're almost always tears that spring from a place of love or beauty. In these cases, the Ace reminds us that the best way to deal with powerful emotions is to let them flow through us—repressing them will only lead to pressure and pain. When the Ace of Cups appears, there's something precious to be gained by allowing ourselves to feel and experience our emotions. By being in tune with our inner world, we can unfold new levels of awareness and connection interpersonally, spiritually, and intuitively. So tune in to your underwater currents of feeling: there's treasures in the depths.

TWO OF CUPS

The Two of Cups invites us to reflect on our emotional relationships and the reciprocity of connection and exchange within them. Most interpretations talk about romantic relationships with

---

* For more on reclaiming emotion and intuition as a radical act, see the High Priestess and Empress chapters.

this card—it's often called the "soulmate card"—but the most important aspect of this card is not romance but *connection*. The Two of Cups can just as easily bring up your connection with your best friend as it can your romantic partner, or it can reference an excellent conversation with a family member, acquaintance, or even a stranger, because this card is about any experience in which something special or profound is shared, no matter how brief. This card isn't necessarily about soul*mates* but soul moments—those whispers of time wherein you brush up against another's soul or your own, where the world mirrors a piece of your truth back to you and you feel loved, seen, or fulfilled.

As special as these moments are, the Two of Cups also cautions us to cherish and tend to our mutually fulfilling relationships, because even the strongest relationships require care and maintenance. Twos are about balance and reciprocity, so this card can appear when we need to check in with the emotional exchange in our relationships and make sure the channels are open and flowing. Sometimes in relationships, we insist on 50/50 splits in all things—chores, finances, movie night selections, emotional labor—but in truth nothing is ever parsed with such rigid equivalence. Instead, rewarding relationships need to be flexible to allow for the ebb and flow of life. Sometimes, one party may have to pick up the slack while the other deals with something challenging, and at other times the balance will shift in the other direction. If things feel disconnected, the Two of Cups says it may be time for a conversation about everyone's needs and whether they are being met, because the Two of Cups' mirroring can also lean in to its less-fun cousin: projection. Take some time to check in with your emotions and those of the people you love and clear up any muddy waters.

THREE OF CUPS

Where the Two of Cups is about interpersonal relationships, the Three of Cups spreads the love into our communities and groups. This card calls up all the ways we support each other emotionally through networks of care: it's the friends who show up to celebrate our successes and comfort our sorrows, the extended family who can always be depended on for a good time or in times of need, and the community that rallies together for protests and potlucks alike. This card can nudge us to reach out when we're carrying our burdens alone, reminding us that we have people who love us and will be happy to help. It also shows up in times of happiness and celebration, reminding us that success for one of us is success for all of us, because in connected communities we all rise together. If you're lacking community right now, this card can encourage you to seek some out: get involved by volunteering in your neighborhood or community center, joining a park sports league, or looking up local spiritual organizations or clubs that match your interests.

On a different note, threes are about growth, expansion, and also *expression*. Like the Three of Wands was the point when our ambitions found tangible expression in the world, the Three of Cups is where the matters of our hearts begin to find their vibrant external expression. Dreams and desires are starting to become real in this card, which is why it's often connected to times of celebration, togetherness, and general merriment. The tricky side of the Three of Cups is that its zing of ecstasy can lead to an emotional crash afterward when the endorphins fade—or to partying a bit *too* hard and setting ourselves up for a wicked hangover. When this card shows up, enjoy the party! But remember that growth takes work and you're growing, baby. Get ready to nurture this newly expansive part of your life with the attention and care it deserves.

FOUR OF CUPS

Remember the emotional crash I mentioned in the Three of Cups? Well, here it is. The Four of Cups shows up when we are feeling emotionally drained, ambiguously let down, and mired in a funk. Sometimes, this card appears when we're feeling dissatisfied and are indulging in a pity party, unaware of the good things that surround us and unwilling to pull ourselves out of our rut. Other times, our ennui arises from a lack of stimulation or excitement, in which case the Four of Cups invites us to stir up those stagnant emotional waters with something that interests us, even if it feels like a chore right now.

On a serious note, this card can show up as an emotional health red flag, signaling a need to take steps to care for ourselves. My partner, who has struggled with depression off and on throughout his life, has an array of practices for when his mood starts dipping, ranging from exercise and good food to listening to upbeat music and taking a trip to the museum. He calls this his "emotional toolkit," and he basically forces himself to use it when he feels the funks creeping in. Most of the time, it helps. Of course, depression and other emotional struggles can't always be remediated with a bag of tricks—or a tarot deck—and in these cases the Four of Cups can direct us toward professional help.

Unfortunately, mental health care is not accessible to many of us, and when it is, it often comes with a long wait-list. Sometimes the best we can do is ask for help from someone we trust or seek out free or donation-based local support groups. Whatever you can do to help yourself out of this emotional swamp is a good thing.

FIVE OF CUPS

With love comes grief. It's an unfortunate fact, and one that most of us try our best to ignore until its reality is upon us. The Five of Cups shows up to help us face it. This card is about grief, loss, despair, sadness, and the rest of the flip side of the heart. If you are currently experiencing a loss, this card witnesses your pain and supports you in feeling your feelings and moving through the grieving process. If you've experienced loss in the past and haven't yet dealt with it, this card can show up to say it's time to do so. The Five of Cups can also unearth our fear of loss itself. A major lesson of this card is that we cannot love with our whole hearts if we're holding back for fear of loss and pain. We cannot fully experience the joy, connection, and belonging of love if part of us is shrinking from the knowledge that one day we may lose it.

My therapist once asked me to sit with the feeling of unconditional love, and I immediately fell to pieces in a mess of tears and hyperventilation. Not because I hadn't been loved in that way—I have—but because I had never let myself *fully feel it* without reservations. Instead of basking in it, I leapt straight forward to the loss part, to the grief that lies at the end of love's rainbow. Over time, I began to understand that we have to accept the eventual pain of loss to fully experience the bliss of loving and being loved. To be truly happy when happiness is here, we have to accept that we will be sad when it leaves. It's easier said than done, but that's the big lesson of the Five of Cups, as well as the reason for the three spilled cups and two full cups that are iconic of the card.

Many interpreters, including me, have said those cups represent being too immersed in our losses to appreciate what we still have. But now I understand that those cups mean something else: they are the reality of the heart's dichotomy. They are the simultaneity of grief and love. By opening ourselves to love, we open ourselves to pain. There's no way around it, and that's okay. To love is to grieve, and to grieve is to love. They are the two sides of the heart, beating together.

SIX OF CUPS

After the loss of the Five of Cups, what we have left is memory. The Six of Cups captures the bittersweetness of memory and nostalgia, which can offer happy reflections or trap us in their longing for days past, preventing us from moving on and living in the present. Alternately, this card can show up to haunt those of us who may be *avoiding* the past. If our memories aren't exactly happy, it's only natural to skirt around them—but that can also leave things undigested and unsettled, waiting to rear back up and mess with our present.

When we talk about "baggage," this is what we mean: the traumas, disappointments, and wounds of the past that still affect our behaviors in the present, even when the harmful situation is ancient history. There are lessons to be learned from our past experiences, and if we integrate them, then we won't have to repeat that history. But if we run from those memories, they usually have a way of controlling us. Sixes are about harmony, so this card asks us to harmonize our emotional reality with our present reality and make sure we're not emotionally stuck in the past. Despite what's happened or may happen in the future, happiness is available to you right now. Make some new memories.

This card of emotional harmony can also be about lighthearted pleasure. The card has an association with children, and it invites us to remember the wonder, imagination, and openness of being a child. In a world filled with stress and responsibility, adults tend to forget how to have good, simple fun. The Six of Cups invites us to remember. There is pleasure to be had in the mundane world, this card says. Allow yourself to experience it.

SEVEN OF CUPS

The internal world can be a playground of imagination and fantasy—or a labyrinth of illusions and fears. The Seven of Cups presents us with both options and many more, sending a plethora of choices dancing through our daydreams. This can be a delightful smorgasbord to sample and savor, or it can be a mess of confusion and indecision. My partner calls this the Weekend Card because it reflects his typical Saturday struggle: Should he go on a hike? Should he bake scones? Should he finally tackle that project he's been putting off? Should he call his mom? Surrounded with so many options and wanting to do them all, he either gets overwhelmed and does none of them, or he tries to do too much and gets mad at himself when he can't do it all. In this case, the Seven of Cups can clue us in to the need to simplify our objectives.

You don't have to do it all! Triage what's most important and go from there.

Alternately, when we have a selection of good choices at our fingertips, this card can show up to give us permission to explore and imagine what each future could hold. Visualizing our options is a great practice to explore the pros and cons, as long as we can do so without indulging in delusions of grandeur and wishful thinking or the opposite: doomsday fantasies and worst-case scenarios. If you're thinking door number one will deliver permanent happiness, you're going to be disappointed. If you're convinced door number two will lead to ultimate despair, you're probably wrong. Few choices are so stark and extreme as that. If your imagination is swinging to these extremes, it's a sure sign that you've been swept up in the Seven of Cups' sly tide of illusion. Bring your sights back to shore and make a choice from firmer ground.

EIGHT OF CUPS

The Seven of Cups presented us with many choices, but the Eight of Cups leaves us with only one. It's a choice we know deep down is the right one, try as we might to avoid it. It's a choice that is as sorrowful as it is correct. The choice is this: move on.

Sometimes, things don't work out despite our best efforts and intentions. We can pour all our love and effort into something, and still its heart won't beat. When this happens, we might stick around longer than we should, clinging to a wilted dream, trying to resuscitate a ghost. We may be afraid of the changes and unknowns that departure will bring into our lives, but the Eight of Cups gently sends us on our way. There are no guarantees that we'll find immediate happiness once we make this change. There is no assurance that we won't get hurt again or have regrets. But that's no reason to stay in a situation that has stopped being good.

The struggle in this card is almost always fear of feeling pain or causing pain, but admit it: you've been hurting for a while now, haven't you? Walking away from something you have loved can feel like breaking your own heart, but at the end of the day, letting go is an act of self-care and self-love. It creates room for whatever unknown thing might come next and makes space for that new journey. The Eight of Cups is where you stop hesitating on the threshold and take those first steps into the night.

NINE OF CUPS

The Nine of Cups is sometimes called the "wish-fulfillment card" because it signals desires attained and dreams come true. Nines represent a climax in their suit, and in the watery realm of emotion this means an apex of happiness, satisfaction, and pleasure, often one that comes as the result of a long emotional journey, an artistic or creative achievement, or a lot of work and investment in internal or relationship realms. On this emotional high note, know that you have something to be proud of and enjoy this period of well-earned happiness.

But, as the saying goes, be careful what you wish for. Sometimes when we attain our heart's desire, we find it's not what we imagined. It's a familiar story: we set our sights on something and tell ourselves that once we get it—marriage, professional success, a family, a house, a waist size—we'll *finally be happy*. But then we arrive and the marriage needs work, the success heaps on the stress, the house leaks, and we're always hungry. In other words: life happens. Capitalism sells us happiness as a commodity, wraps it in a bow as the American Dream, and incentivizes it with corporate perks and the eventual paradise of retirement. While these things can deliver the momentary dopamine burst of surface pleasure, they cannot on their own grant us the real thing. The work of this card is to identify our *authentic* longings, our heart's true wishes, not what the world, our parents, our friends, or the TV tells us we should desire. Locating your genuine desire is a radical act of self-reclamation, and following that yearning has the power to revolutionize your life—and maybe even the world.

TEN OF CUPS

In the Ten of Cups, we arrive at the completion of our emotional journey. This is the moment when we know what it means to be truly happy. If you've been following along through the Cups suit, you know that true happiness is knowing that happiness is not a constant. The Ten of Cups is frequently chalked up to happy endings: it's the credits at the end of the rom-com, snapshots of the seemingly picture-perfect wedding scrolling down the screen. But that's not reality—and it's not the end. After our happy milestones, life still rolls on. We can't stay in euphoria forever like a fly trapped in amber. That's not living.

The joy of the Ten of Cups is not externally sourced, not based in objects and achievements. Rather, it's rooted in a sense of internal stability and satisfaction that arises from being true to our authentic selves. This is self-love and self-knowledge, not as a spa day or a mindfulness retreat, but as an integrated and lived reality. The Ten of Cups happens when we love ourselves enough to be compassionate and accountable, when we trust ourselves enough to know we'll figure life out even when it's hard, and when we feel our happiness enough to let it guide our choices. This card is often depicted with a rainbow, which we can take as a nod to the queerness and diversity of love. The rainbow can also represent all the colors of our emotions and the spectrum of life's experiences. Love and grief, joy and despair, anger and amusement: all of them are caught up in that rainbow. So perhaps the Ten of Cups is not just about the *happiness* end of that spectrum but about embracing the sheer vivid experience of the whole thing. The secret of the Cups is in learning to move and dance and rejoice through it all, rain or shine, storm or rainbow.

ACE of SWORDS

THE SWORDS OF THE
TWO-EDGED MIND

Domains: thoughts, reason, perception,
communication, mental health, truth

The Swords are the suit of the mental realm, telling the story
of our thoughts and perspectives, our analysis and discernment,
our anxieties and obsessions. Like the blade that symbolizes the
suit, the mind can be honed to a fine edge of clarity and precision,
or it can be blunted with confusion, delusion, and misinformation. Like the element of air to which it corresponds, the mind is
the medium through which we see the world. It's how we build
our narratives, communicate with each other, and tell our stories.
All of this makes the Swords a very powerful and very fraught suit.

The stories we tell ourselves about who we are are important.
They don't create the world all by themselves—that would ignore
the very real environmental factors and systems of oppression that
affect people's lives—but our narratives do have a huge influence
on how we move through the world. They are a large part of how
we make decisions, form our identities, and choose our roles in
life. In a radical tarot, the Swords are a pivotal suit for healing the
trauma of living in an unjust world, for unlearning controlling

ideologies and harmful beliefs, and for reclaiming our power and prioritizing our mental health.

ACE OF SWORDS

The Ace of Swords represents that coveted and controversial thing: truth. As the pure element of air, this Ace is absolute clarity of perception, bringing epiphanies, insights, and lightbulb moments of understanding. If you've been searching for answers or feeling lost and uncertain, this card is excellent news, heralding a new focus and sense of direction. It can reference turning over a new leaf in your attitude, perspective, or identity. But like the Sword that symbolizes the suit, truth can be a two-edged thing. It can cut through the bullshit and free us from our misconceptions, or it can confront us with sharp news that is hurtful or hard to bear. Sometimes it does both. That's the two-edged blessing of truth: it can hurt, but it also liberates. This Ace has historical associations with power—the sword is mighty, after all—but unlike some traditional meanings of the card, I don't believe this power necessarily has anything to do with force or violence. That's a misuse of the power of truth and the mind, and it will show up later in the suit. Instead, the Ace of Swords reminds us that knowledge is perhaps the most powerful thing of all, and how we wield it makes all the difference.

TWO OF SWORDS

The Two of Swords meets us at a difficult crossroads where we aren't sure which road to take. Unlike the Seven of Cups, which can mean confusion or indecision due to an abundance of attractive options, the Two of Swords usually indicates indecision due to a *lack* of them. We don't like any of the choices on our table, so we do our best to avoid the decision entirely, usually making things worse for ourselves in the process. On the flip side, this card can appear when we are racking our brains to pick apart every potential outcome, strategize every fallout, or divine information that simply isn't there for us to have. In other words, this card shows up when we're looking to external sources to make a tough decision for us, and its message is this: no one else can make this decision but you, so you might as well get to it.

Alternately, the Two of Swords can reference being "in two minds" about something. We see the good and the bad, we love it and we hate it, and our decision flips every few hours. Here, the clarity of the Ace of Swords has gotten twisted into confusion and waffling. Some interpreters say the solution to the Two of Swords' dilemma is to make a logical choice using our brains instead of our emotions, but I think this card calls for just the opposite. This particular stalemate is almost always caused by overthinking or perfectionism. There will never be a clear winner or obvious choice at this crossroads, but we must pick a path anyway. What we need in the Two of Swords is not more thinking but a little faith. Twos are about balance, after all. Logic and reason are intelligent but so is the heart. Make sure you're listening to both.

THREE OF SWORDS

The iconic sword-pierced heart on the Three of Swords communicates its meaning clearly: this is a card about heartache. Here is the territory of anguish, hurt, regret, and shame—emotions that may seem more at home in the heart's suit of Cups, but their presence in the suit of the mind gives a hint to their cause and their resolution: our thoughts. When we get hurt, our minds spin into action in defense of our emotions. We throw ourselves into work and distractions to avoid feeling our feelings, leaving our wounds to fester untended under a bandage; or we worry over our injury with what-ifs and if-onlys and could-have-beens, picking at the scab so it never heals. This card is about how our thoughts, in trying to protect or help us, can end up doing the opposite.

Unfortunately, we can't exactly control our thoughts. Trying *not* to think about something is a sure way to think about it. At the same time, focusing on "love and light" and "good vibrations" is not the magic fix it's billed to be; in fact, it can function dangerously as avoidance, repression, and spiritual bypassing.

This card is less about *controlling* our thoughts and more about cultivating *awareness* around what they're doing, how they're impacting our emotional well-being, and how to work with them in a more helpful way. It's about supportively facing the source of our pain and working to pull out those thought-swords so our wounds can finally heal. Often, we'll discover deeper areas in need of healing under the surface. For example, if you're hurting over a breakup, maybe it's also bringing up childhood wounds around feeling unloved, unwanted, or not good enough. If you're obsessively beating yourself up after making a mistake, maybe your anguish is rising from a deeper fear of being unworthy or undeserving of love, care, and forgiveness. Once you identify the nature of the wound, you can set your mind to healing.

FOUR OF SWORDS

Following on the heels of the Three of Swords, the Four of Swords highlights the need to create time and space for rest and healing. This is a radical card in the era of 60-hour work weeks, constant content creation, and the reign of the grind. It gives us permission to pause, withdraw, seek solitude and tranquility—or just take a nap. Rest is important for obvious reasons: without it, we'll burn out energetically and break down mentally. But rest and relaxation are vital for bigger reasons than simply recharging our productivity battery. When we're busy and exhausted all the time, our brains struggle to keep up and can't do the deep processing necessary for learning, synthesizing information, and emotional growth. But when we sleep or engage in restorative activities, whether that's a walk in the neighborhood, a novel in the bathtub, or binge-watching a series on the couch, our brains are free to process the happenings of the day and sort out our thoughts and emotions in the background. Through relaxation and enjoyment, we become more aware of and in touch with our real thoughts, needs, and desires.

Relaxation is its own kind of radical resistance to systems of oppression, which historically have enforced unsustainable levels of productivity to keep the nonruling classes biddable and too exhausted to revolt.[175] Rest makes us more empowered, informed, and connected to one another and less likely to settle for poor treatment from employers and governments. Taking time and space for ourselves is a radical reclamation of our own agency, brain space, independent thought, and self-direction. It promotes clarity and self-awareness, which in turn support us in questioning the systems that control us and in seeking our own truths. When this card comes up, take a break and rethink your relationship to work, productivity, and labor. With some clarity and distance, the world can look a whole lot different than you think.

FIVE OF SWORDS

The Five of Swords is about cruelty, vindictiveness, and nasty fights. You know the kind: the ones that start trivial and brew into a storm of insults, cutting words, and trauma triggers. Before you know it, you're screaming or frosting each other out and you can't remember why the fight started in the first place. Not that anyone cares, because now this fight is about one thing only: winning. This card says to put down your swords. The classic image shows one person with a smug look on their face, hoarding five swords while two people walk away in defeat. You don't want those swords, believe me. Nobody likes that guy. This card is about knowing when enough is enough and breaking the cycle. It can mean taking a loss or letting the other person continue with their mean tactics or smug righteousness, but this fight isn't worth it. There's no victory for you here because victory will come at too high a cost.

But the Five of Swords has an even more difficult side. This card can bring up the very real and serious territory of emotional and psychological abuse, trauma, harassment, hate speech, discrimination, oppression, and anything else that involves abuse of power. Fives are about challenges, and in the suit of the mind, a major and devastating challenge lies in the warped perceptions that cause some people to believe they have the right to hurt others. Unfortunately, this is not a card about justice or changing hearts and minds. This is a card about getting yourself away from harm. But walking away isn't always possible, especially when the harm is institutional or systemic. In these situations, the Five of Swords reminds us that we cannot change other people, but we can protect ourselves. We can set boundaries around how much time and attention we afford them. We can delete Twitter, block their number, and decide to be unavailable to certain kinds of bullshit. Mostly importantly, we can refuse to allow their cruelty to rob us of our future of love, trust, generosity, and belonging.

This card may advise us to put down the sword, but that doesn't mean we are defeated. It means we refuse to use their tactics, engage on their terms, or become like them. It means we preserve ourselves to fight another day, or not to fight but to *live* and *thrive* despite them. The world is bigger than this battlefield, after all. The Five of Swords says it's time to leave the fight and live instead.

SIX OF SWORDS

If the Five of Swords is about walking away from harm, the Six of Swords is the transition that comes after. This is a card about leaving a bad situation on the hope that there's something better. A card of the in-between spaces, it speaks to departure, liminality, and journeys undertaken of necessity and faith. It holds us in the unknown gulf between leaving and arriving. That's why this card is often illustrated with a boat: this is a place of motion, change, and tides. It's the wild expanse between the previous shore and the next one, when you're not where you were but not yet where you want to be. It's the messy, confusing, painful, magical territory of transition, of *becoming*.

In a queer context, the word *transition* gains whole new meaning. It speaks to the medical or surgical transitions that some of us go through as well as to the huge and ever-unfolding transitional experiences of simply being queer. These can include coming out, exploring your gender and/or sexuality, finding the clothes and haircut that help you feel like you, changing your name or pronouns, figuring out how to date people, disclosing (or not) your gender or sexuality over and over at every party or new job or social interaction—the list goes on. Some of these transitional periods can be wonderfully exciting, affirming, and healing, but a lot of them can also be just plain hard.

The Six of Swords shows up to witness that we're in the boat, out to sea, and scared we won't find land. It says, "Yeah, it sucks sometimes, but look at you, you're on the way." It says, "Yes, you're in the middle and there's no map, but you're not drowning today." Whatever changes and transitions are happening in your life, this card is an ally for you in your journey, encouraging you onward even when it stings, even when you feel alone, even when the doubts and fears stir the waters. There's a shore out there for you, the Six of Swords says, and it's better than the one you're leaving. Keep paddling.

SEVEN OF SWORDS

The Seven of Swords is about the acrobatic powers of the mind, encompassing its nimble powers of cleverness, creative thinking, strategizing, and wit, as well as its more devious capacities of dishonesty, cunning, manipulation, and subterfuge. Guidebooks tend to focus on the negative side of this card, trumping the whole thing up to lies, trickery, deceit, even theft. Indeed, this card can call us on dishonesty, asking us to consider *why* we feel the need to lie. But I don't think it passes any judgment. If we have good reasons to "deceive"—not being ready to disclose something private, for instance—then this card asks us to check in with those reasons and consider if they're still necessary. It can also be a flag to make sure you're not lying to *yourself.* If our reasons for deception are faulty, unnecessarily selfish, or cowardly, the Seven can encourage us to come clean. In general, the motto of the Seven of Swords is this: honesty is not always the best policy, but unnecessary dishonesty is the *worst.*

But I've got a different take on the Seven of Swords to share, and it's not about deception. It's about thinking outside the box. This can be a card of forging your own path and marching to the beat of your own drum, and sometimes that means flouting authority and breaking the rules. I admittedly have a soft spot for this card because it's a card for the nonconformists, weirdos, and self-proclaimed freaks. It's a card for the rabble-rousers and anarchists, a card for anyone who's ever been told to stop being who they are and get back in line. In the RWS version, a person tiptoes away from a military encampment, arms full of swords, apparently in the act of stealing the weapons. Whether their thievery is a bad or a good thing depends entirely on your perspective. Are you in the military camp, marching on orders? Or are you with Robin Hood's band of Merry Men, robbing from the rich to feed the poor? The Seven of Swords acknowledges that the "proper channels" are sometimes designed to discourage the already disenfranchised, uphold the status quo, and make change nearly impossible.

When this card shows up, it acknowledges that a little dishonesty can be a good thing when it means protecting yourself, and you don't owe your truth to just anybody, anyway. It can even call for some civil disobedience. When faced with an obstacle, sometimes we need to go around or under instead of through. When institutions aren't built for us, when the mainstream shuns us, we build our own networks and communities. We get creative. *That's* the Seven of Swords.

EIGHT OF SWORDS

If the previous card is a mental Houdini, the Eight of Swords is the mind's handcuffs from which we have to escape. This card shows up when we're feeling trapped, blocked, and powerless. This is the suit of the mind, however, so this captivity is more about *perception* than it is about reality. When this card appears, whatever has us feeling imprisoned is at least partially based in our own self-defeating thinking or limiting beliefs. This card comes up a lot when we're holding on to narratives of persecution and self-pity, telling ourselves that everyone is out to get us, that the system is rigged, and that there's nothing we can do about it. But here's the thing: it may be true that people are out to get you, and it's *definitely* true that the system is rigged, but this card says that you *can* do something about it. I see this mindset happen in the queer community all the time because there *are* so many obstacles we have to face, some people *are* truly out to get us, and in some arenas we really do have very little power.

When you're marginalized, it can be easy to adopt a victim mentality and give up what power you have to the narrative that you have no control over your life. The truth lies somewhere in the middle. There are so many things outside our power to control, but there are so many things within our power too. The Eight of Swords is about waking up to the difference. It's about liberating ourselves from our mental prisons, self-defeating thought spirals, and oppressive ideologies so we can liberate ourselves in the real world.

NINE OF SWORDS

The Nine of Swords reflects one of the most difficult aspects of the mental realm: anxiety, fear, worry, and despair. This is the nightmare card, accompanying sleepless nights and troubled dreams that follow us into the daytime. The good news with this card is that a nightmare is only that: a phantasm of the mind, a mental ghost. This doesn't mean it's *all* in our head—nightmares often arise from very real daily worries, after all—but this card does tend to show up when we're letting our anxieties get the better of us. That being said, when our brain is supplying us with *panic! doom! danger!* commands, it can be hard or impossible to simply snap out of it. When mental illness or trauma are present, we often have little to no control over how our brains respond to a given stressor. But when the Nine of Swords appears, it indicates that there may be another way to manage our mental health or handle this anxiety-inducing situation.

As a person with generalized anxiety and complex PTSD, the Nine of Swords has shown up to both acknowledge my heightened nerves and triggered thoughts and to support me in regulating and soothing myself. Something I learned during the pandemic was that bringing attention to my body and its safety in the present moment—not sick, not homeless, not hungry—helped assuage the constant waves of anxiety and ground me in reality. Now when my thoughts start to spin in a doomsday spiral, I'm able to acknowledge that my brain is trying to protect me from danger in its own way, and I remind myself that I am safe. There is no earthquake, no tsunami. My loved ones are healthy. There's a roof over my head. For me, these comforts help separate anxiety from reality. That distinction is what the Nine of Swords is about. This is the card where we learn to manage our worries and fears—not *cure* them, because frankly there's always something to worry about. Maybe the world will end tomorrow; maybe it won't. In the meantime, we can do our best to live right now.

TEN OF SWORDS

The Ten of Swords is when we mentally bottom out. This card appears when our brain chemicals are circling the drain, when our nerves are so fried that we can't function and our emotions are so massive that we go numb. This card says: if all you can do today is feed yourself and stare at the ceiling, that's enough. This card says: just hang on. Like the person on the RWS card, we're flattened, prone, pinned by the pointy end of the truth. If we've been in denial, here is where the truth breaks through. If we've been in avoidance, here's where it all catches up. This is where we end up if we let the Nine of Swords possess us completely, if we turn our own nightmares into reality like a self-fulfilling prophecy. This is the rock bottom we hit when we've run from our own snarled minds too long, numbing our thoughts with substances, projecting our demons onto others, running from connection, self-destructing, hurting those we love. Like a little Death mixed with the Tower, here we meet a long-in-coming and devastating release.

But release can be a catharsis, and defeat can be a relief. The endings this card references may be sad, anguished, resigned, difficult, but above all else they are necessary. The Ten of Swords confronts us with one of the most challenging and most mature tasks of the mind: accepting a reality that we don't want to be true. The mind rebels, bargains, denies, rages, blames, avoids. The Ten of Swords is where it settles. Where it accepts. Here, we admit there is no other option but to surrender, let go, and find out what comes after this ending. If we can do that, we may be able to find some peace in all the chaos, a little hope amid the strife. In the end, the Ten of Swords is not about death but about *survival*. Buried in this card, in you, in us, beneath the black clouds and the mud and the swords, there is a bedrock of resilience and perhaps stalwart hope. There is the bone-deep knowledge that as hard as this is, as much as this hurts, you *will* survive this. You *will* figure out what's next waiting on the other side of the night.

ACE of PENTACLES

THE PENTACLES THAT BUILD THE WORLD

Domains: resources, wealth, labor, routine, the body, material reality, values

The Pentacles, also called Discs and Coins, are the suit of the material realm. I prefer the name Pentacles over Coins, since the latter makes it too easy to reduce this entire wonderful suit to mere currency. The Pentacles are about so much more than money: they're the suit of our bodies, the tangible work we do in the world, our pleasure and labor, the skills and crafts we practice and hone. They tell the story of how we carve out a home in the world, the story of where we come from, what kind of families we build, and what we leave behind us when we go.

The suit of earth, the Pentacles are the literal ground beneath our feet: the soil and the roots, the pebbles and mountains. This is also the stuff of the Earth: our natural resources and all the living things that the Earth births, feeds, and supports. On a planet undergoing catastrophic climate change, the Pentacles are more important than ever. And, yes, they're also about money. In a radical tarot, we can work with the earth suit to revolutionize the way we interact with the environment, our own bodies and communities, and the institutions and systems that support or harm all of the above. Instead of the money suit, the Pentacles can be the suit of workers' rights, of body and sex positivity, of wealth redistribution, of the Indigenous Land Back movement, of climate justice, and of envisioning different and better ways of building a society—a home—on this planet, together.

ACE OF PENTACLES

The other three Aces bring opportunities in the realms of inspiration, emotion, and insight, but the Ace of Pentacles is where potential becomes reality in the tangible world. This is an opportunity you can touch and hold. This is a seed with roots, ready to grow. As the essence of the suit of earth, this Ace signals a newness in the realm of work, home, wealth, comfort, pleasure, and material reality. If you pull this card at the start of a project, a career, or a relationship—all things that classically fall in the realms of the other suits—the Ace of Pentacles says that this thing has the potential for staying power and long-lasting success. This is good, rich soil for you to plant your future in.

The Ace of Pentacles can also speak to our bodies and our relationship to them, and it can herald a positive change in how we care for and nourish our bodies, how we connect to our sensuality and pleasure, or how we embody our gender and sexuality. As the first card in a suit, Aces are not only beginnings but changes. They accompany shifts and transitions, and they ask us to be willing to change to pursue the potentials they lay out for us. Beautiful new things don't usually fall in our laps without effort; instead, we have to reach out, become available, make ourselves rich soil for the seeds we want to grow. That's also what the Ace of Pentacles is about: becoming our own fertile ground for the future we want to create.

TWO OF PENTACLES

The Two of Pentacles is about finding balance amid life's wild and rocky fluctuations. It shows up to say, *life happens*. Sometimes we're smooth sailing on the yacht of our accomplishments, and other times it's all we can do to keep our head above water—and sometimes these highs and lows happen within the same week, same day, same moment. The good news is that we have the capacity to mourn our losses and celebrate our joys at the same time. That's what the Two of Pentacles is about: our ability to hold and balance opposites. These opposites may be roles we have to play at work and at home, responsibilities that pull us in multiple directions, needs that compete with our ambitions, or the plain and simple fact that life can be magnificent and it can be difficult, and oftentimes it's both at once. If we can learn to accept the bad along with the good, learn to be flexible and adaptable to life's fluctuations, then finding the balance will become much easier.

THREE OF PENTACLES

The Three of Pentacles is about the good work we do in this lifetime. It references the beautiful things we are building, the valuable contributions we're making, and the worthy work we're dedicated to. It can also reference things that we are building *together* as a people or a community, from free neighborhood gardens to mutual aid funds, from global protest movements to local beautification projects. As a card of community, if it shows up when you're feeling stunted or stuck it can suggest seeking out the help and skills of others to complement your own.

As a three, this card can mark an expansion in our material work, skill, and labor or in the results of it, possibly signaling growth opportunities, collaborations, or new expressions of our work to explore. Threes frequently appear in spiritual and religious contexts, so the Three of Pentacles carries a connotation that the work we are doing, the thing we are building, has a higher purpose. This work is not merely motivated by profit, but by a cause or a mission, and it can remind us to stay true to those values while we're growing. Growth is where so many projects go off track, after all. Whether with a business, co-op, activist network, or individual, when the success starts coming, people can change. Core values get forgotten under the glare of fame, profit, and expectation. The bottom line becomes more important than the mission statement. When the Three of Pentacles appears, it's a good sign that you're doing something worthwhile in the world. Don't forget your roots. Keep growing in line with your values.

FOUR OF PENTACLES

One way of looking at the Four of Pentacles is what can happen if we let the growth of the previous card warp our values and make us materialistic and greedy. More often than not, I see this card come up when we're too afraid of risk and vulnerability to allow much growth at all. The Four of Pentacles is about the urge to scrounge, hoard, guard, and protect. In the suit of earth, this guardedness may arise around money, material possessions, and professional opportunities, but it also frequently shows up around relationships, trust, and other sensitive personal areas. It all tracks back to the same place: the fundamental need for safety and security. Whenever we've been hurt or disappointed, no matter how far in the past, we tend to guard that area possessively. We meter out our trust like a finite resource. We declare, "Never again!" while we bury our hearts like gold in the backyard. I can't believe I'm about to use a financial metaphor, but the problem is this: gold buried in the backyard may stay safe and precious, but it will never compound interest. Investing—whether with your money, your heart, your reputation, your time, or your energy—requires risk. It requires stepping outside your comfort zone. It requires a willingness to take a loss but the belief that you'll make a gain instead.

Whatever your situation, the Four of Pentacles is here to say you don't need to be so afraid. Fours are numbers of stability, and in the earth suit this means you're in a good place right now. A place from which you can allow yourself a little vulnerability, a little risk. If you don't, it'll be like planting a tree in a pot that's too small: you're going to become root-bound and stunted, or else you're going to break the pot eventually. This card says, "Go ahead and break the damn pot." Let those roots snake into deeper soil. Let those branches spread toward the sun. A seed locked in a vault will never grow.

FIVE OF PENTACLES

Fives are challenges, and in the suit of earth, this card is an earthquake. The Five of Pentacles is about instability and uncertainty, about steady ground opening beneath our feet. The Five of Pentacles can bring up real and tangible instability in our lives—job insecurity, housing instability—but it does not signal impending doom every time it shows up on the table. More often than not, the Five of Pentacles brings up smaller issues that feel like big tremors. It has shown up for me not once but twice to reference spider mites in my houseplants—not a big deal in the grand scheme of things, but a thing that leaves me feeling frantic and unsettled in my own home. Homes are the one place in the world where we should feel peace and security, so this card shows up frequently when that fundamental need is being challenged, whether by financial changes, domestic issues, rude neighbors—or spider mites. By the same token, the Five of Pentacles can reference feeling unsafe or insecure in our own bodies, bringing up health struggles as well as bodily violations. I've seen it show up when my PTSD is triggered and when I'm feeling gender dysphoric, as well as during struggles to access transgender health care.

The Five of Pentacles has a special relationship with people from marginalized groups because we are more likely to experience poverty, employment and housing insecurity, violence and discrimination, and barriers to health-care access—but also for a less obvious reason. Like the Seven of Swords, the Five of Pentacles is a card of outsiders. It's a card for the marginalized and disen-franchised, the exiled and shunned, the oppressed and ignored. Anyone who has been turned away from a business, snubbed by a server, or harassed by a stranger because of who they are knows this card. Anyone who has been rejected by their family or com-munity because of their gender identity or sexual orientation knows this card. The Five of Pentacles speaks to us about the pain of being othered, of being denied belonging, of not being able to go home. And in that vein, it asks us to find where we do belong.

I appreciate Pamela Colman Smith's version of this card because it shows two people, injured and in rags, walking in the snow out-side a church. The implication is that they are either heading to the church doors to seek shelter, or they have been turned away from this place of sanctuary and cast out into the cold. What I like about this image is that there are two people. They are huddled together, supporting each other. Even in their exile and hardship, they are not alone. That's the medicine of the Five of Pentacles. It reminds us that there is help out there, maybe not in the usual and established places, maybe not in the mainstream or in our families of origin, but in fellowship with other people like us. There is community on the margins, and it's often more caring and connected than the communities that have barred us entry. Find your people, this card says, and you'll find home.

SIX OF PENTACLES

After the struggles of the Five of Pentacles, this next card is a welcome reprieve and a potential solution. Sixes are where the challenges of the fives recalibrate toward harmony, and in the Six of Pentacles this finds its expression in sharing and generosity. This is a card about helping each other when we're down and lifting each other up when we rise. Guidebook definitions tend to lean on charity as an interpretation, but in a radical tarot we can cast our net much broader than that. On the collective scale, this card brings up questions of income inequality, wealth redistribution, reparations, and generational poverty and wealth. If we're in a place of financial comfort, it asks us to take a hard look at our spending and start funneling some of it into mutual aid and community care. If we're in a place of financial want, it encourages us to ask for help and not be ashamed of it.

This card also extends well beyond the financial realm to bring up topics of trust, generosity, and sharing at large. The thrust of this card isn't so much about money for money's sake but about having a true investment in the *common good*. Under the highly individualistic form of capitalism that reigns today, the Six of Pentacles encapsulates the radical idea that our happiness and well-being do not hinge on how much wealth we hoard individually but on how much connection and mutual support we foster communally. Building relationships of mutual care within our communities means that we are each in the position of both helper and helped. Whether it means pooling our funds to help pay someone's rent or medical bills, organizing a casserole train to provide meals during a family's time of need, helping friends with childcare or elderly neighbors with yard work, or lending and borrowing household tools, helping each other means we have greater access to resources and a much deeper sense of stability and welfare. It means we will help when and to the extent that we can, and likewise there will be someone available to help us when we need it. That's the kind of generosity that creates abundance.

SEVEN OF PENTACLES

If you recall the sevens in the other three suits, you may have noticed that they tend to present a secondary challenge. Not one as up front and harrowing as in the fives, but more of a sideways challenge of perspective. The Seven of Pentacles brings us yet another tricky matter to ponder: success versus failure. And the distinction is not as clear as it may seem.

In the RWS deck, this card shows a farmer leaning on a shovel, gazing at a bountiful crop. Conventional interpretations usually have to do with one's proverbial harvest bearing fruit, a.k.a. your labors are finally paying off. However, I always thought the farmer looked more pensive, exhausted, and troubled than proud or jubilant. So, which is it?

When the Seven of Pentacles comes up, the reality is usually somewhere in between. This card reflects the fact that sometimes our successes are laced with disappointment. Sometimes, we get what we want and are left feeling drained and empty, the result not worth the price. Other times, success in one area of our lives comes at the cost of fulfillment in another part. The harvest starts coming in but doesn't yield the crop we expected. This card calls for a second look at our successes and disappointments. We are so thoroughly conditioned that our worth is equal to our productivity that when we fail or the product of our efforts comes out imperfect, we are buried by embarrassment and shame. We need to shift that mindset. Failure is one of the best ways to learn, improve, and innovate, and imperfection can yield surprising creativity. Maybe some adjustments will steer this thing back on track, maybe it's time to call it a loss, or maybe you can apply your lessons here to something new. You can only make the call by taking a good, long, measured look at your crop and the process you took to grow it.

EIGHT OF PENTACLES

One of the most straightforward cards in the deck, the Eight of Pentacles is about one thing: good, old-fashioned hard work. It shows up when we have something more to learn and calls for patience and diligence, because the results referenced in this card don't come quick or easy; they're the work of years, if not of a lifetime. This card asks about the *process* of our work. It goes hand in hand with the Three of Pentacles, which asks us what we're working for and *why*. The Eight of Pentacles is the *how*. Are we doing a good job? Are we enjoying it? Are we focusing on the process or rushing toward the end? The Eight of Pentacles is the kind of work that may seem tedious, laborious, or boring as sin to some, but is nourishing and pleasurable to those who love it. Sink into the process, this card says. Luxuriate in it. Appreciate the experience of the process for what it is, not only for what it produces.

Of course, our work is not *always* enjoyable. Sometimes it requires sweat, back pain, and elbow grease. When that's the case, this card says to bear down and do it anyway. Diligence, grit, and attention to detail are the name of the game in the Eight of Pentacles, because when we put in the hours, it will show. When this card appears, know what you're working toward is worthy of your efforts—and know the work isn't done yet. Hone your skills, do your research, and show up for your craft. Building something great is one part talent and three parts diligence, and you've got it in you. Get to work.

NINE OF PENTACLES

At the climax of the suit of earth, the Nine of Pentacles is a card of abundance, luxury, and achievement. When it shows up, it means that you've arrived in a place of plenitude that is entirely of your own making, so allow yourself to enjoy it! This is not the only card of success in the deck, but what sets this one apart is its connotations of independence, self-reliance, and responsibility. When the Nine of Pentacles appears, this success isn't a flash in the pan as it might be in the Six of Wands, but a success that's grown slowly and been nurtured attentively by our own hands. It doesn't burn itself out in a showy blaze; it creates seeds to sow for future endeavors. There's a particular flavor of strength and grit in this card that speaks to overcoming obstacles and beating the odds. There's also an adultness about it, the kind of self-knowledge and self-control that only comes of experience. The Nine of Pentacles highlights our ability to run our *own* lives by our *own* devices. This life is ours to build and no one else's, a fact that comes with great freedom but also responsibility.

In the RWS card, a person walks through a garden with a falcon perched on their wrist. If you look closely, the falcon is wearing a little hood. That's because it is captive, a predator trained for hunting. At first glance, the image seems to be one of luxury, power, and leisure: the person is in control, promenading through their lands, with a predator at their service. But if we dig deeper we might ask ourselves, *at what price?* The falcon might symbolize a side of ourselves that functions best under constraints—my tendency to come up with ideas for new projects in the middle of ongoing ones and get sidetracked, for example. Or it might symbolize a place where we're exercising *too much* control, keeping ourselves on too tight a leash in a way that is hampering either our potential or our happiness.

When it comes down to it, it's up to us to decide how to comport ourselves in this life. In this card of independence and pleasure, abundance and responsibility, we have to figure out our own best mix of freedom and self-control. The Nine of Pentacles asks you to define success, abundance, and pleasure on your own terms. This garden is yours to tend.

TEN OF PENTACLES

The Ten of Pentacles is traditionally a card about, well, tradition. As the conclusion of the earth suit, it makes sense that this card would be about things bigger than us that last long after we are gone. But most guidebooks confine the deep roots of this card only to the realms of family, wealth, or personal legacy—an obviously capitalist interpretation. As we've progressed through this suit, one of our focuses has been questioning the money-obsessed values of our culture that have put our planet and society at the breaking point. The Ten of Pentacles is where this work culminates.

This card asks us to reconsider the systems and institutions that instill those values, especially the patriarchal and capitalist systems that are usually reflected in the traditional Ten of Pentacles, and to do our part in building different and better ones.

Instead of generational wealth, we might take the Ten of Pentacles to be about broadening our conception of kin beyond the confines of the nuclear family, expanding it to include friends, neighbors, community, and the land itself and the creatures that live on it with us. This card about ancestry and heritage might instead be about becoming good ancestors for future generations. As a card about legacy, it might not be about getting our name on a university building but about having a meaningful positive effect on the world, no matter how small. As a card of tradition, it might be about ending traditions of oppression and harm, continuing traditions of cultural value, and creating new traditions for a newly becoming world. In the Ten of Pentacles, the seed of the Ace has become a full-grown tree, one that can live and provide shade and shelter for a long time. This card asks us to cultivate roots that go so deep they twine with others. Roots that share nutrients. Roots to hold up the hillside.

PART 4

THE
COURT CARDS

THE KING IS DEAD.
LONG LIVE THE _____

The Court Cards, also called face cards, are some of the toughest cards for newcomers to get a grip on. Do we read these as other people or as aspects of ourselves? What even is a Page, anyway? The Courts are also some of the most problematic cards, wrapped up as they are in gender norms and feudal hierarchy. The traditional thought process, where Kings are the highest-ranking member of the suit, is patriarchal to say the least. Queens are often treated as being emotional while the Kings are rational, reducing the Courts to a gender stereotype puppet show.

Some modern decks have tried to address the problem by changing the feudal titles to more relatable titles based on family roles: usually father, mother, brother, and sister. While well-intentioned, I find this method falls prey to the same pitfalls of the original, reaffirming patriarchal heads of house and going a step further by layering hierarchical gender roles onto the positions of Knight as brother and Page, the traditionally lowest-ranked card, as sister. Furthermore, it presents the picture-perfect nuclear family, down to the matched set of children, one of each binary gender, further shutting out nonbinary, two-spirit, agender, and other gender-nonconforming people; ignoring the existence of gay, lesbian, and other queer families; and potentially alienating people who come from single-parent or nontraditional homes. While I think the idea of the Court Cards as a family unit or a close-knit group is useful, I think we can find ways to reframe this set of cards without further ingraining the issues that make them problematic in the first place.

In *Fifth Spirit Tarot,* I chose to tackle this quandary by juxtaposing the traditional card titles (King, Queen, etc.) with queered imagery, purposefully troubling the gendered assumptions we make, not just about the titles but about the roles of the cards themselves. A cisgender man can be the nurturing Queen of Pentacles, a butch lesbian the empathic Queen of Cups, a trans woman the executive King of Pentacles, a nonbinary person the mentoring King of Cups.

Other decks have renamed the Court Cards entirely with non-gendered titles. Cedar McCloud's *The Numinous Tarot*, for example, adopts the titles Dreamer (Page), Explorer (Knight), Creator (Queen), and Mystic (King). This kind of renaming allows the cards to represent anyone of any gender, breaks them out of their stereotypical functions, and muddles hierarchy in lovely and expansive ways. In the following pages, I offer my own alternate titles for the Courts: Students for Pages, Seekers for Knights, Sages for Queens, and Stewards for Kings. I also suggest a name for each of the 16 cards that can help connect with its personality or way of being. Each of these offers a foothold into the card's spirit, or the way they interact with the world of their suit.

In the way I use them, Court Cards seldom represent real-life people (i.e., the King of Pentacles showing up to represent your boss at work); instead, they represent embodiments of the nature of their suit. They show up to speak to us about the way we're engaging with the energetic realm of the Wands, the emotional realm of the Cups, the mental realm of the Swords, or the material realm of the Pentacles. The Seeker of Air (Knight of Swords), for instance, seeks clarity or understanding and is driven by the power of their mind, so I dubbed them "the Genius." The Seeker of Water (Knight of Cups), on the other hand, seeks connection or emotional fulfillment and is driven by the power of their heart, hence "the Romantic." If the former appears in a reading, it might tell you to pursue your objective with intelligence and focus, while the latter might tell you to let your heart be your guide. The Court Cards can offer approaches or perspectives to consider as we work with the suits' domains in our daily lives.

In order to understand the Court Cards in a truly queered and radical way, we need to unlearn both the hierarchy and the gender norms embedded within them. New titles can help as we make this transition, but we'll never truly get there unless we also confront our own biases and assumptions buried underneath the card titles. We need to untangle reason and authority from being inherently masculine, for example, and emotion and nurturance from inherently feminine. We need to stop thinking of Pages (Students) as being inherently lesser, at the bottom of the hierarchy, and Kings (Stewards) as being the best, at the top. We learn throughout our lives, do we not? Even in positions of leadership, still we keep learning—if we don't, we'll make pretty poor leaders. The Major Arcana is a circle, and so are the Ace through Ten cards, so why not the Court Cards as well? They may seem a linear progression—even in the way I will lay them out in the following pages—but in fact the Court Cards are ways of being, ways that are cyclical and relational, ways we all embody and express at different times, simultaneously or in combination. As we will see, there is no order of greatness or hierarchy of better or worse, only various, equally valuable manners of interacting with the subject of their suit.

PAGE of WANDS

THE PAGES: STUDENT EMBODIMENT

Attributes: curiosity, open-mindedness, playfulness, creativity, exploration, growth

If we track the role of Page back to its medieval roots, pages were messengers, errand-boys, or apprentice footmen in service to a noble household. The job was taken by young people who hoped to learn, excel, and leverage it into a higher position, kind of like college kids with internships today (except pages were actually paid). A page was also a role of personal service to a knight, where the page would clean the knight's clothing and weapons, attend him, and do odd jobs in exchange for training in combat and courtly manners. In other words, pages were in the occupation of learning, training, and apprenticing. In the tarot, Pages capture this energy of *beginning* and everything that goes with it: the excitement, interest, and ambition as well as the ignorance, mistakes, and experimentation. They are *Students* of the area of their suit, learning how to engage with it, mold it, and work with it.

Updating this card for a radical tarot means reframing it outside the feudal hierarchy, but even more than that, it requires reconsidering our orientation to the status of learning, beginning, or being a novice, something that is not very prized in our hierarchy-climbing society. It means opening our minds—itself a very Student-like action—to the revolutionary power of being an amateur. In an essay on punk and queer performance, José Esteban Muñoz writes that the kind of "amateurism" that finds home and expression in those spaces "signal[s] a refusal of mastery and an insistence on process and becoming."[176] It is through this lens that the Page or Student becomes radical and powerful. In a society that demands perfection, the amateur embraces imperfection and experimentation. They do not rush toward mastery but savor the process of learning and discovery. When they engage with something, they do it for the joy of curiosity and the pleasure of play. Students know there is no shame in being new, in making mistakes, or in admitting ignorance. In fact, they know that mistakes and ignorance are an integral part of the process of learning and growing.

The radical work of the Pages is *exploring unknown possibilities.* Their superpower is that they approach everything with the open-mindedness of a beginner, the pleasure of a dabbler, and the eagerness of an enthusiast. There's a reason that most revolutions are powered by young people. They have the beginner's genius of fresh perspective, the student's inquisitiveness to ask *why*, the optimist's belief that better is possible, and the idealist's refusal to settle for less. They haven't yet become set in the ways of the world. They are new and uncharted. They are unafraid of the end and eager for the beginning. That's the radical power of the Pages, and that's where we begin.

PAGE OF WANDS, STUDENT OF FIRE: THE EXPLORER

The Page of Wands is full of big inspiration, big energy, and big ideas. They court their creative spark with curiosity and are unafraid to take risks in trying something new. As a Student of Fire, they never met an adventure they didn't take advantage of. Whether in travel, philosophy, spirituality, or art, the Page of Wands adores exploration, inspiration, and experimentation. They live in a space of creativity, whipping up the kind of art, outfits, and ideas that could be avant-garde or could be abject failures—to the Page of Wands, either is a success. The point is in the process and the triumph in the experience. Daring, bold, inventive, the Page of Wands invites us to court what lights us up. Via play, study, trial and error, this card is about learning to work with the spark of our creativity, passion, and purpose. This Page can show up when we're feeling uninspired to remind us to have fun. Go to a museum, watch a favorite movie, check out a new hiking trail, do something a little adventurous, because any spark needs fuel to catch into a blaze.

PAGE OF CUPS, STUDENT OF WATER: THE DREAMER

The Page of Cups is the Student of the heart's waters. They show up when it's time to explore our emotions from a place of curiosity instead of judgment, to indulge in imagination and fantasy without self-censorship or shame. There is so much to be discovered in the underwater realms of the subconscious, intuition, and dreams, if we don't mind getting wet. A true dreamer, the Page of Cups is brave enough to be idealistic and strong enough to believe in love. No stranger to flights of fancy and whimsy, this card has big "believes in fairies" energy and doesn't care about being deemed uncool for their unabashed sincerity. When they show up, the Page of Cups can suggest artistic exploration such as journaling, doodling, or music as avenues of self-discovery. Often appearing when our hearts are getting too calloused and crusty, this Student of Water invites us to rinse off the dust by engaging in imagination, play, and possibility. There's nothing wrong with believing in magic, this card says. There is something to be learned in the realm of emotion, intuition, or connection if we can be open-minded—and open-hearted—enough to receive it.

PAGE OF SWORDS, STUDENT OF AIR: THE SCHOLAR

The Page of Swords or Student of Air is a true student in every sense. The object of their curiosity is knowledge, truth, and understanding. They approach the world with an open but also analytical mind, seeing—and arguing—all sides of an issue. This Student never met a puzzle they could resist trying to solve, and they delight in intellectual challenge. This is the card of late-night café conversations and lively debates, of playing devil's advocate and summoning the devil, just to see if you can. The Page of Swords' ideas and thought experiments are not always sound, but they are inventive! This Page shows up when we're embarking on a new journey of understanding, or when our thoughts and opinions have become too rigid and need some shaking up. If you think you know it all, the Page of Swords says, "Think again!" Be open to new or differing perspectives, think critically and creatively, and never stop learning.

PAGE OF PENTACLES, STUDENT OF EARTH: THE MAKER

As a Student of Earth, the Page of Pentacles is a creator. Their fascination is with how things work, how they grow, how they become real. This is the energy of taking apart clocks to see what makes them tick, of chemistry experiments in the kitchen, of learning to make sourdough or sew your own clothes. Like the Page of Wands, the Page of Pentacles is also a card of creative self-expression, but in this suit the focus is on self-defined beauty and embodiment. The Page of Wands experiments with self-expression to explore themself; the Page of Pentacles does it to *embody* themself. They invite us to play with what makes us feel good, with what nurtures us, with what makes us feel at home in our own skin. The Pages or Students are all about the process of becoming in their various ways, but the Page of Pentacles handles perhaps the most tangible becoming of them all because their work is in the material realm. Whether this card references the beginning of a business or the exploration of a gender identity, rearranging the furniture or crafting something beautiful with your hands, the Student of Earth says to do it with a sense of wonder and possibility, because you're making something real.

KNIGHT of CUPS

THE KNIGHTS: SEEKER EMBODIMENT

Attributes: passion, devotion, action, movement, direction, purpose, change

When you hear the word *knight*, you probably think of medieval knights marching into battle, chivalric knights on a holy quest, or fairytale knights out to slay the dragon and save the maiden. In a radical tarot, the Knights have nothing to do with violence, conquest, and military games, nor do they have to do with storybook narratives of male heroics and female helplessness, but they *do* bear a similarity to chivalric knights. While romantic chivalry was plenty patriarchal, its emphasis on honor and devotion resonates with the tarot's Knights, who are defined by their dedication to the subject of their suit. The Knight of Cups is devoted to love, connection, and beauty; the Knight of Swords to truth, knowledge, and clarity; the Knight of Wands to passion and purpose; the Knight of Pentacles to craftsmanship and sustainability. It is this devotion that drives the Knights into action—they are fighting, searching, working for a cause. The literary genre of medieval romance (not to be confused with the hot and steamy romance genre as we know it today) was filled with stories of epic quests, wherein a knight would be honor bound to complete an objective or perform a service, often at great personal risk to themselves. This purpose-driven action in pursuit of a goal is why I call the Knights *Seekers*.

Seekers are passionate about their purpose. Their devotion drives them to take action and make moves, so these cards speak to us about the manner in which we pursue our goals. Quickly or slowly, tenderly or studiously, patiently or with great haste, each Seeker has their own pace and process. As they pursue their purpose, Seekers create ripples of change. They go after what they believe in with single-minded focus. They aren't afraid to make sacrifices for their cause, and their devotion is unmatched. In other words, the Seekers hold the energy, focus, and dedication we need to do the radical work of *creating change* in our lives and in the world.

KNIGHT OF WANDS, SEEKER OF FIRE: THE VANGUARD

The vanguard is on the forefront of change, and that's exactly where the Knight of Wands wants to be. They are an innovator and a trailblazer with a performer's energy, grabbing attention and setting fires of inspiration wherever they go. They are the kind of person who is wholly and *loudly* themself, and they don't care what anyone thinks about it—they only have eyes for their purpose. This Seeker of Fire takes bold and creative action in pursuit of their passions, giving them a definite performance-art-meets-frontline-protest vibe. They know what they want and where they're going, and they're not afraid of making some trouble to get there. Each Knight or Seeker speaks to a particular pacing and style of movement, and the Knight of Wands says to move quickly, confidently, and boldly, and do it with *style*. Don't be afraid to take some risks and ruffle some feathers, because you've got the fire of inspiration on your side.

KNIGHT OF CUPS, SEEKER OF WATER: THE ROMANTIC

The Knight of Cups is the quintessential romantic knight, wearing their heart on their sleeve and ready to do anything for love. Informed and enthusiastic consent should be a watchword with this card, because the fire of devotion mixed with strength of emotion can spell trouble otherwise. Of course, this card does not *have* to reference romantic love or connection; it also can reference pursuit of a different kind of love, the love of a cause or an ideal. The Seeker of Water is the prototypical bleeding heart, ready to fight for the rights of others, go door-to-door for a cause, and make sacrifices for what they believe in: making the world a better place. The cynical may call this Knight an idealist, but the conviction of their beliefs and the openness of their heart is this Seeker's strength. The Knight of Cups advises acting and creating change in ways that are aligned with the heart and prioritize compassion and connection. Their pace of movement flows like the tides, sometimes fast and sometimes slow, depending on what feels right. In all things, they say to let your heart lead the way.

KNIGHT OF SWORDS, SEEKER OF AIR: THE GENIUS

The Knight of Swords has a reputation in the tarot world. They can be a bit blunt and brusque in their communication, which some might perceive as unfriendliness, but it's only because they prioritize clarity of message, say it like they see it, and refuse to lie. As a Seeker of Air, this Knight is motivated in pursuit of mental clarity, information, answers, and truth. Their strength is their laser focus and tenacious attention, which can border on obsessive but also gives them the ability to hunt down any answer that can be found and solve any thought puzzle that can be solved. This is the energy of investigative journalists, whistleblowers, research scientists, astrophysicists. This Knight is the champion of truth, and their quest is to find the truth and bring it to the people, whatever that truth may be. In other words, this Seeker's radical work is about *changing minds* in the service of truth and justice. They will pursue it doggedly with unmatched attention, come what may. When they show up, the Seeker of Air says to move fast as lightning and focused as an arrow. They advise aggressive, strategic, and precise action. Stay sharp, be smart, and act quickly in the pursuit of truth.

KNIGHT OF PENTACLES, SEEKER OF EARTH: THE ARTISAN

Some other knights are all about the flash, the romance, the victory prize, but this knight plays the long game. Steady and dependable may not be glamorous, but it gets the job done. The Seeker of Earth makes this knight sound like a lost astronaut searching for home, and in a way that's not far off. The thing that this Knight seeks is a home, a stable and nourishing place to set down roots and grow. If you haven't found a literal or metaphorical home yet, this card says steady persistence will get you there, though it may come in agonizing baby steps. If you have found home, this card is all about the hard work of cultivating of it. Like a homesteader plowing fields and churning butter, the Knight of Pentacles takes on the essential labor of making a place comfortable, sustainable, and lovely. Like an artisan honing their craft, they take fine things and make them even finer. When it shows up, this card says to put in the hours, pay attention to the details, and not rush it. Good things sometimes take time. The movement of this card is slow, steady, and thorough, so have patience, even when it's frustrating, because the good work you're doing is worth it.

QUEEN ᵒf PENTACLES

THE QUEENS: SAGE EMBODIMENT

Attributes: wisdom, experience, intuition, insight, depth, holism, liminality, connectivity

I don't need to tell you what a Queen is. We've already touched on the role of women in the tarot a number of times, but suffice it to say that in a modern, radical tarot, the Queens have nothing to do with royal wifehood or the birthing of heirs. While there have been several real-life queens who have ruled in their own right, and even more who have been the brains and power behind the throne, our Queens aren't about rulership either. (Neither are our Kings.) The Queens of the tarot have, in typical gender norm fashion, frequently been chalked up to *having emotions*, even though *everyone* of *every* gender has emotions. Learning how to work with our emotions is one of the more challenging things about being a human, and one of the most powerful things once we know how to do it. Yet we diminish this essential skill to a weakness, one that considers people who feel their emotions instead of repressing them unfit to lead. On the contrary, repressing emotions is a sure way to be subconsciously ruled by them, while paying attention to and handling emotions allows us to heed them as the powerful source of information they are. That, in part, is what the Queens are all about.

Sometimes when we're trying to break out of stereotypes we flee in the farthest opposite direction from the territory of our marginalization. Instead of owning emotions for the strengths they are, we might insist that we are as "rational" and "cold-hearted" as men—falling into yet another trap of binary gender roles. I admit that I was guilty of that at one point myself and discovered that I had a fair amount of internalized misogyny to work through. The Queens of the tarot can be incredible allies in the work of disentangling submissiveness from femininity, dominance from masculinity, and emotions from being gendered at all. They invite us into exploring the intelligence of emotion and the intuitiveness of reason, into the strength of feeling into the spaces where we have been afraid to venture, into the hugeness of our capacity to embody gentleness *and* strength, feeling *and* rationality, analysis *and* intuition. Like the tides, the Queens know we are each changeable and cyclical; we can flow between states on different days, in different roles, and at different points in life. Whether high tide or low tide, it's all the ocean. And it holds depths.

I struggled to come up with an adequate name for the Queens until I remembered the DBT concept of "wise mind." We may tend to relate wisdom to a faculty of the logical brain, but here's the thing: emotions come from the brain too. Wisdom is not a product of the rational "thinking" mind only, nor is it of the emotional "feeling" mind only. Wise mind is where the two overlap. This liminal and intersectional space of wisdom, where the rational mind and emotional mind meet, where both/and takes precedence over either/or, is the territory of the Queens. That's why I've called them *Sages*.

QUEEN OF WANDS, SAGE OF FIRE: THE ARTIST

Fire is associated with creativity, vitality, spirituality, and passion, so this Queen is *hot stuff.* The Queen of Wands is the Sage of Fire, holding the wisdom of what lights us up and makes us burn. They know the power of fire to inspire, motivate, illuminate. They know how it can sway and influence. How a painting can stir thoughts and awaken feelings. How a performance can move a person to tears or laughter or action. How the body responds to a song with a foot tap, a hip sway, a mosh pit, a raised fist. This Sage bridges the gap between the fire realm of inspiration and expression and the water realm of emotion and imagination, creating a potent artistic brew that grabs eyeballs and steals hearts. The Sage of Fire is a magic worker, casting illusions that reveal truths, unknotting emotions like a tangle of hair now flowing freely. Their joy is in creating experiences for others to explore themselves, fuel their passions, feel their feelings, find their catharsis. They invite you to plumb your emotional depths and transmute the raw stuff of life into something beautiful. This card also has a performance aspect because the Sage of Fire is about holding and sharing a *vision*. Through their art and alchemy, they allow people to both see and *feel* what's possible for them, for the future, for the world. That's powerful stuff, indeed.

QUEEN OF CUPS, SAGE OF WATER: THE EMPATH

The Queen of Cups is intimately in touch with their own emotions and has the emotional intelligence to understand those of others. They are highly empathic, but I don't mean that in the New Age, psychic-adjacent way that it's tossed around today. I mean it in the sense of empathy, the ability to connect with and compassionately feel for others. The word *compassion* comes from the Latin root *pati*, to suffer, and the prefix *com*, or together, literally meaning to "suffer together." The ability to suffer with another person even when you don't have to is a truly radical act of connection and love. This Queen refuses to turn away from another's suffering for the sake of their own comfort, refuses to become calloused to the pain and injustice of the world, because they know that when one of us suffers, we all do. They know that an individual cannot single-handedly heal the pain of the world, but keeping the heart open to connection and compassion is vital or else all motivation for change is lost. It's easy to develop emotional overattachment or codependency when swimming in these heady waters, so it's important to stay clear on where other people's emotions start and where yours end.

QUEEN OF SWORDS, SAGE OF AIR: THE JUDGE

The Queen of Swords is where the heart and mind meet. Of all the Sages, this one is the clearest example of wise mind, bringing both their emotional intelligence and logical intelligence to the table. The Queen of Swords knows much information can be gleaned from paying attention to our feelings: information about what makes us feel good and bad, what soothes us and triggers us, what makes us generous, and what makes us defensive. Our behavior is dictated far more by emotion than it is by logic and reason, so it pays to be in touch with our emotional currents and work with them—not against them—to steer the proverbial ship. This card can also appear when it's time to pick up the archetypal sword and cut ties with someone, set boundaries, or hack through some bullshit. The Sage of Air's wisdom can give us more agency in our lives and equip us to make conscious decisions that are informed by both our rational and emotional realities. The radical work of this card is in defying the mind/heart dichotomy and insisting that *both* are equally valid and vitally necessary for an awakened life.

QUEEN OF PENTACLES, SAGE OF EARTH: THE CURATOR

The Queen of Pentacles has a relationship to self-care, sensuality, nurturance, and abundance, but these attributes have been well covered in other tarot books. Here, I'll highlight a quality of this card that gets less attention. One of the big things the Pentacles suit deals with is the concept of *value*—not value in terms of money, but value in terms of what we give importance and priority to. Maybe we value money (it's hard not to), but we probably also value lots of other things: our relationships, our free time, our work, our integrity. The Queen of Pentacles asks us to check in with what we value and make sure we're carrying those values through to our daily, material lives, because often what we think or say we value is out of synch with what our actions suggest. If, for example, I say I value my relationships and home life but I spend all my time working, I'm acting out of alignment with my values. If I say all bodies are beautiful but I continually criticize and shame my own, then I'm not extending my own values to myself. This Sage's wisdom bridges the gap between inwardly held values and outwardly manifest reality. When we're not living our professed values, this Sage supports us in taking a deep look at why we're struggling to uphold those values or what we're valuing over them. The Queen of Pentacles invites us to define our core values, if we haven't already, because spending time considering and clarifying them will make it easier to carry those values through into material reality in our actions, choices, and behaviors. Defining our values is a radical thing, because when we live in alignment with our authentic values, we live happier, more fulfilling lives.

KING of SWORDS

THE KINGS: STEWARD EMBODIMENT

Attributes: responsibility, accountability, leadership, service, discernment, management

Our primary examples of authority and leadership in the last many thousands of years tend to be oppressive, extractive, and tyrannical, or else lukewarm, smarmy, and incompetent. Too often, authority is synonymous with oppression and control. In our capitalist society, leaders are usually in it for fame, fortune, or power, rather than for service or accountability. However, leadership and authority do not *have* to be bad. An authority is also a person who possesses extensive knowledge and expertise in an area. Leaders can be inspirational and can influence positive change. Power, too, does not have to be abusive. Each of us has power over ourselves and our own lives. We have collective power with one another to enact meaningful change. Arguably, all the Courts hold power in their own ways. The Queen of Wands? Huge power of influence. Page of Cups? The essential power of imagination. Knight of Pentacles? The only way anything gets done around here. What we talk about when we talk about power is actually *dominance*, and dominance is only cool when it's consensual—if you know what I mean.

Let's reimagine the Kings outside of the structures of patriarchy, dominance, and supremacy. In a radical tarot, what if authority was not about command but about rigorous consideration, thoughtful discernment, and constant learning? What if leadership was not about dominance and control but about responsibility, accountability, and above all else, service? It's an oft forgotten and frequently trampled tenet of democracy that leaders only hold power at the will of the people, so what if power was decentralized and shared? Through this lens, leadership is not about consolidating power, but about *spreading* it. Authority is not about command but about guidance, not about control but about caretaking, not about rulership but about service.

To help ease this transition in reframing the Kings, I suggest the title *Steward* in its place. A Steward is a person who cares for, looks after, or manages a domain. Steward can be an official position—park rangers, estate managers, and librarians are all career stewards of a sort—but we also act as Stewards all the time in our own ways. If you pick up litter on the street, that's an act of Stewardship. If you talk to your kids about LGBTQIA2S+ rights, that's an act of Stewardship. If you pick up groceries for an elderly neighbor, if you volunteer to drive people without transportation to the voting booth, if you take accountability when you make a mistake, if you protest an oil pipeline on Indigenous lands—all meaningful acts of Stewardship. In a radical tarot, the Kings aren't despots—they're custodians, organizers, and caretakers. They know their power is a privilege, and their privilege is service.

KING OF WANDS, STEWARD OF FIRE: THE LEADER

The King of Wands is the Steward of Fire. It's their privilege and their duty to tend the flame and keep it alight. With fire's relationship to spirit, passion, inspiration, and purpose, this can mean that you find yourself in a position of caretaking the heart and soul of something deeply meaningful. Maybe it's a social movement, a spiritual group, or a local community project, but whatever the case, people look to you for guidance and inspiration.

When this card comes up, know that you hold the power to influence outcomes and motivate people for good. And remember that you may be carrying the torch right now, but this isn't about *you*, it's about that purpose, that cause, that flame that you serve. It's your job to keep it burning and lift it high for all to see, but don't get lost in the glare.

If you're not in a public-facing role, this Steward can call on you to step up into the responsible service of your passions or your spirituality. How are you tending to your own spark of life, your own spiritual flame? What can you do to more responsibly caretake it? Consider how your beliefs and opinions might be influencing those around you in meaningful ways. If you're a parent, for instance, what do your behaviors or the things you say about yourself or others teach your children? How can you be a better leader by example?

KING OF CUPS, STEWARD OF WATER: THE COUNSELOR

As the Steward of Water, the King of Cups is the responsible caretaker of the emotional realm. I've always thought of them as a counselor or therapist, someone who is a trustworthy guide and support in tough emotional waters. Their emotional intelligence means they know when to offer advice, when to ask questions, and when to just listen.

When this card shows up, it reminds you of your capacity to be a good Steward of your emotions. It can also appear when you're called to be a good friend in someone's time of need, offer wise counsel, or provide compassionate aid. In the Steward's capacity as a leader, this card can be about visibly being a person with feelings—a radical act in a society where emotions are perceived as weakness. Men owning and talking about their feelings, for example, is instrumental in turning back the tide of toxic masculinity, which teaches boys to repress and ridicule emotionality. Lastly, this Steward knows the power and utility of talking about our emotions with honesty and courage. They may call on you to broach a sensitive topic with someone you care about, to communicate your feelings, or to hold compassionate space for another.

KING OF SWORDS, STEWARD OF AIR: THE ADVOCATE

As the Steward of the suit of Air, the King of Swords is the keeper of the mental realm, acting in the diligent service of truth and peace. The Swords are a tough suit, filled with thought snarls, warped perceptions, and power imbalances, but we can work with the Steward to manage, clarify, and rectify all those challenges. In a suit about communication, the Steward streamlines and clarifies to ensure understanding. In a suit about thoughts, the Steward ponders, analyzes, researches, and makes sure all sides are heard before coming to conclusions. In a suit about truth, the Steward is a watchdog, a fact-checker, a critical thinker, upholding honesty and transparency in a world of spin and misinformation. And in a suit about power, the Steward advocates for those who are powerless, wields their privilege to fight oppression, and amplifies the voices of the unheard.

In a way, the King of Swords has the most difficult position of all the Kings, because this card is so often about being accountable even when it's hard, being honest even when it's scary, about being visible even when it's intimidating. As the Steward of the mental realm, this King can also be about seeking or receiving mental health treatment, advocating for the mentally ill and for mental health resources, or fighting the stigma of mental illness by spreading awareness and information. Lastly, in the domain of truth and communication, this King can ask you to share your story. Whatever it may be, your story has a place in the world and an audience that will connect with it. Don't be afraid to share your truth, because your truth is valid and meaningful, and someone out there might need to hear it.

KING OF PENTACLES, STEWARD OF EARTH:
THE GARDENER

The King of Pentacles is the Steward of Earth, offering support in taking care of what we've planted. As a gardener, the Steward of Earth knows when to fertilize and when to prune, when to harvest and when to dig up the bulbs for winter. Their role is not to keep a thing frozen in time, nor to sustain it in unnatural and unceasing growth, but instead to care for it through all its cycles of change and transition, of growth and decline. That's something we tend to forget—or ignore—when we connect this card to capitalistic conventions of profit, legacy, and wealth accumulation, as so often happens when we hear its other name, the King of Coins. The constant growth that is demanded under capitalism is not only unsustainable, it's destructive. We have forgotten when to build and when to demolish, when to work and when to rest, when to let a plant go to seed.

The Steward of Earth is about reconnecting ourselves to this wisdom and letting it guide our actions. We have an opportunity in the Steward of Pentacles to plant different values: to nurture the Earth instead of destroying it, to cultivate more ease and rest amid the productivity grind, to prioritize pleasure and generosity instead of perfection and greed. This leadership is patient and wise. It's steady and thorough. It's grounded in values of sustainability, accountability, community, and care.

A good gardener knows what to fertilize and what to pull out by the roots. Remember what *radical* means? Of the roots. In a radical framework, the roots are the values that give the whole system nourishment, stability, structure, and meaning. The health of the roots affects the whole organism. So be a good steward and tend to the roots. And remember: what you nurture, grows.

PART 5

READING TAROT RADICALLY

READ THE CARDS, CREATE THE FUTURE

First things first: there's no "right" way to do a tarot reading. There's no right way to shuffle, no right way to flip over the cards, no right way to read reversals or not read reversals. There's also no right way to acquire your first deck—the long-standing rumor that you must be gifted your first tarot deck is mystical misinformation at best, and a gatekeeper strategy at worst. You can absolutely buy your first deck—I did. Twice. The only wrong way you can read tarot, in my opinion, is if you give up your power to it. Here, we'll take a practical look at how to read the cards—not for telling the future but for *creating* it.

1. ASK GOOD QUESTIONS

A reading consists of four main parts: the question, the shuffle, the spread, and the interpretation. Formulating the question is important because it establishes the subject matter of the reading, but also because it gives you a chance to refine what you're *actually* looking for or wanting from a reading. I stay away from yes/no questions because tarot is a tool for exploration, not precision, and anyway, life is seldom so binary. If you want to ask a yes/no question, like "Will I get the promotion?," what you're really looking for is a sense of security in knowing the future. A natural desire, but one that's impossible to satisfy because the future is not set in stone. Since the tarot's purpose is to examine the present in order to help shape the future, a better question might be "How can I best set myself up for success at work?" Or even "What do I need to know about work?" During the course of the reading, you might discover that what you're really concerned about is a sense of security or a fear of rejection. Or maybe you don't actually like your position and need to look for a new one. With this deeper information about what's going on beneath the surface, you can better support yourself in making conscious decisions about what's best for you. I find that *why* and *how* questions yield the richest readings, along with open-ended inquiries like the "What do I need to know" example.

2. SHUFFLE IN (SOME) CHAOS

Then comes the shuffle. I like to shuffle while I'm mulling over my question because I find the act of shuffling meditative and relaxing. Like all meditative things, the shuffle helps loosen the mind, makes space for thoughts and feelings to drift up from the subconscious, and facilitates making creative connections—a conducive mental space for any tarot reading. If you're new to shuffling, it probably won't feel at all meditative at first. That's okay! Be patient with yourself. With experience, you'll find the shuffle that works best for you—it's probably the one that lets you sink into a rhythm. A question I get asked a lot is, "How do you know when to stop shuffling?" For me, the answer is "When it feels right." Infuriating, I know, but it's a sense that you'll develop over time. If you find yourself shuffling endlessly, try declaring a stopping point. Tell your cards, "Three more shuffles and we'll be ready." And then stick to it.

When it's time to put cards on the table, there's also no right way to pull cards from the deck. Some people pull directly from the top of the deck, while others cut the deck in the middle and draw from there. Others like to fan the cards on the table and pick at random or with the help of a pendulum. Experiment with various methods, and eventually you'll find the one that feels best to you.

3. INTRODUCE SOME ORDER

The next part of a reading is the spread. A tarot spread is simply an arrangement of cards where each position has a specific meaning or purpose. Some spreads are designed for a specific kind of question or subject matter, such as decision spreads, and some are more general and suited to a wide variety of questions. When choosing a spread, pick one that suits your question and doesn't feel overwhelming.

There are an infinite variety of spreads out there with varying levels of complexity, from two-card spreads to 78-card spreads. (Yes, there are spreads that use every card in the deck.) I find that there's a point where a spread becomes so large and complex that it stops being helpful, but some people love spending hours sinking into a giant spread.

If you're just starting out, stick to the smaller spreads. I used a simple four-card spread for everyday guidance when I was learning. At the beginning of every week, I'd ask, "What do I need to know about the week ahead?" and draw one card for the overall outlook, one for the week's challenge, one for the week's blessing, and one for the week's advice. I'd record the cards and journal about them throughout the week as anything relevant came up. At the end of the week, I would look back and see how the cards showed up in my day-to-day. This helped me reverse engineer their meanings in a personal and practical way as I developed my own relationship with the cards.

It's a good idea to choose your spread before you start shuffling, but sometimes I make my spreads up on the fly *as* I'm shuffling. Give yourself the freedom to do this too! The cards—and your intuition—will tell you where to go and what to do next. Either way, knowing what positions you're using before you start putting cards on the table is usually a good idea.

4. FIND THE PATTERNS

Once you've shuffled and laid the cards on the table, it's finally time to read them! Reading tarot is not an exact science; it's more like an art. It's intuitive and interpretive, a dance whose rhythm you discover as you go. At the same time, it's analytical, using the part of your brain that notices patterns and solves puzzles. The act of interpretation bridges the visual realm of the cards and the linguistic realm of making meaning, involving both sides of the brain in its dance. (Remember when I told you the tarot was non-binary? It's both/and, not either/or. It's synthesis, not separation.) Reading a spread is kind of like looking at one of those Magic Eye posters from the '90s where a 3-D image rises from the pixelated fuzz: you have to kind of relax your eyes and let them cross a little to see the picture emerge. You don't *literally* need to cross your eyes when reading a spread, but it helps to zoom out and loosen up to allow connections between cards to emerge. The meaning comes from the juxtaposition of card and spread position, but also from the spaces *between* the cards, from the overlap of meaning, from the buzz of intuition hovering like a static field. It comes from the places where things meet, from where a paper card meets imaginative possibility, from the margins, not the center.

Sometimes when you lay out the cards, an answer will jump out immediately, clear as day. If this feels like an "aha" moment, where something surprising suddenly seems obvious, then you're onto something. If this instead feels like a lead weight or a deflation, it's probably confirmation bias. When interpreting, be aware of your own tendencies toward either worst-case scenario dooms-day thinking or everything's-fine wishful thinking. If your conclusions feel like there's a lot of emotion attached, it's probably your fears reading the cards for you. Likewise, if your reading feels coldly logical, you're probably not allowing space for intuition and the unexpected to come through.

I've mentioned the DBT concept of "wise mind" before, and that's helpful here too. Wise mind is the mental space where you're able to consider emotional input from your feelings as well as logical input from facts and analysis without giving undue power to either. This is the space I look for when I'm reading—that nonbinary space of head *and* heart, reality *and* possibility. Intuition is often cast as an illogical or emotional thing, but that couldn't be more wrong. Intuition is instead a sense that arises from this in-between, wise mind space, both logical and emotional and something else altogether: a calm and quiet sense of *understanding*. As you spend more time reading tarot, you'll develop this intuition muscle and it will become easier to find this wise, centered space, both when reading and during the ups and downs of daily life.

5. CREATE THE FUTURE

The goal of a reading is not to tell the future, make predictions, or make your decisions for you. A reading is instead a safe space for reflection, exploration, and self-knowledge. It's a space for uncovering what's going on underneath your surface, for figuring out what's pulling your strings, for bringing your tenderest hopes and deepest fears into the light of day so you can address them consciously. You will rarely leave a reading with a clear and tidy answer—that's not the point. Instead, you'll leave with a new array of self-knowledge, with a sense of acceptance or understanding, and *that* can give you the information and impetus you need to change your life.

The tarot provides a way to look at the past to understand how it's affecting the present, and to look at the present to understand how it's creating the future. We might pull cards in a "future" position, but this does not suggest a future set in stone but rather a potential trajectory to contemplate in conjunction with our agency to make change in the present. This is what makes the tarot so liberatory: it naturally empowers each of us to consciously create change. It gives us back our agency and our awareness. It puts the power to direct the future into our hands.

So, grab your cards and don your Fool's cap. It's time to change the World.

CONCLUSION

When I say that tarot saved my life, people usually think I'm being dramatic. But I mean it. Before tarot found me that second time, I was living a half-life of unexamined choices and compulsory roles, of dulled emotions and tepid dreams. I was a ghost of the fully alive person I could be—who I am now, who I am still becoming. But tarot didn't save my life all by itself. I had to help. I had to step up to the table, ask the hard questions, and face down the scary cards. I had to tear up the foundations of my Towers, dance with my Devils, and howl my wildness at the Moon. I had to be bold enough to divine a future of my own creation and brave enough to risk a Fool's leap into the unknown.

Tarot is radical and revolutionary because it introduces us to ourselves by reconnecting us to emotion and intuition and empowering us to self-direct our lives. It invites us to examine our beliefs and values, and it opens our awareness to new perspectives. It cultivates a marginal consciousness where we can consider things slantwise and from many directions, a queer vantage from which new possibilities, new portals, new realities can emerge. Across its history, tarot has refused to be pinned down and codified into just one thing, not in iconography or archetype, correspondence or magical system. Like nature, like thought, like water, it adapts and slithers. It moves and becomes anew.

I wrote this book in the hopes of sharing the way I use tarot, the way that saved my life, with other people like me. I wrote it for the queer kids and teen witches who will hide this book in their bedrooms, who search for themselves in secret because they can't in the open, who intrepidly chase that magic spark. I wrote it for the adults who have lived through some shit and survived, who are rich with complexity, who stay awake with nightmares, who are bruised and weary and still hopeful. I wrote it for anyone who has ever felt lost, clueless, and unworthy, who has made mistakes and fears the next step, who dreams that there is more to life than this. (Spoiler alert: there is.)

I wrote it for you too, reading this, even if you're nothing like me. *Especially* if you're nothing like me. (Though I suspect we have more in common than you think.) Tarot is a conversation— between you and the cards on the table, between reader and querent, between my interpretations and yours, and between every other person who reads the cards, past, present, and future. The conversation is ongoing, and you are a part of it. If this book does only one thing, I hope it invites you to engage in the conversation by questioning your assumptions, breaking the rules, reimagining your cards, and discovering your *own* radical tarot. Tarot is a revolutionary tool, but only if you use it like one.

So here at the end, my benediction for you is this: May you be bold enough to challenge your Emperors and question your Hierophants, daring enough to listen to your High Priestesses and open to your Empresses, soft enough to befriend your Strength and unspool your Deaths, and hopeful enough to topple your Towers and follow your Stars. May the Sun's warmth shine within you and the Hermit's lantern brighten your path. May the Lovers ride beside you as you steer your Chariot through life's bends, and may you not fear the Devil because the Moon is on your side. And when you finally hear Judgment's trumpet, may you have the Magician's magic and the Hanged One's wisdom, Justice's discernment and a Fool's faith to rise to the call. May the Wheel roll ever in the direction of your best future, dear friend, and may Temperance lift you on wings past every border, because a new World is on the horizon.

Tarot always meets us in the present, at the nexus of yesterday and tomorrow, in this most maximum moment of potential energy for change. Here, now, on this perpetual ledge between the known and the unknown, is where we create the future.

It's time to begin.

ACKNOWLEDGMENTS

This book truly would not exist without my spouse and partner in all things. Aaron, thank you for listening to my zany late-night tarot ramblings, reading every chapter as soon as the proverbial ink was dry, and putting homecooked meals in front of me when I'm too in the zone to remember to eat. Thank you for loving me through all my changes and for believing in me with unabashed enthusiasm. But most of all, thank you for reading my cards after the Renaissance fair. The moment you crashed into my life, I swear I tripped through a portal into an alternate and *way better* reality. You made the magic real.

Thank you to my mom, Donna Burgess, for reading me poetry at bedtime and keeping *The Power of Myth* on your bookshelf. You were the first person to introduce me to the magic and divinity in all things, to *everything which is natural, which is infinite, which is yes*. Thank you to my dad, Dean Burgess, for modeling that strength and gentleness, seriousness and humor are not opposites but companions, for being endlessly interested in and supportive of me, and for always trying to understand. And thank you to my brothers, Andrew and Mark: the resilience, compassion, and thoughtfulness you both exude pushes me to be a better person. I'm so thankful you're my family.

To Coleman Stevenson, thank you for your friendship, advice, and generosity, and for demonstrating that one can build an exceptional life out of tarot, writing, and art. You gave me the courage to build my own. Thank you to Erik Arneson for many a conversation (slash debate, slash banter session) about tarot, ceremonial magic, grimoires, gods and goddesses, occult miscellany, and the mysteries of the universe—over many, many beers, of course. To Sara Mulholland D'Antoni, my platonic true love and first comrade in the resistance (damn the man!), thank you for all the history and civics lessons, for the cathartic rants about politics, and for making me laugh about the bleakest things.

To my other lovely friends who are never afraid to wade into deep conversational waters about tarot, magic, gender (what even is it?), love, and life, especially Joseph, Iris, Kelsey, and Hazel. Thank you for making me think and making me cackle in equal measure. To Jenny, who convinced me over drinks at a Belmont Street bar one night in 2018 that I had something worthwhile to offer the tarot world, thank you for lending me your enthusiasm, optimism, and faith. You tipped the first domino.

A massive thank-you to my agent, Kelly Van Sant, the most wonderful advocate and adviser a radical queer witch could hope for, and to my incredible and thoughtful editor, Anna Cooperberg. Both of you believed in me patiently and persistently well before I typed the first word of this manuscript, and I don't know if I would have had the audacity to write a book like this without that belief. What an incredible gift it is to work with you both.

Thank you to everyone at Hay House, including eagle-eyed copyeditor Lea Galanter, Kathleen Reed, Tricia Breidenthal, Nick Welch, the amazing design team that cooked up the cover with me, and all the many people who had hands on this book behind the scenes.

This book wouldn't be what it is without the amazing tarot community I've found online. So many of you have inspired and touched me with your ideas, words, art, or just by being you. I don't have the room to name you all, but I must particularly and wholeheartedly thank Cassandra Snow, Lane Smith, and Nick Kepley. You have each inspired me, challenged me, lifted me up, and made me think about tarot in new ways. Cassandra, you're *the* trailblazer in queer tarot as far as I'm concerned. This book exists in your footsteps. Lane and Nick, thank you for sharing your wild, queer, nonbinary, liberatory visions for tarot with me. Let's fuck shit up.

Lastly, thank you to the Fool, the Tower, and the Star, the patron saints of this radical little book. You taught me that the heart of resistance, of defiance, of revolution, is hope.

ENDNOTES

Introduction

1. *Rider Waite Tarot Deck* instruction booklet (Stamford, CT: U.S. Games Systems, Inc., 1991).

Chapter 1

2. Audre Lorde, "Uses of the Erotic," *The Selected Works of Audre Lorde*, ed. Roxane Gay (New York: W. W. Norton, 2020), 32–33.
3. *Merriam-Webster*, s.v. "radical," accessed February 20, 2023, https://www .merriam-webster.com/dictionary/radical.
4. Credit for this magical talisman of a question goes to Black trans actress and LGBTQIA2S+ advocate Laverne Cox, who ends every episode of her podcast, *The Laverne Cox Show*, by asking her guest, "What else is true?"
5. I am indebted to the works of many, but especially Asali Earthwork, creator of Tarot of the QTPOC (Queer Trans People of Color) resource at https://www .asaliearthwork.com/tarot-of-the-qtpoc; Cassandra Snow, author of *Queering the Tarot*; Cedar McCloud, author and creator of *The Numinous Tarot*; and Courtney Alexander, writer, artist, and creator of the *Dust II Onyx* tarot.
6. Cassandra Snow, *Queering the Tarot* (Newburyport, MA: Red Wheel/Weiser, 2019), 4.

Chapter 2

7. Ronald Decker, Thierry Depaulis, and Michael Dummett, *A Wicked Pack of Cards: The Origins of Occult Tarot* (New York: St. Martin's Press, 1996), 40–42.
8. My understanding of tarot numerology is indebted to the work of Rachel Pollack, *Seventy-Eight Degrees of Wisdom*, rev. ed. (San Francisco: Weiser Books, 2007); Mary K. Greer, *Tarot for Your Self: A Workbook for Personal Transformation* (North Hollywood, CA: Newcastle Publishing, 1984); and Faith Javane and Dusty Bunker, *Numerology and the Divine Triangle* (Atglen, PA: Whitford Press, 1979).
9. Lorde, *Selected Works*, 173–4.
10. Sonya Renee Taylor, *The Body Is Not an Apology: The Power of Radical Self-Love*, 2nd ed. (Oakland, CA: Berrett-Koehler, 2021), 36.

Chapter 3

11. Nick Kepley frequently discusses the limitations and harms of the masculine/ feminine duality and of using gender as a shorthand on their Instagram (https://www.instagram.com/insearchoftarot/), notably in their Gender in Tarot series from 2020–2021, and on their podcast, *In Search of Tarot* (https:// anchor.fm/in-search-of-tarot/).
12. Arthur Rosengarten, *Tarot and Psychology: Spectrums of Possibility* (St. Paul, MN: Paragon House, 2000), 113.

13. Walt Whitman, "Song of Myself," *Leaves of Grass*, 1892 version, https://www
.poetryfoundation.org/poems/45477/song-of-myself-1892-version.
14. Rachel Pollack, *Seventy-Eight Degrees of Wisdom*, revised ed. (San Francisco:
Weiser Books, 2007), 22.

The Fool

15. Helen Farley, *Cultural History: From Entertainment to Esotericism* (London:
Bloomsbury Academic, 2009), 83.
16. Charles Taylor, *A Secular Age* (Harvard University Press, 2009), 46.
17. Farley, 82.
18. Yoav Ben-Dov, *The Marseille Tarot Revealed: A Complete Guide to Symbolism,
Meanings, and Methods* (Woodbury, MN: Llewellyn, 2021), 201.
19. *Meditations on the Tarot: A Journey into Christian Hermeticism* (New York:
Tarcher/Putnam, 2002), 605.
20. Arthur Edward Waite, *The Pictorial Key to the Tarot* (Stamford, CT: U.S. Games
Systems, Inc., 1994), 152.
21. José Esteban Muñoz, *Cruising Utopia: The Then and There of Queer Futurity*,
10th anniversary ed. (New York: New York University Press, 2009), 26–7.
22. Ibid, 22, 25.

The Magician

23. Sallie Nichols, *Tarot and the Archetypal Journey: The Jungian Path from Darkness
to Light* (Newburyport, MA: Red Wheel/Weiser, 2019), 69.
24. Pollack, 31.
25. Ibid.
26. *Meditations*, 41.
27. Nichols, 50, 53.
28. Ibid, 52.
29. adrienne maree brown, *Emergent Strategy: Shaping Change, Changing Worlds*
(Chico, CA: AK Press, 2017), 59.
30. Ibid, 53.
31. Muñoz, 121.

The High Priestess

32. Paul Huson, *Mystical Origins of the Tarot: From Ancient Roots to Modern Usage*
(Rochester, VT: Destiny Books, 2004), 83–4; Farley, 55.
33. Farley, 52, 57.
34. Ibid, 55–7.
35. Muñoz, 65.
36. Silvia Federici, *Caliban and the Witch: Women, the Body, and Primitive
Accumulation*, 2nd rev. ed. (New York: Autonomedia, 2014), 33.
37. Maria Minnis, "Reimagining Love and Light with the High Priestess,"
MariaMinnis.com, accessed June 29, 2022, https://www.mariaminnis.com/
blog/anti-racism-with-the-tarot-reimagining-love-and-light-with-the-high-
priestess.
38. *Meditations, 40, 41.*
39. Ibid, 30.
40. Online Etymology Dictionary, "conscious," accessed June 28, 2022, https://
www.etymonline.com/word/conscious.

The Empress

41. Robert M. Place, *The Tarot, Magic, Alchemy, Hermeticism, and Neoplatonism* (Saugerties, NY: Hermes Publications, 2017), 385.
42. Pollack, 45.
43. Lorde, 30, 32–3.
44. Ibid, 34.
45. Devon Price, *Laziness Does Not Exist: A Defense of the Exhausted, Exploited, and Overworked* (New York: Atria Books, 2021), 106.
46. Lorde, 31.

The Emperor

47. brown, 84–6.
48. Ibid, 87.
49. Tyson Yunkaporta, *Sand Talk: How Indigenous Thinking Can Save the World* (New York: Harper One, 2020), 68–71.
50. Ibid, 96.
51. Misha Magdalene, *Outside the Charmed Circle: Exploring Gender & Sexuality in Magical Practice* (Woodbury, MN: Llewellyn, 2020), 255–6.

The Hierophant

52. Magdalene, 112.
53. Octavia Butler, *Parable of the Sower* (London: Headline, 2019), 43.
54. Lorde, 32–3.
55. Ibid, 173.
56. Alice Sparkly Kat, *Postcolonial Astrology: Reading the Planets through Capital, Power, and Labor* (Berkeley: North Atlantic Books, 2021), 13.

The Lovers

57. bell hooks, *All About Love* (New York: William Morrow, 2001), 165.
58. Muñoz, 68.
59. Taylor, 36.
60. Lorde, 173.
61. hooks, 185

The Chariot

62. Rickie Solinger, *Pregnancy and Power: A Short History of Reproductive Politics in America* (New York: NYU Press, 2005), 89.
63. Huson, 98.
64. Jessica Dore, *Tarot for Change: Using the Cards for Self-Care, Acceptance, and Growth* (New York: Penguin Life, 2021), 63.
65. Pollack, 68.
66. brown, 70.

Strength

67. Aradhna Krishna, "How Did 'White' Become a Metaphor for All Things Good?" *The Conversation*, July 6, 2020, https://theconversation.com/how-did-white-become-a-metaphor-for-all-things-good-140674; Hope Johnson, "DARKNESS and LIGHT: Updated Personal Perspectives," *Unitarian*

Universalist Association, October 9, 2020, https://www.uua.org/southern/blog/darkness.
68. Taylor, 65.
69. Ibid, 66.
70. Nichols, 205.
71. Ibid.
72. Timothy Morton, "Guest Column: Queer Ecology," *PMLA*, Vol. 125, No. 2 (March 2010), 275–6.

The Hermit

73. Ben-Dov, 145; Place, *Tarot, Magic, Alchemy*, 421–2.
74. Farley, 68.
75. Huson, 104.
76. My understanding of these three paths is a merger of theories from Rachel Pollack, Sallie Nichols, the anonymously authored *Meditations on the Tarot* (thought to be by Valentin Tomberg), and Lindsay Mack.
77. Place, *Tarot, Magic, Alchemy*, 424.
78. Ibid.

The Wheel of Fortune

79. Joseph Campbell and Bill Moyers, *The Power of Myth* (New York: Doubleday, 1988), 118.
80. Lindsay talks about finding one's center with the Wheel frequently in her classes and her podcast *Tarot for the Wild Soul*. See Lindsay Mack, "93. Staying in our Center with Wheel of Fortune," November 17, 2019, in *Tarot for the Wild Soul*, produced by Lindsay Mack, podcast, MP3 audio, 59:21, https://podcasts.apple.com/us/podcast/93-staying-in-our-center-with-wheel-of-fortune/.
81. Rebecca Solnit, *Hope in the Dark: Untold Histories, Wild Possibilities,* 3rd ed. (Chicago: Haymarket Books, 2016), 78.
82. Bayo Akomolafe, *These Wilds Beyond Our Fences: Letters to My Daughter on Humanity's Search for Home* (Berkeley: North Atlantic Books, 2017), 12.
83. Nichols, 186.

Justice

84. Charles W. Bardsley, *Curiosities of Puritan Nomenclature* (London: Chatto and Windus, 1888), retrieved from *The Public Domain Review*, https://publicdomainreview.org/collection/curiosities-of-puritan-nomenclature-1888#0-0.
85. Yunkaporta, 40.
86. James Baldwin, "As Much Truth As One Can Bear," *New York Times Book Review*, January 14, 1962, Section 7, https://www.nytimes.com/1962/01/14/archives/as-much-truth-as-one-can-bear-to-speak-out-about-the-world-as-it-is.html.
87. Pollack, 91.
88. Baldwin, "As Much Truth," *New York Times*.
89. Pollack, 92.

The Hanged One

90. Ben-Dov, 157.
91. Farley, 71.
92. Ibid, 70–2.
93. Huson, 115.
94. Nichols, 216.
95. Huson, 113.
96. Brené Brown, "Listening to Shame," March 2012, TED video, 14:20, https://youtu.be/psN1DORYYV0.
97. Lorde, 60.
98. Lorde, 177.

Death

99. Huson, 36–7, 117–8; Farley, 75.
100. Place, *Tarot, Magic, Alchemy*, 445–6; Nichols, 230; Ben-Dov, 161.
101. Kat, 95.
102. Éliphas Lévi, *Transcendental Magic: Its Doctrine and Ritual*, trans. Arthur Edward Waite (United Kingdom: William Rider & Son, Limited, 1923), 476.
103. Akomolafe, 218.
104. hooks, 80–81.
105. Nichols, 229.
106. Oscar Wilde, *De Profundis* (London: Methuen & Co., 1913; Project Gutenberg, 2007), https://www.gutenberg.org/files/921/921-h/921-h.htm.
107. Nichols, 228.
108. Akomolafe, 285.

Temperance

109. Waite, 124.
110. *Merriam-Webster*, s.v. "temperance," accessed February 22, 2022, https://www.merriam-webster.com/dictionary/temperance.
111. *Merriam-Webster*, s.v. "temper," accessed August 14, 2022, https://www.merriam-webster.com/dictionary/temper.
112. Place, 451; Huson, 121; Ben-Dov, 165; Farley, 67.
113. Place, 451.
114. adrienne maree brown, *Pleasure Activism: The Politics of Feeling Good* (Chico, CA: AK Press, 2019), 15.
115. Ibid, 16.
116. Place, 340–50, 451.
117. Pollack, 106–7; Nichols, 258.
118. Dore associates DBT's "wise mind" with the Hermit, which is a very cool perspective. Dore, 91.
119. Sophie Strand, *The Flowering Wand: Rewilding the Sacred Masculine* (Rochester, VT: Inner Traditions, 2022), 113.

The Devil

120. Ben-Dov, 171; Huson, 125; *Meditations*, 403.
121. Huson, 32–34.
122. Federici, 17.
123. Ibid, 194.

124. Ibid, 186, 194.
125. Ibid, 197.
126. Ibid, 198.
127. Ibid, 200.
128. Elisabeth Schüssler Fiorenza, "A Critical Feminist Biblical Hermeneutics of Liberation," *Theologies of the Multitude for the Multitudes*, ed. Rita Nakashima Brock and Tat-siong Benny Liew (Claremont Press, 2021), 115.
129. Sumi Cho, Kimberlé Williams Crenshaw, and Leslie McCall, "Toward a Field of Intersectionality Studies: Theory, Applications, and Praxis," *Signs* 38, no. 4 (2013): 797, https://doi.org/10.1086/669608.
130. *Meditations*, 408.
131. Alejandro Jodorowsky, *The Way of Tarot: The Spiritual Teacher in the Cards* (Rochester, VT: Destiny Books, 2004), 214–17; Snow, 48–50.
132. Rosengarten, 101.
133. Federici, 177.

The Tower

134. Robert M. Place, *The Tarot: History, Symbolism, and Divination* (New York: Tarcher/Penguin, 2005), 155.
135. King James Bible, Rev. 8:7, https://kingjamesbibleonline.org/Revelation-Chapter-8/#7.
136. Huson, 131.
137. *Merriam-Webster.com*, s.v. "chaos," accessed August 21, 2022, https://www.merriam-webster.com/dictionary/chaos.
138. Farley, 84.

The Star

139. Ernst Bloch, "Can Hope Be Disappointed?" *Literary Essays,* Trans. Andrew Joron and others (Stanford, CA: Stanford U. Press, 1998), 340.
140. Solnit, 4.
141. Ibid, xiii–xiv.
142. Muñoz, 1.
143. Ibid.

The Moon

144. Farley, 76.
145. Waite, 140.
146. Mary K. Greer, "The Moon Card: Between a Dog and a Wolf," *Mary K. Greer's Tarot Blog*, September 17, 2021, https://marykgreer.com/2021/09/17/the-moon-card-between-a-dog-and-a-wolf/.
147. Akomolafe, 284.
148. Morton, "Guest Column: Queer Ecology," *PMLA* 125, no. 2 (2010): 276. http://www.jstor.org/stable/25704424.
149. Ibid, 277.
150. Dore, 109.
151. Akomolafe, 284.

The Sun

152. Kat, 34.

153. brown, *Pleasure Activism,* 13.
154. Taylor, Prologue to *The Body Is Not an Apology,* 2nd ed., xvii.
155. ALOK Vaid-Menon, interview with Justin Baldoni, Liz Plank, and Jamey Heath, "ALOK: The Urgent Need for Compassion," *The Man Enough Podcast,* July 26, 2021, YouTube video, 7:50 to 7:57, https://youtu.be/Tq3C9R8HNUQ.
156. ALOK Vaid-Menon, *Beyond the Gender Binary* (New York: Penguin Workshop, 2020), 25.
157. "ALOK: The Urgent Need for Compassion," 28:53 to 29:31.
158. Alice Walker, *Possessing the Secret of Joy* (New York: Harcourt, 1992), 279.

Judgment

159. Yunkaporta, 68.
160. Wren Sanders, "Theorist Susan Stryker on One of Her Most Groundbreaking Essays, 25 Years Later," *Them* (November 14, 2019), https://www.them.us/story/susan-stryker-groundbreaking-essays-25-years-later.
161. Yunkaporta, 68.
162. Sanders, "Theorist Susan Stryker," November 14, 2019.
163. Arundhati Roy, *War Talk* (Cambridge: South End Press, 2003), 75.

The World

164. Huson, 151.
165. Akomolafe, 250.
166. Place, *The Tarot,* 165.
167. Solnit, 79.
168. Muñoz, 121.
169. Ibid, 97.
170. Ibid, 121.
171. Solnit, 80–1.
172. Ibid, 95.
173. Butler, 3.

The Wands That Spark Creation

174. Erik is the host of the *Arnemancy* podcast on tarot, magic, Hermeticism, and occult philosophy, which can be found at https://arnemancy.com/.

The Swords of the Two-Edged Mind

175. Price, 23–5.

The Pages

176. Muñoz, 106.

BIBLIOGRAPHY

Akomolafe, Bayo. *These Wilds Beyond Our Fences: Letters to My Daughter on Humanity's Search for Home.* Berkeley, CA: North Atlantic Books, 2017.

Anonymous. *Meditations on the Tarot: A Journey into Christian Hermeticism.* Translated by Robert Powell. New York: Tarcher/Putnam, 2002.

Baldwin, James. "As Much Truth As One Can Bear." *New York Times Book Review,* January 14, 1962, Section 7. https://www.nytimes.com/1962/01/14/archives/as-much-truth-as-one-can-bear-to-speak-out-about-the-world-as-it-is.html.

Ben-Dov, Yoav. *The Marseille Tarot Revealed: A Complete Guide to Symbolism, Meanings, and Methods.* Woodbury, MN: Llewellyn, 2021.

Bloch, Ernst. "Can Hope Be Disappointed?" In *Literary Essays,* translated by Andrew Joron and others, 339–45. Stanford, CA: Stanford University Press, 1998.

brown, adrienne maree. *Emergent Strategy: Shaping Change, Changing Worlds.* Chico, CA: AK Press, 2017.

———. *Pleasure Activism: The Politics of Feeling Good.* Chico, CA: AK Press, 2019.

Butler, Octavia. *Parable of the Sower.* London: Headline, 2019.

Campbell, Joseph and Bill Moyers. *The Power of Myth.* New York: Doubleday, 1988.

Chang, T. Susan. *Tarot Correspondences: Ancient Secrets for Everyday Readers.* Woodbury, MN: Llewellyn, 2019.

Cronon, William. "The Trouble with Wilderness; or, Getting Back to the Wrong Nature." WilliamCronon.net. Accessed July 29, 2022. https://www.williamcronon.net/writing/Trouble_with_Wilderness_Main.html. Originally in William Cronon, ed., *Uncommon Ground: Rethinking the Human Place in Nature.* New York: W. W. Norton, 1995.

Crowley, Aleister. *Magick in Theory and Practice.* New York: Dover, 1976.

Decker, Ronald, Thierry Depaulis, and Michael Dummett. *A Wicked Pack of Cards: The Origins of the Occult Tarot.* New York: St. Martin's Press, 1996.

Decker, Ronald and Michael Dummett. *A History of the Occult Tarot.* United Kingdom: Duckworth, 2002.

Derrida, Jacques. *Points . . . : Interviews, 1974–1994.* Edited by Elisabeth Weber. Translated by Peggy Kamuf and others. Stanford, CA: Stanford University Press, 1995.

Dore, Jessica. *Tarot for Change: Using the Cards for Self-Care, Acceptance, and Growth.* New York: Penguin Life, 2021.

Farley, Helen. *A Cultural History of Tarot: From Entertainment to Esotericism.* London: Bloomsbury Academic, 2009.

Federici, Silvia. *Caliban and the Witch: Women, the Body, and Primitive Accumulation*. 2nd rev. ed. New York: Autonomedia, 2014.

Giles, Cynthia. *The Tarot: History, Mystery, and Lore*. New York: Fireside, 1992.

Gray, Eden. *A Complete Guide to the Tarot*. New York: Bantam, 1972.

———. *Mastering the Tarot: Basic Lessons in an Ancient Mystic Art*. New York: Signet, 1971.

Greer, Mary K. *Tarot for Your Self: A Workbook for Personal Transformation*. North Hollywood, CA: Newcastle Publishing, 1984.

hooks, bell. *All About Love: New Visions*. New York: William Morrow, 2001.

Huson, Paul. *Mystical Origins of the Tarot: From Ancient Roots to Modern Usage*. Rochester, VT: Destiny Books, 2004.

Javane, Faith and Dusty Bunker. *Numerology and the Divine Triangle*. Atglen, PA: Whitford Press, 1979.

Jodorowsky, Alejandro and Marianne Costa. *The Way of Tarot: The Spiritual Teacher in the Cards*. Translated by Jon E. Graham. Rochester, VT: Destiny Books, 2004.

Kaplan, Stuart R. *The Encyclopedia of Tarot*, vol. 1. Stamford, CT: U.S. Games Systems, Inc., 1978.

———. *The Encyclopedia of Tarot*, vol. 3. Stamford, CT: U.S. Games Systems, Inc., 1990.

Kat, Alice Sparkly. *Postcolonial Astrology: Reading the Planets through Capital, Power, and Labor*. Berkeley, CA: North Atlantic Books, 2021.

Lévi, Éliphas. *Transcendental Magic: Its Doctrine and Ritual*. Translated by A. E. Waite.
London: William Rider & Son, 1923.

Lorde, Audre. *The Selected Works of Audre Lorde*. Edited by Roxane Gay. New York: W. W. Norton, 2020.

McCloud, Cedar. *The Numinous Tarot*. Card deck. Numinous Spirit Press, 2018. https://numinousspiritpress.com/numinoustarot.

Morton, Timothy. "Guest Column: Queer Ecology." *PMLA* 125, no. 2 (March 2010): 273–82. https://www.academia.edu/1050754/Queer_Ecology.

Muñoz, José Esteban. *Cruising Utopia: The Then and There of Queer Futurity*. 10th anniversary edition. New York: New York University Press, 2009.

Nichols, Sallie. *Tarot and the Archetypal Journey: The Jungian Path from Darkness to Light*. Newburyport, MA: Red Wheel/Weiser, 2019.

Papus. *The Tarot of the Bohemians*. Translated by A. P. Morton. London: Chapman and Hall, 1892. https://www.sacred-texts.com/tarot/tob/tob16.htm.

Place, Robert M. *The Tarot: History, Symbolism, and Divination*. New York: Tarcher/Penguin, 2005.

———. *The Tarot, Magic, Alchemy, Hermeticism, and Neoplatonism*. Saugerties, NY: Hermes Publications, 2017.

Pollack, Rachel. *Seventy-Eight Degrees of Wisdom*. Revised edition. San Francisco: Weiser Books, 2007.

Price, Devon. *Laziness Does Not Exist: A Defense of the Exhausted, Exploited, and Overworked*. New York: Atria Books, 2021.

Rosengarten, Arthur. *Tarot and Psychology: Spectrums of Possibility*. St. Paul, MN: Paragon House, 2000.

Salisbury, David. *Witchcraft Activism: A Toolkit for Magical Resistance*. Newburyport, MA: Weiser Books, 2019.

Snow, Cassandra. *Queering the Tarot*. Newburyport, MA: Red Wheel/Weiser, 2019.

Solnit, Rebecca. *Hope in the Dark: Untold Histories*, Wild Possibilities. 3rd ed. Chicago: Haymarket Books, 2016.

Strand, Sophie. *The Flowering Wand: Rewilding the Sacred Masculine*. Rochester, VT: Inner Traditions, 2022.

Taylor, Sonya Renee. *The Body Is Not an Apology: The Power of Radical Self-Love*. 2nd ed. Oakland, CA: Berrett-Koehler, 2021.

Waite, Arthur Edward. *The Pictorial Key to the Tarot*. Stamford, CT: U.S. Games Systems, 1994.

Yunkaporta, Tyson. *Sand Talk: How Indigenous Thinking Can Save the World*. New York: Harper One, 2020.

ABOUT THE AUTHOR

Charlie Claire Burgess (they/them) is a queer and nonbinary tarot reader, tarot teacher, deck creator, writer, artist, and witch. They are the creator and illustrator of *Fifth Spirit Tarot*, which, when first self-published, swiftly became one of the most beloved queer tarot decks available. They host *The Word Witch* podcast, which guides the listener through tarot from an inclusive perspective and features interviews with tarot readers, deck creators, witches, magicians, and healers who are creating magic from the margins. They are also a short story writer—their stories have appeared in literary journals and anthologies, and have received a Pushcart Prize Special Mention (2014) and notable mentions in two *Best American* anthologies.

Hay House Titles of Related Interest

YOU CAN HEAL YOUR LIFE, the movie, starring Louise Hay & Friends
(available as an online streaming video)
www.hayhouse.com/louise-movie

THE SHIFT, the movie,
starring Dr. Wayne W. Dyer
(available as an online streaming video)
www.hayhouse.com/the-shift-movie

***

TAROT MADE EASY: How to Read and Interpret the Cards,
by Kim Arnold

TRANSIENT LIGHT TAROT: An 81-Card Deck and Guidebook,
by Ari Wisner

THE WANDERING STAR TAROT: An 80-Card Deck and Guidebook,
by Cat Pierce

All of the above are available at your local bookstore,
or may be ordered by contacting Hay House (see next page).

***

We hope you enjoyed this Hay House book. If you'd like to receive our online catalog featuring additional information on Hay House books and products, or if you'd like to find out more about the Hay Foundation, please contact:

Hay House, Inc., P.O. Box 5100, Carlsbad, CA 92018-5100
(760) 431-7695 or (800) 654-5126
(760) 431-6948 (fax) or (800) 650-5115 (fax)
www.hayhouse.com® • www.hayfoundation.org

———

Published in Australia by: Hay House Australia Pty. Ltd.,
18/36 Ralph St., Alexandria NSW 2015
Phone: 612-9669-4299 • *Fax:* 612-9669-4144
www.hayhouse.com.au

Published in the United Kingdom by: Hay House UK, Ltd.,
The Sixth Floor, Watson House, 54 Baker Street, London W1U 7BU
Phone: +44 (0)20 3927 7290 • *Fax:* +44 (0)20 3927 7291
www.hayhouse.co.uk

Published in India by: Hay House Publishers India,
Muskaan Complex, Plot No. 3, B-2, Vasant Kunj, New Delhi 110 070
Phone: 91-11-4176-1620 • *Fax:* 91-11-4176-1630
www.hayhouse.co.in

———

Access New Knowledge.
Anytime. Anywhere.

Learn and evolve at your own pace
with the world's leading experts.

www.hayhouseU.com

Free e-newsletters from Hay House, the Ultimate Resource for Inspiration

Be the first to know about Hay House's free downloads, special offers, giveaways, contests, and more!

 Get exclusive excerpts from our latest releases and videos from *Hay House Present Moments*.

 Our *Digital Products Newsletter* is the perfect way to stay up-to-date on our latest discounted eBooks, featured mobile apps, and Live Online and On Demand events.

 Learn with real benefits! *HayHouseU.com* is your source for the most innovative online courses from the world's leading personal growth experts. Be the first to know about new online courses and to receive exclusive discounts.

 Enjoy uplifting personal stories, how-to articles, and healing advice, along with videos and empowering quotes, within *Heal Your Life*.

Sign Up Now!

Get inspired, educate yourself, get a complimentary gift, and share the wisdom!

Visit www.hayhouse.com/newsletters to sign up today!